The Birth of the Torah

The Birth of the Torah

by
EDWARD ZERIN

APPLETON-CENTURY-CROFTS

New York

First edition

Affiliate of
MEREDITH PRESS
Des Moines & New York

MANUFACTURED IN THE UNITED STATES OF AMERICA FOR MEREDITH PRESS

VAN REES PRESS • NEW YORK

Dedicated to my teachers at the Hebrew Union College-Jewish Institute of Religion, who inspired and guided me in the study of Torah.

Foreword

ARCHAEOLOGY and the science of Bible study are in-
fant sciences in the world of scholarship; the
Bible is an ancient book in the field of religion.

Recent archaeological findings and scientific studies have
shed new light on biblical times. What impact have these findings had on the thoughts and attitudes of those who study and
treasure the Holy Scripture?

This book deals primarily with the first five books of the
Jewish Bible, or the Old Testament, as the Christian world
calls it. Together, these five books constitute what the Jewish
people call the Torah. The purpose of this volume is to describe how scholars in the fields of archaeology and the science of Bible study conceive of the birth of the Torah.

It should be pointed out, however, that if one wishes to understand the role of the Torah in contemporary Jewish life he
will need to carry the story beyond the limits of the present
volume. The Torah represents but the first, although a most
important, phase in the total literature of Judaism.

The birth of the Torah, as we shall see, took place during
the fifth century B.C.E. Although the official list or canon of
books to be included in the entire Jewish Bible was not formalized until 90 C.E., the last of the Bible books was completed,
scholars hold, in the second century B.C.E. Even as the Bible
was being completed, however, the laws of the Torah were
being extended. In 220 C.E., all interpretations and new laws

of the previous four centuries which sought to explain the teachings of the Torah were collected into sixty-three different books, divided into six "orders" or main parts and called the Mishnah or the "review" of the Torah. The Mishnah sought to make the laws of the Torah relevant to the early post-biblical generation. The next extension of the Torah was the Gemara, which in 550 C.E. brought together additional interpretations and laws developed since the completion of the Mishnah. The combined writings of the Mishnah and Gemara made up the Talmud and were so arranged that each paragraph of the Mishnah was followed by that portion of the Gemara which represented the extension of the Torah law. In addition, commentaries, codes, and responsa literature were written throughout the succeeding centuries. Today, if one seeks to know the significance of the Torah for modern Judaism, he must be familiar not only with the Torah in its own historic development but also with the literary development in the twenty-five centuries which followed the birth of the Torah.

Acknowledgments

The Birth of the Torah grew out of many years of study and teaching. It came to fulfillment, however, only with the help of many persons.

To my teachers, who inspired me, I am deeply indebted. To my students—whether at Drake University, at the Central Presbyterian Church, or at Temple B'nai Jeshurun, Des Moines, Iowa—a debt of personal gratitude is gratefully acknowledged.

To Dan Levin, who patiently read the manuscript, I express my appreciation for his numerous suggestions which sharpened my own focus on many important issues.

To my secretary, Mrs. Joseph E. Fugate, I owe much because of her patience and devotion in typing the manuscript.

For me, this has been a labor of love.

DR. EDWARD ZERIN

Temple B'nai Jeshurun
Des Moines, Iowa
May 18, 1962

Contents

The Birth of the Torah

CHAPTER I

Archaeology and the Science of Bible Study

THROUGHOUT the ages, men have asked questions about the authorship of the Five Books of Moses. The traditionally recognized concept was that God had revealed either by dictating or by presenting in written form, or both, these Five Books, or the Torah as they are called in Judaism, to Moses at Mount Sinai. This Torah was infallible, authoritative, and sacred. In time, however, people began to raise questions about the Torah. Often these questions were raised by religious people who believed in the truth of the Bible; nonetheless, they were puzzled about some of the things they found. For example, they asked:

1. How could Moses, who is supposed to have written down the Five Books of Moses, have written about his own death and the events which followed, as found in Deuteronomy 34: 5–12?

2. If the world is governed by natural law, how can one explain the miracles of the Bible; e.g., the crossing of the Red Sea?

3. If God is a spiritual God of the entire world and cannot be seen, how can one explain such a phrase as "the hand of God" which is used throughout the Bible, and the numerous

other phrases of the Bible which describe God in human forms?

4. If geology tells us that the world is millions and millions of years old, how can one believe the story of creation?

Because these individuals still believed that every word of the Torah was divinely revealed, they tried in every way possible to reconcile the truth of the Torah with what their reason and experience told them should be true. They developed, as a result, explanations which to them sounded reasonable and, therefore, acceptable. This method is called "harmonization." The following outline illustrates some of the ways by which people have tried to harmonize reason and experience with regard to the above questions:

1. Obviously no person can write about events after his death; however, Moses did write the entire Torah with the exception of this one passage, which was written by Joshua after Moses had died.

2. The world is governed by natural law; however, even before creation took place, God had provided for the appearance of these miracles at a given time. Consequently, the appearance of the miracle did not break God's conception of natural law. The miracle was but the "natural" occurrence of an event. God is not an arbitrary God who interferes with the normal processes of the universe, once these have been established by Him.

3. The Bible spoke the language of men; therefore, when the Bible referred to the hand of God, it did not mean specifically a hand as human beings conceive it. The term "hand of God" was a *symbol* of the power of God.

4. The world may in truth be millions of years old as man counts time; however, when the Biblical writers referred to

a day of creation they may very well have referred to a day in terms of God's conception of time. Each of the six days of creation may very well have been millions of years long, according to the reckoning of men.

Religious people throughout the ages have used the *power of reasoning or logic* to help square what they read in the Torah with what they found in the *experiences of their lives.*

With the advent of science, however, a new method was developed for the examination of ancient documents. This new approach was the *historical method,* and, when it was applied to the Torah, the result was the emergence of the *science of Bible study.* Instead of trying to explain away by the power of reason the difficulties of the Torah, the new method suggested a completely different approach. For example, certain questions were asked and answered about the Torah:

1. Who wrote the Torah?
2. When was the Torah written?
3. How was the Torah written?
4. Why was the Torah written?
5. For whom was the Torah written?

As a result of the approach of the science of Bible study, certain conclusions about the origin and development of the Torah were reached:

1. *Who:* Moses was not the author of the entire Torah. Many people participated in the writing of the Torah.

2. *When:* Nor was the Torah written all at one time. The Torah was written over a period of nearly a thousand years, with the earliest identified written parts going back to approx-

imately 1250 B.C.E. and the last part being written about
400 B.C.E.

3. *How:* In the beginning, parts of the Torah were handed
down both by word of mouth and in written form. Many
years later, these traditions were edited and new ideas added.
This editing process took place at least four different times.
The first time, the ancient materials were collected by a set
of editors living in Judah, in the south of Canaan, sometime
during the tenth to the ninth centuries (950–850 B.C.E.).[1]
These editors are referred to as the "J School" because they
used the name "Jahweh" or "Yahweh" for God. A little later,
another group of arrangers, living in the northern part of
Canaan, produced a second written version of the tradition.
Since they used the name "Elohim" for God, they are known
as the "E School." The third written version arose in response
to a religious reform that swept through Judah in the year
621 B.C.E. These editors are identified as the "D School" because they supposedly discovered a series of long-lost laws
that in Greek eventually came to have the name Deuteronomy.
The fourth interpretation of the tradition took place around
the years 550–450 B.C.E. These writers came to be known as
the "P School" because it is believed that they were priests.
Finally, the editions of all these four schools were put together
and edited by the P School. The result was the Torah as we
know it today.

4. *Why:* The Torah represented a constitution which
guided the lives of our ancestors in ancient times. It set forth
the laws and rules by which the people were to live. In fact,
the Torah may be called a collection of four different constitutions. Each constitution came into being to meet the specific
needs of different periods of Jewish life. Finally the constitutions were put together to make them seem like one final
constitution.

5. *For Whom:* Each constitution was a guide of laws and rules by which *the people of that particular time* were to live.

The historical method is not an exclusively Jewish point of view. It is shared alike by Gentiles and Jews and is applied to both the Old and New Testaments. In fact, the science of Bible study was developed first at the University of Paris in 1733 by Professor Jean Astruc. He was a non-Jew interested in tracing what seemed to him to be duplicating or contradictory stories in the book of Genesis. Since then, many Gentile scholars have pursued the line of study set forth by Professor Astruc. The climax came in 1876 with the development of the Documentary Hypothesis by two German scholars, Graf and Wellhausen. It was they who first set forth a complete theory about the four basic documents that make up the Torah. These documents, or Constitutions as we have called them, were the products of four schools of writers or editors known as J, E, D, and P. The followers of Graf-Wellhausen are known as modernists, in contrast to the traditionalists, who continued to believe in the Mosaic authorship of the Torah. Many Jewish scholars have followed in their footsteps and have adopted the modernists' teachings as their own. Because of their use of the historical method, Gentile and Jewish modernists are no longer called upon to harmonize contradictory passages in the Torah. To the contrary, the contradictions for them serve as invaluable clues to the discovery of the JEDP schools.

... the key to reading the Bible is to read it with the historical method—to see it as a series of books written by men, albeit extraordinary ones, in a given time and place. We are then never called upon to justify the Biblical text against our deepest beliefs and hopes. We do not have to blind ourselves to those occasional passages where the Bible is untrue to our highest insights, nor do we have to make separate compartments in our mind to believe simultaneously in the primitive scientific statements of several thousand years ago and those we learn from today's laboratories. What is more, we can see the Bible against its time and come to recognize more clearly not just what it naturally shared of it, but where it stepped outside it and spoke with a voice that still rings with meaning in our own hearts.[2]

Since 1876, the views of the early modernists have been superseded by those of the contemporary modernists. Here, too, the views are shared by Gentiles and Jews alike. The transition from the views of the early to the contemporary modernists came about with the development of the science of archaeology as a partner with the science of Bible study for the understanding of Scripture.

Modern archaeology has had a tremendous impact on biblical scholars. While archaeological findings, in general, have tended to support the modernist point of view, the discoveries have led even the modernists to make certain revisions in their theories. The concept of JEDP is a case in point. Formerly, it was believed that the editors of the J school, which was regarded to be the earliest school, had resource only to oral traditions. Now we know that the earliest editors had available to them considerable written as well as oral materials. Moreover, contemporary modernists now look upon JEDP as parallel schools, each using materials which had been preserved from very early times, rather than as consecutive schools, one building on top of the other.

Similarly, some early modernists held that the patriarchs—Abraham, Isaac, and Jacob—never existed. They contended that these persons were the creation of later writers who invented them to fit in with the writer's purpose. Today, the historical background of the patriarchs is too well known to deny their existence. Again, early modernists believed that the concept of ethical monotheism—the belief in only one God who demanded justice of His people—was a late invention.

Today, many modernists feel that the ethical elements of monotheism were present in the religion of ancient Israel almost from the beginning. In addition, the evidence now seems to indicate that even among the polytheistic religions, which believed in many gods, the gods were looked upon as the rulers of the entire world. The idea of a universal god or gods who ruled the universe was part of the belief of many religions. In a fourth point, too, the position of the early modernist is not followed today. Formerly, it was held that the real unity of the ancient Israelites was not achieved until the time of King David and King Solomon. This was more than two hundred years after the Exodus from Egypt. Now, scholars hold that this sense of unity had progressed quite far by the time of Joshua, the successor to Moses. Thus, the contemporary modernists believe that the sacred traditions and institutions of ancient Israel are much older and more authentic than they were thought to be by the early modernists. They go back to the earliest period of Jewish life in Canaan, to the time of Joshua and the Judges, as well as to that of Moses in the Sinai desert-wilderness.

The new trends in Bible scholarship can be summarized as follows:

It is generally agreed today ... that a new approach to the Biblical traditions is required. The older critics, it has long been realized, proceeded too largely on the assumption that the Hexateuch (The Five Books of Moses and the Book of Joshua) was the product of a purely literary activity, which came into being by the editing together of written documents. They conceived their task, therefore, almost exclusively as that of unraveling these various strands that they might study each in isolation. While the possibility was granted by some of them that the documents might contain older material, this recognition was in practice allowed little play; the documents were evaluated as the creations of the ages in which they were written, and this led inevitably to the discounting of their worth as historical sources. But no sooner did new archaeological discoveries begin to pour in than it became evident that a new evaluation was in order, for it began to be clear, in the light of parallels, that at least some of the material of the Hexateuch did not originate with the authors of the documents at all, but had been adapted by them from traditions much more ancient. As early as the turn of the century, indeed, certain scholars had begun to turn their interests from documentary analysis to the study of individual units of tradition within the documents. The pioneer was H. Gunkel, who was the first to apply the methods of form criticism to Biblical studies, and who early gave attention to certain traditions in Genesis in the light of Babylonian parallels. He was followed in this by H. Gressmann, who applied similar methods to the study of the traditions of Moses. . . .

It is today quite evident that to date the documents by no means dates their contents or passes verdict on their value, and that documentary analysis is only the beginning of the critic's task. As one observes, for example, the remarkable way in which the Patriarchal narratives of J and E—though presumably written down in the tenth century and after—reflect conditions that obtain a half millennium or more earlier no other conclusion is possible. Attention must be given, therefore, to the history of the traditions in their pre-literary form. It has become clear that while one may assign to the various documents absolute and relative dates, their material can be ranked in no neat chronological progression, nor can the documents themselves be used to support an equally neat picture of the evolution of Israel's religion. But this has meant that Wellhausenism, in its classical form, has all but ceased to exist, while the Documentary Hypothesis itself has been forcibly placed in a new light.[3]

Archaeology is defined by *Webster's New World Dictionary* as "the scientific study of the life and culture of ancient peoples, as by excavation of ancient cities, relics, artifacts, etc." [4] While archaeology deals with the past, it is, comparatively speaking, a brand-new science. It is less than one hundred years old and has come into its golden age only within the last twenty-five to fifty years.

Ancient man would build one city right on top of another. Whenever a city was destroyed, the people would construct their new homes on top of the old rubble heap. Very often, they did not bother to clean up the old site and usually left much pottery lying around. By examining these pottery fragments, the modern archaeologist has been able to tell not only how many cities had been built on one place but also when these cities had been constructed. In the year 1890, the father of modern archaeology, Dr. W. M. Flinders Petrie, was able to identify the remains of eight ancient cities by tracing the shapes, materials, and kinds of pottery which he found on one site. He accomplished this feat by digging down nearly two hundred feet through a mound of debris, known as a tell.

While Petrie discovered the method of archaeology, the significance of his work was not established until many years later. In 1921, the American archaeologist Dr. William F. Albright, two other Americans, and two Arabs driving two donkeys loaded with equipment set out from Jerusalem for a walking tour of the region of northern Palestine. They did not use the well-traveled paths. Instead they climbed over tells and ruins, living simply on the food of the natives: unleavened bread, cheese, eggs, and leben, or fermented milk. For nearly two years, Dr. Albright and his party paid special attention to the different types of pottery dug from the various levels of the ancient cities. From this evidence, he was able to date the exact years in which the tells had been inhabited.

Pottery fragments tell us not only the dates but also the names of ancient cities. They are the clues to the geography as well as the chronology of Bible times. Because of the many empires and cultures which centered in Palestine, place names had changed frequently during the course of the centuries.

For example, there had been a controversy for many years whether the Arabic name "el-Jib," given to a town just eight miles north of Jerusalem, was the same as the Biblical name "Gibeon." In 1956, however, the matter was settled. In the course of clearing the debris from a large rock-cut pool just inside the city wall, the archaeologist Dr. James Pritchard found two jar handles inscribed with the name "Gibeon" in ancient Hebrew script. Later, other handles were found to confirm that el-Jib was the site of the Biblical Gibeon.

Not only bits of pottery but also fragments of papyrus are of great importance to the archaeologist. Until 1947, it was believed that the oldest known Bible manuscript came from the period of 900 C.E. In fact, one archaeologist had stated most emphatically: "There is, indeed, no probability that we shall ever find manuscripts of the Hebrew text going back to a period before the formation of the text which we know as Massoretic." [5] (The Massorites were Jewish scholars who in the ninth century C.E. gave the Hebrew Bible its present form by putting in punctuation marks. Since the original Hebrew text contained only consonants, they also added vowels in order to preserve what they thought to be the correct reading.) But the impossible did come to pass. The discovery of the Dead Sea Scrolls has brought the modern reader much closer to the original text of the Bible, by pushing back by nearly one thousand years the date of the earliest known manuscripts of the Bible.

The story of the actual discovery of the Dead Sea Scrolls in a cave is in itself a fascinating account. The late Professor Eliezer Sukenik of the Hebrew University in Jerusalem, the first to recognize the antiquity and significance of the scrolls, has left for us in his private journal an account of this event:

They [the Arab bedouins] had been moving with their goats along the north-western shore of the Dead Sea. While searching for a stray goat, they had stumbled across an opening in the rocks overlooking the sea. It excited their curiosity. They threw stones into the cavern and were surprised to hear a strange sound, as if the stones had hit and broken a piece of pottery. But they were too busy with their flocks to investigate, and so they returned the following day. Crawling into the cave they found themselves in a narrow crevice. On the floor were eight earthenware jars, five on one side, three on the other. Several of these jars were still covered with upturned dishes. Inside the jars they found bundles of leather, some wrapped in linen. While groping inside the jars, they accidentally broke some. For several weeks they had wandered about with the bundles, showing them occasionally to friends in their tribe who had visited them in their tent. They then decided to come to Bethlehem, the commercial centre of the Bedouin from the Judaean desert, and see whether they could get some money for their find.[6]

Since the original discovery, other caves have been explored, and hundreds of fragments of scrolls have been discovered. Archaeologists believe that the original cave was a storehouse for an ancient library of the first century C.E., in which many manuscripts of much older date were preserved. The explorations now indicate that this barren Dead Sea area had been the site of a kind of Jewish "monastery," called Khirbet Qumran, which flourished in parts of the first century B.C.E. and the first century C.E. Among the Dead Sea manuscripts found was a leather scroll about twenty-four feet long containing fifty-four columns of text. The Arab bedouin had discovered a manuscript of the Book of Isaiah which was, by nearly one thousand years, the oldest copy of the Book of Isaiah in existence.

Since the earliest Bible manuscripts now known go back only to the first or second century B.C.E. (Dead Sea Scrolls), how do we know what the Hebrew language looked like when

the Bible itself was written? Here, too, archaeology can help
us.

On a hot summer day in June, 1880, a boy was wading with
some of his friends in a pool of water located just south of the
old city of Jerusalem. Gradually he made his way up a tunnel
from which the waters of the pool were coming. Suddenly his
foot slipped, and he fell into the cold water. While getting up,
he noticed that a series of letters had been cut into the stone
walls of the tunnel. Later investigation showed that the boy
accidentally had discovered six lines of writing in ancient
Hebrew script. While the existence of the tunnel had been
known for a long time, no one had ever noticed the story of
the building of the Tunnel of Siloam, as this passageway was
known, which had been engraved on a smooth portion of the
wall. This discovery not only revealed the first example of
ancient Hebrew writing but also helped to identify a tunnel
built by King Hezekiah of Judah in the seventh century B.C.E.,
which is mentioned in the Bible (II Kings 20:20).

A second and even more dramatic discovery of ancient Hebrew writing was made in 1935 by the English archaeologist
Dr. James Starkey, as he dug in a tell. One day his workmen,
while excavating some black rubbish, uncovered small pieces
of broken pottery which contained strange writing. These
fragments were washed carefully in filtered water so that only
the dirt was removed. Soon more than one hundred lines of
old Hebrew script were available. This discovery is known as
the Lachish Letters and comes from the time of the prophet
Jeremiah, who died in the sixth century B.C.E. These letters
were samples of military correspondence written by a Jewish
officer serving in a northern Palestinian outpost to his commander in Lachish.

Archaeology also helps us to explain many of the statements
in the Bible which have puzzled men for centuries. For exam-

ple, there are times when the Bible uses figures and numbers which seem unbelievable. One such Bible passage deals with the number of horses and chariots which King Solomon owned. In the Book of I Kings (10:26-29), it tells that he had no less than a "thousand and four hundred chariots, and twelve thousand horsemen." [7] Is such a figure realistically possible? Most people have questioned its authenticity. However, in 1928, an archaeological expedition came upon an amazing discovery in an excavation of the ancient city of Meggido. While digging in the fourth layer from the top, the expedition uncovered a large area composed of five units of stables. In front of the stables was a huge water tank, which could have provided for each of the 150 horses stabled there as much as eighteen and a half gallons of water a day. Other nearby excavations showed that as many as 450 horses could be stabled and 150 chariots accommodated comfortably in Meggido. As soon as one recalls that King Solomon had built, according to the Bible, many "Cities for his chariots," the discovery at Meggido makes the numbers found in the Bible very real and understandable. [8]

Likewise, archaeology also tells us things about which the Bible itself is often silent, or, at the most, gives only a hint. For example, archaeological finds have brought to light an unknown language called Ugarit. One day in the spring of 1928, a peasant was plowing his field in the area of Rash Shamra, which is on the northern coast of Syria. Suddenly his plow struck a large stone. The farmer lifted up the stone and found that it belonged to a tomb. The tomb itself contained pottery, including several small vases that were unbroken. The discovery of the cemetery prompted archaeologists to explore further. Soon, a whole city, including a library containing many clay tablets inscribed in an unknown language, was uncovered. When the tablets were translated several years later, the archaeological world realized that an entirely new branch of studies had been discovered. It was called Ugarit after the ancient name of the town in which the texts had been found.

The discoveries of Ugarit also revealed new information about the religion which the Israelites found when they entered Canaan. Now we know, for example, that the Canaanites had a Bible whose poetry resembles some of the writings of our present book of Psalms. They also had a highly organized system of gods and goddesses as well as a priesthood. No longer are we dependent today for our knowledge of what idol worship was like on the few scattered references in the Bible. The Ugaritic texts tell us in great detail the beliefs and practices of the fourteenth century B.C.E. Canaanites.

While archaeological discoveries help to clarify the meaning of many passages in the Bible, the Bible, too, has been a valuable help to the archaeologist. For example, Dr. Nelson Glueck, president of the Hebrew Union College-Jewish Institute of Religion, is a strong believer in the use of the Bible for achaeological purposes, and, as a result, he has unearthed many famous archaeological treasures, not the least of which is King Solomon's Copper Mines.

For many years, no one had found justification for the biblical statement that Palestine at one time had been "a land whose stones are iron and out of whose hills you can dig copper" (Deut. 8:9). Dr. Glueck, nevertheless, set out to discover whether or not there really were copper mines. The Bible gave him his clue. In the Book of Numbers 21:9, it is said that Moses had healed the people of Israel with a copper serpent. This event was supposed to have taken place in the Wadi Arabah, in the desert regions of Southern Palestine. It was reasonable, therefore, assumed Dr. Glueck, that copper could be found in the region even now. In 1932, he began his work. In a few years, he not only had discovered copper in the Wadi Arabah but also had rediscovered the ancient city of Ezion

Geber on the Gulf of Aqabah. This city was King Solomon's port, from which his ships sailed to carry on commerce in Africa and Asia. Ezion Geber was also the site, as Dr. Glueck has shown, of the largest copper smelter of ancient times. "The ores already partly 'roasted' at the mines in the Wadi Arabah were sent to Ezion Geber for further refinement. From that southernmost city of Solomon's power came ingots and finished metal articles for home consumption and for the foreign export trade." [9]

In summary, it may be concluded that in light of the discoveries of archaeology today's modernists, in contrast to those of yesterday, tend to place greater emphasis upon the trustworthiness of the Bible narrative. It is important to point out, however, that archaeology seeks neither to prove nor to disprove the religious message of the Torah, or for that matter of the entire Bible. The Bible is not a history book. On the other hand, it is equally apparent that the religious message of the Bible cannot be understood properly outside the framework of history. The purpose of archaeology is to give us a clearer picture of the historical setting within which the birth of the Torah, that special part of the Bible with which we are concerned, took place. Archaeology does not presume to teach theology.

Dr. Nelson Glueck has stated the issue succinctly when he wrote:

The truths of the Bible expressed in commandments and prophecy, in legend and law, in history and myth, in unvarnished and biographical sketches and compressed genealogical tables, and some of them repeated in different versions not only in different books but in the same chapters, are not susceptible to proof of any kind. They can neither be buttressed nor invalidated archaeologically. New discovery may perhaps modify or fill out a particular account in the Biblical annals, but it can never replace or refute or corroborate its religious worths. The discoveries by archaeological exploration and excavations in Bible lands have a relevancy to historical events in the Bible, but in no wise affect its religious propositions or ethical decrees, which are applicable to all peoples in all lands at all times.

From this point of view, there is no relationship between archaeological discoveries in Bible lands and the Bible itself, or between the finds of archaeology and the teachings of Judaism. Archaeology helps us understand better the land in which the Bible evolved, in which Judaism emerged and developed. It gives us more information than is otherwise available either in the pages of the Bible or elsewhere about the historical situations which evoked revolutionary religious doctrines, in harmony with the genius of developing Judaism.[10]

CHAPTER II

Mesopotamian Beginnings

ALTHOUGH scientists believe that our earth is from two to three billion years old and that man has lived on the earth for approximately one million years, modern civilization is a comparatively new event in world history. The transition between primitive and modern civilization occurred only six thousand years ago in the valleys of the Tigris and Euphrates Rivers in Asia Minor and of the Nile River in North Africa.

In both Mesopotamia and Egypt, the lands surrounding the valleys were drying up and forming deserts. Nature was forcing men who had roamed these lands for hundreds of thousands of years to come together in large groups near the rivers. To become civilized, these men needed three things: protection from marauders, ways of getting food, and protection from each other.

In the Tigris-Euphrates region the high hills to the north and the desert to the south provided some protection. In the Nile Valley the great deserts and the Mediterranean Sea gave men safety from invaders for a long time. Likewise, it was easy to obtain food in both regions without cultivation. Thus, men could live for a few years without planting anything and without raising their own animals. This was very important. Now, instead of worrying about the next meal, men could plan their food supply over a long period of time by developing new ways of growing plants and taming animals. This new security gave the people of these two regions the time to devote themselves to the third requirement for civilization. Protection from each other was the one necessity which nature could not supply. Men had to supply it themselves. At last, men had the opportunity to invent government, a system of laws by which people living in larger cities and spread out over wider areas could co-operate with each other for their mutual welfare.

In these two cradles of civilization the beginnings of Jewish history also took place.

In Mesopotamia the people made rapid strides in organizing their way of life. For example, improved agriculture permitted the support of an increased population while developed urban life made possible new advances in the arts and crafts. The Mesopotamians invented the wheel and the arch, and their metalworking and gem-cutting reached heights of excellence seldom surpassed. Trade and cultural contacts reached far and wide. Likewise, they developed the world's first system of writing. Numerous examples of their wedge-shaped or cuneiform letters have been discovered by archaeologists, giving evidence of what must have been an abundant literature. In the Tigris-Euphrates River Valley, the foundation for a science of mathematics also was laid.

In the fields of government and religion, too, a high degree of organization was evident. First of all, Mesopotamia was organized into a system of city-states, most of which were quite small. Although one city-state was able at times to conquer another, no one city-state ever succeeded in asserting itself over all the others. Apparently the idea of uniting all the city-states was regarded as a sin against the gods. Second, the city-state was a government ruled by a god; the city and its

lands were the god's estate; the temple, his home. All community activities were based, therefore, upon religion; even the economic life was organized about the temple with its gardens, fields, and storehouses. The people, each in his place, were the god's retainers, workers on his estate. Third, each city was ruled by an earthly city-king or city-priest of the local temple. Although the offices of the city-king and the city-priest were not identical, the authority which each exercised was often for all intents the same. Each ruled as the earthly representative of the god and managed the estate. Where there was both a king and a priest, the authority of the priest generally was subordinated to that of the king.

According to Mesopotamian traditions, the authority of the city-king came down from heaven at the beginning of time. Recent archaeological evidence indicates, however, that the government originally was composed of a city assembly. From these beginnings there emerged gradually the city-king, first as an emergency measure and later as a permanent institution. Nevertheless, the tradition was maintained that the city-king held his authority as a result of divine election.

Finally, the religion of Mesopotamia represented a highly developed polytheism. The people believed that there were many gods, some of whom were males and some females. These gods represented the phases of nature, such as the sky, stars, storms, etc., and they were worshiped by the bringing of sacrifices. Religion in Mesopotamia was also anthropomorphic because it was believed that the gods not only existed i the image of man but also had human needs. For example, tl gods and goddesses also were represented by human-shap idols, and the priests who ministered in the temple would br these human-like figures food and wine three times daily.

At the head of the pantheon or organization of the gods Enlil, lord of the storm. While the cults of the various were carried on in the cities where it was believed the

their seats and where each god's prestige rose or fell with that of the city with which he was identified, the gods themselves were not conceived to be mere local gods. Their existence as well as their functions were recognized by all the peoples of Mesopotamia. There was, however, an order among the gods, and frequently disputes ensued. Whenever a war broke out between the city-states, it was attributed to the fact that a legal battle also was going on in the state of the gods. The victory in battle of one city-state over another represented the endorsement of that city's claim by Enlil, the king of the gods. Calamity on earth also reflected the anger of the gods because of some affront. It was the function of the priests to serve the gods, to calm the gods in their anger and thus maintain peace and stability.

Because of the comparatively advanced stage of civilization found in the Tigris-Euphrates River Valley, it was inevitable that many wandering groups of people were attracted to the area from the south hill country and the desert regions. Some came as invaders; others settled peacefully.

Among the many people who settled in the Tigris-Euphrates Valley was a group of wandering tribes called Habiru. The Habiru actually were a mixed group made up of no one people. They represented a social class of semi-nomads who lived in Mesopotamia but who were unable to become completely a part of an organized community. They would wander from one area to another, for example, settling in each one only temporarily. The Habiru would support themselves by pasturing their flocks or by serving as skilled craftsmen, such as smiths and musicians. They were not necessarily always peaceful in their activities. At times some of the Habiru would seek to make their living by raiding caravans and weak, outlying communities, or by hiring themselves out as mercenaries.

It is believed by many scholars that some of the Habiru were

the early ancestors of the Jewish people. These scholars point, for example, to the similarity between the names of Habiru and Hebrew (Gen. 14:13). Moreover, archaeological evidence tells us that the Habiru tribes were living in the very regions and in the same period of time associated with Abraham. This fact, say the scholars, testifies further to the kinship between the people who are called the Habiru and the Hebrews.

Not all the Habiru tribes, however, became part of the Jewish people. Some of the Habiru groups became the ancestors of what came to be called, many hundreds of years later, the Arab people. Only those groups who moved ultimately into the land of Canaan, which is called today Israel and Palestine, and who associated themselves with the traditions of Abraham in Mesopotamia and later of Moses in Egypt came to be regarded as the founders of the Jewish people.

Three terms are used as names for the Jewish people. The earliest ancestors were called Hebrews. When the Hebrews under Moses, as we shall see, entered into a covenant or agreement with their God, Yahweh, they came to be called Israelites. The term Hebrew continued in use, however, being retained as the name by which the Israelites referred to themselves whenever they spoke with foreigners. The term "Jewish people" came into use during the Greek period following the conquest of Jerusalem by Alexander the Great in the year 332 B.C.E.

The period of history connected with Abraham is known as the period of the patriarchs. A patriarch is a father, and the term applies to Abraham and his descendants, Isaac and Jacob, who, according to the tradition of the Bible, are considered to be the fathers or the founders of the Jewish people. The patriarchal period refers, however, in its broadest sense to the period of Jewish history beginning with Abraham and continuing until the Hebrews began to live in Egypt. Some scholars say that the age of the patriarchs lasted from 1850–1720

B.C.E.; others believe that it covered a longer period, from approximately 2000 to 1720 B.C.E.

When Abraham came upon the scene of history, the civilization of the Tigris-Euphrates River Valley already was in a state of decline. After nearly fifteen hundred years of growth, Mesopotamian civilization had begun to decay because of the numerous invaders who gradually were able to overrun the country. As a result, many people began to move from place to place in search of better living conditions. This situation must have fashioned the pattern of Abraham's life, too. It must be remembered that Abraham was a man of considerable wealth and prestige (Gen. 13:2). He needed to live where his cattle and flock could have adequate grazing area. He also needed to live near cities where he could carry on his business. Both of these requirements called for a peaceful setting. The political situation in Mesopotamia at this time was rather chaotic. The invading groups permitted neither the peaceful pasturing of flocks nor the successful transaction of business. It is against this background that we must view the migrations of Abraham and of the early Hebrews.

Tradition tells us that Abraham moved with his father, Terach, from the city of Ur in southern Mesopotamia to Haran in the northern part of the country. Some writers associate the city of Ur, however, not with southern Mesopotamia, but with a different city of Ur found in northern Mesopotamia. Others believe that Abraham's home was in the city of Haran itself. The Bible tells us that when Abraham sought a wife for his son, Isaac, he sent Eliezer, his servant, to Haran, "unto my country, and to my kindred" (Gen. 24:4). Nonetheless, the fact remains that Abraham chose to leave his childhood home and to live in the land of Canaan.

It is possible that Abraham left Mesopotamia not only because of the political unrest in the Tigris-Euphrates River

Valley but also because of his dissatisfaction with the religious teachings of his time. The belief may have begun to develop that if the god they worshiped were truly God, he could not be pictured like a man or woman, nor could he have human needs. The thought may have begun to grow, moreover, that only one god should be worshiped. Abraham, perhaps, could no longer accept the official and highly organized polytheistic and anthropomorphic teachings about the gods and goddesses of his Mesopotamian world. The Torah itself gives us one of the clearest examples of Abraham's situation. The origin of the story of the sacrifice of Isaac (Gen. 22) may be nothing less than a patriarchal protest against the sacrifice of human beings which was practiced widely in the Tigris-Euphrates River Valley. Therefore, despite the superior culture of the cities of the Tigris-Euphrates River Valley, it may very well have been that Abraham and some of the early Hebrews chose to reject this culture with its unacceptable religious teachings. They may have preferred to live in the southern as well as the hill country of Central Canaan where they could be free not only to pursue in greater peace their business as a shepherd people but also to develop their own ideas about God.

What the exact nature of the religion which Abraham and the other Habiru groups practiced was is not certain. Some scholars have suggested that originally in Mesopotamia Abraham and many of the Habiru worshiped a moon god called Sin. For example, they claim that the name of Laban, who, the Torah tells us, was the brother of Rebekkah, comes from the same root as the Hebrew word for moon (Gen. 24:29). It is more probable that Abraham and the other Habiru tribes, like many other people of the time, worshiped their gods under the name of El, and that there were many such Elim, or gods. One such El was Shaddai, who was the god of the mountain. Therefore, in saying that Abraham and some of the early Hebrews chose to develop their own ideas of God, we must not assume

that Abraham and his followers understood the idea of the one
God as we understand it today.

Some scholars tell us that the patriarchs neither had a father-
son relationship nor were worshipers of the same god. They
point out that not one but many families may have become
dissatisfied with the polytheistic and anthropomorphic religious environment of Mesopotamia. Each of these families or
clans, as a result, began to worship its own god, generally the
god of its leader or patriarch. This ancient practice has been
called by some modern scholars "practical monotheism" or
"implicit monotheism." [1] In time, these groups migrated to different parts of the land of Canaan, where they worshiped at
the already established local shrines. The various patriarchal
gods took on the names of the gods of these respective holy
places. It is interesting to point out, however, that only the
names of the patriarchal gods were changed in the process of
the migrations. The scholars tell us that the clans continued
to worship their respective gods at the sanctuaries in Canaan
in the same manner as they had previously in Mesopotamia.
Later on, these same scholars tell us, even as the separate stories
of the patriarchs were worked into one tradition so the different one-gods also were unified into one God. This tendency accounts for the fact that Yahweh is referred to by many
different names in the Torah.

What seems to have been unique, however, in the relationship between the patriarchs and the one-god was not necessarily the fact that God was one but the idea that the bond between this one-god and the patriarchs was in the form of an
agreement called a covenant or, in Hebrew, a *brit*. There was
a personal relationship between the patriarch and his god. The
patriarchs apparently treasured their covenant relationship because they believed that their respective covenants held forth
for them the promise of a land inheritance and the attainment
of a posterity which would become a great nation, both of

which were essential for their survival as semi-nomads (Gen. 15). This relationship was guarded zealously not only by the individual but also by the family connected with this god. The god of the patriarchs was both a personal god and a patron god of the clan.

The religion of the early Hebrews, however, was not free from what today is called primitive thinking. Despite any objections which the patriarchs may have had to the religions of Mesopotamia, they also had anthropomorphic aspects in their god-concept. For example, the Teraphim which the Torah tells us Rachel stole from her father Laban were nothing less than statue-like representations of his household gods (Gen. 31:30–34). Even more important, however, was the fact that these statues were also the symbols of a man's right to an inheritance. This meaning of the Teraphim became very clear in 1919 with the discovery of a series of clay tablets in the ancient city of Nuzi in Mesopotamia. The tablets tell that if a man has no male children he may adopt his son-in-law, who becomes the heir and receives his property and the household goods. Later, however, if a son is born, this son can inherit the family wealth, and it is he who receives the Teraphim. As a result of these discoveries, it has become quite obvious why it was of great importance for both Laban and Rachel to possess the Teraphim. Laban wanted to protect any son who might be born to him. Rachel, on the other hand, wanted to protect herself and her husband Jacob in any eventuality. By possessing these Teraphim, Rachel felt that both she and her husband not only would have a successful life under the protection of the god but also would be the sole inheritors of Laban's property.

At one time the question was raised among scholars whether Abraham, Isaac, and Jacob were real persons. Although no document ever has been unearthed referring specifically to these three patriarchal ancestors, the weight of archaeological evidence is such today that no one questions the fact that at least the life and times described in the Genesis stories are reliable.

One of the foremost archaeological expeditions to shed light upon the historical background of the patriarchs was undertaken by Dr. Nelson Glueck. During the years 1932–39 he made a systematic survey of Southern Jordan east and south of the Dead Sea. Today this area is a sparsely settled desert-like region. Yet the Bible tells us that when the shepherds of Abraham and Lot quarreled and could not live together, Lot chose the regions of the Jordan River because he "lifted up his eyes, and beheld all the plain of the Jordan, that it was well watered everywhere" (Gen. 12:10). As a result of his careful study, Dr. Glueck has shown that in the centuries before 2000 B.C.E., many villages were in existence in this now barren area. Moreover, his findings indicate that for some mysterious reason the inhabitants suddenly abandoned their homes and took up their wanderings again. Dr. Glueck also has explored the Negev region of modern Israel. Although today it, too, is an uninhabited, parched wasteland, he found abundant evidence that during the period of Abraham hundreds of communities dotted the terrain. Several centuries later, the Negev region, like the Jordan valley, suddenly lost its settlers and returned to a vast empty wilderness. Since Abraham with his large family and extensive flocks could have prospered only in a settled area where he could engage in cattle business and in a land which offered fertile pasture for his herds, Dr. Glueck concludes that "our explorations of the Negev and Transjordan indicate that the time of Abraham could not have been later than the nineteenth century B.C.E." [2]

Dr. Glueck has described his explorations in the Transjordan and the Negev as follows:

Either the Age of Abraham coincides with the ... period between the twenty-first and nineteenth centuries B.C. or the entire saga dealing with the Patriarch must be dismissed, so far as its historical value is concerned, from scientific consideration.... We have been able to establish through archaeological exploration that that period was preceded and followed, respectively, both in the Negev and in Transjordan, by an extended break in the history of permanent, sedentary, agricultural civilization.

Abraham's experiences in the Negev and Sinai did not occur in a vacuum. An Abraham of the eighteenth to the eleventh centuries B.C. would have found the Negev to be an almost unrelievedly harsh and uncultivated wasteland. His heavily laden, slowly moving and unarmed caravan would have fallen speedy prey to vulturelike nomads; nor could he have sojourned there, as we are told he did (Genesis 20:1), without incurring the danger of being cut off and destroyed by them.

The background of the Biblical narrative implies on the contrary the existence in the Negev during the Age of Abraham of villages and camps, and, above all, of conditions of general peace. It assumes the presence of a friendly population that received him and his retinue with hospitality and passed him on from place to place until he reached his journey's goal. It takes for granted that he found among them a common language, common customs and in general a common way of life....

... We found the pottery evidence of the Age of Abraham in the Negev startling and exciting. At every one of the numerous settlements there ... we found fragments of the easily recognizable and strikingly unique types of pottery which are characteristic of this period.

... The amazing uniformity of this pottery ... emphasizes that the Negev was then ... what its geography compelled it endlessly to remain, a crossroads of trade and travel between continents.... The benefits that the Negev enjoyed in this respect were a mixed blessing. The same routes which opened the cultivable areas of the Negev to civilized settlement in times of peace were also the ones invariably followed periodically by invading armies.... The Bible recounts a savage incursion in the time of Abraham which extended from Syria southward through the length of Transjordan and westward through the Negev to Sinai and back.

. . . Among the chief protagonists listed in Genesis 14 are Amraphel, Aryoch, Chedorlaomer and Tid'al, described as the Kings of the East. Under the leadership of Chedorlaomer, they spread havoc wherever they went. Mentioned too are Bera, Birsha, Shinab, Shemeber and one other whose name was not remembered. They ruled over the Dead Sea cities of Sodom, Gomorrah, Admah, Zeboyim and Zoar, and sought to shake off their servitude to Chedorlaomer and his confederates. A battle took place in the vale of Siddim which was "full of bitumen pits" (Genesis 14:10), when the might of the four was being pitted against the strength of the five, to the discomfiture of the latter. Many fell, others fled, and some were taken captive. "And they took Lot, Abram's brother's son, who dwelt in Sodom, and his goods, and they departed" (Genesis 14:12).

. . . "And when Abram heard that his brother was taken captive, he led forth his trained men, born in his house, three hundred and eighteen, and pursued as far as Dan. And he divided himself against them at night, he and his servants, and smote them and pursued them unto Hobah, which is on the left hand of Damascus. And he brought back his brother Lot and his goods and the women also and the people" (Genesis 14:14–16).

The rebellion of the small kings of the cities on the east side of the Dead Sea against what must have been the extortionate rule of absentee suzerains was brutally crushed. This comparatively minor insurrection was thereupon utilized as a pretext to settle old scores and to raid and ravage with unleashed ferocity for as much booty as could possibly be won. An old order was crumbling. From southern Syria to central Sinai, their fury raged. A punitive expedition developed into an orgy of annihilation. I found that every village in their path had been plundered and left in ruins, and the countryside laid waste. The population had been wiped out or led away into captivity. For hundreds of years thereafter, the entire area was like an abandoned cemetery, hideously unkempt, with all its monuments shattered and strewn in pieces on the ground.

The sorry tale is compressed in the Bible into a few bald sentences ... (Genesis 14: 1–7).

... The peaceful journeys of Abraham from Canaan to Egypt and back again ... emphasize the importance of the Negev ... as a land providing possibilities for settlement and that of Kadesh-barnea (Kadesh) as a well-known dwelling and camping place and as a junction of important roads and, furthermore, the connection of Abraham with them are neatly capsuled in Genesis 20: 1, which reads:

"Thereupon Abraham journeyed from thence (Zoar of the Cities of the Plain) to the land of the South (the Negev) and dwelt there between Kadesh and Shur (east of the Nahal Mizraim), and he sojourned at Gerar (Tell Abu Hureireh on the northern border of the Negev)." [3]

Dr. Glueck's conclusions have been supported further by the findings of Dr. William F. Albright of Johns Hopkins University. Dr. Albright, after excavating two sites at the southern tip of the Dead Sea, concluded that the cities of Sodom and Gomorrah, which the Bible mentions were destroyed in the days of Abraham (Gen. 19: 27–28), were abandoned around the same time Dr. Glueck believes the Jordan River Valley settlements had begun to decline. Dr. Albright also believes that the cities of Sodom and Gomorrah today lie buried beneath the shallow waters of the southern tip of the Dead Sea. Archaeological explorations have shown that the Jordan River Valley is a natural earthquake fault, with continuing disturbances not uncommon. In fact, the Biblical description of the destruction of these two cities is reminiscent of a catastrophe similar to an earthquake (Gen. 19: 24–28) and may explain why the Dead Sea shifted its course and covered over with its salty waters these ancient cities.[4]

While there are some scholars who disagree with Dr. Glueck's findings, contemporary thinking about the historicity of the patriarchs has been summarized in these words:

We shall never be able to prove that Abraham really existed, that he did this or that, but what we can prove is that his life and times, as reflected in the stories about him, fit perfectly within the early 2nd millenium, but imperfectly within any later period. This is one of the most important contributions which archaeology has made to Old Testament study during the last four decades.[5]

CHAPTER III

The Egyptian Sojourn

THE Nile River valley is the second great region in which modern civilization emerged. In Egypt, as in Mesopotamia, the rich agricultural lands of the river-valley and the natural fortifications of the terrain freed men to develop a method of government, without which no great civilization can exist.

The Egyptians, like the people of Mesopotamia, developed a system of writing called hieroglyphics. They invented paper from the papyrus reeds; pens from reed quills; and ink made of soot and oil or thin glue. Likewise, they developed different metals for tools and weapons; flax, linen, and wool for garments. They created beautiful jewelry, pottery, and musical instruments. They were also master builders, and constructed the pyramids, one of the seven wonders of the ancient world.

In the organization of government, the Egyptian state differed greatly from that of Mesopotamia. First of all, Pharaoh was a god. He was not a mortal who had been selected by divine election nor a human who had been deified. From his very birth he was the visible manifestation of a god among his people. During his lifetime, therefore, it was his responsibility to protect his people. After his death, he lived on in the world of gods and was succeeded by his son, who also was a god. Second, the word of Pharaoh was law. While no law code was ever developed in Egypt, Pharaoh's arbitrariness was mitigated by the fact that as god of his people he was obligated to uphold *ma'at* (justice). The Egyptians, moreover, looked upon this system with favor, because in the authority of their god-king they saw a means of maintaining the peace and security of the land. Finally, "though the lot of the peasant must have been unbelievably hard . . . no rigid barriers existed to prevent men of the humblest origin from rising to the highest positions, if fortune favored them." [1]

In religion, the people of the Nile River valley, like those of the Tigris-Euphrates, were polytheists, believing in the existence of many gods; however, unlike the Mesopotamians, they never developed an orderly pantheon or organization of gods. Many of the Egyptian gods were depicted in animal form, such as Horus the falcon and Apis the bull; at the same time, the animal never became the god but merely represented the form in which the mysterious divine power became known. While the prestige of the local gods might fluctuate with that of the cities where their cults were being practiced, the high gods of Egypt, like those of Mesopotamia, were honored all over the land and were recognized as the rulers of the entire world.

Less than a century before the period of history associated with Moses and the escape of the Hebrews from Egypt, a young pharaoh (1370–1353) declared Aton (the Sun Disk) to be the sole god and changed his own name from Amonhotep IV to Akhenaten or Akh-en-aton (the Splendor of Aton). While the Aton cult closely approximated monotheism, scholars are inclined to feel that Akhenaten's action was not motivated entirely by religious considerations, namely the abolishing of polytheism. Instead, they believe that a combination of factors may have motivated him. It is possible that economic reasons, as well as the growing power of the priests of Amon who ruled at Thebes and who were opposed to the Pharaoh, were behind the religious reformation. Akhenaten, however, failed in his attempt to eliminate polytheism. Immediately after his early death, possibly by assassination, the Aton cult was set aside, and the old religious forms were reinstituted with a vengeance. The new religion had been not only too difficult for the people to understand but also too unconcerned with the social problems of the masses of the people. What is significant for the story of the birth of the Torah, however, is the fact that tendencies in the direction of monotheism were not unknown in Egypt during the centuries when the Hebrews lived in Egypt.

According to tradition, the Hebrews came to Egypt during the time of Joseph, the son of Jacob. The Bible (Gen. 37–50) tells that Joseph was one of twelve sons and that his ten older brothers despised him because of his feelings of superiority. Consequently, they sold him into slavery and told their father that he had been killed by wild animals. They even splattered Joseph's coat of many colors with blood as evidence. Joseph, however, was brought to Egypt, where because of his ability to interpret dreams he became governor of Egypt, second only unto Pharaoh. Foreseeing a famine, he had large bins built to store the excess grain in years of plenty. Then followed seven years of famine which extended to lands as far away as Canaan. Only in Egypt was there food, and among those who came to Egypt to buy food were Joseph's brothers. In time, Joseph and his brothers were reconciled, and Jacob came with his family to live in the land of Goshen, on the borders of the Nile River.

The key to understanding the history of the Hebrews in Egypt, however, is found not in the Joseph story of the Book of Genesis, but in the passage of the Book of Exodus where it is written (1:8–11):

Now there arose a new king over Egypt, who knew not Joseph. And he said unto his people: "Behold, the Children of Israel are too many for us; come, let us deal wisely with them, lest they multiply, and it come to pass, that, when there befall us any war, they also join themselves unto our enemies, and fight against us, and get them up out of the land." Therefore, they did set over them taskmasters to afflict them with their burdens. And they built for Pharaoh store cities, Pithom and Raamses.

Two questions immediately come to mind. First, if Joseph were governor of Egypt, second only to Pharaoh, why did the new king not know about Joseph? Second, why, after being invited to live "in the best of the land" (Gen. 47:6), were the Hebrew people enslaved?

The Bible only hints at the answers to these questions. The answers themselves come from the discoveries of archaeology. Inscriptions and papyri tells us that in 1720/10 B.C.E., Egypt suffered one of her rare invasions from the outside. Internal strife in Egypt between the competing XIIIth and XIVth dynasties, each of which wanted to rule, so weakened the military strength that a group of people from Asia, using horses and chariots for the first time, easily overran the Nile River Valley and gradually established themselves as the rulers of Egypt. These people were called the Hyksos, a term which originally meant "foreign chiefs" or "chiefs of a foreign country"; however, later the Egyptians interpreted the name Hyksos to mean "Princes of the Desert," or "Shepherd Kings." Scholars believe that the early ancestors of the Jewish people came to Egypt during the Hyksos rule. Both were shepherd people, coming from the distant east and settling in the Nile River Delta area known as Goshen. It was during this same period, therefore, that Joseph presumably became governor of Egypt, second only unto Pharaoh, and that Jacob and his family descended into Egypt.

The Hyksos ruled Egypt for more than 150 years (1720/10–

1560/50). Then a revolt led by Egyptian nobility who had taken refuge in Southern Egypt expelled the Hyksos. Scholars tell us, however, that the Hyksos had carried out in their day a social revolution which was to have far-reaching effects long after their time. Before the Hyksos came to Egypt, the land was owned largely by powerful nobles. The Hyksos may have broken up these large estates. The scholars draw their evidence from two sources: (1) the story of Joseph's compulsory purchase of all the land for Pharaoh (Gen. 47:13ff.), and (2) the fact that under the XVIIIth dynasty, after the expulsion of the Hyksos, records show that the land was administered by a bureaucracy and, most significantly, that the peasants had become the serfs of Pharaoh. Although the scholars are not certain that this social revolution was the result of Hyksos policy, they are inclined in this direction because of archaeological evidence which describes how the Hyksos brought about an equally great social upheaval in Canaan.

The new social climate of Egypt provides us with a possible, and perhaps very plausible, explanation for the enslavement of the Hebrews. Although some of the Hebrews may have left Egypt with the defeated Hyksos, the great majority of them undoubtedly remained in Goshen where they continued their semi-nomadic way of life. During the next three centuries, under the XVIIIth and XIXth dynasties (1550–1224 B.C.E.), Egypt was to undergo a period of intense nationalism, marked internally by a series of oppressive policies. As the Pharaohs sought to expand their empire abroad and to undertake ambitious building projects at home, they had need for large and cheap sources of labor. The fact that the peasants now were regarded as the serfs of the Pharaoh instead of the nobility undoubtedly fitted in well with Pharaoh's plans. It is possible to assume further that the Pharaohs, once having had their appetites whetted by the availability of free peasant labor, were not content to limit their sources of manpower. Consequently, the Hebrews, who had enjoyed the right to settle and to conduct their business under the more liberal Hyksos policy, were gradually enslaved under the new oppressive Egyptian attitude. At first only small groups were put into forced labor. This number was supplemented, in time, by the addition of other Habiru groups captured by the Egyptians in Canaan. Finally, there arose with the XIXth dynasty a new Pharaoh "who knew not Joseph." Some scholars, however, while acknowledging Raamses II as the pharaoh of the Exodus, claim that the Pharaoh "who knew not Joseph" belonged to the XVIIIth dynasty, following the expulsion of the Hyksos. Raamses II wanted not only his capital city moved to the delta region of the Nile but also tombs and treasure cities built. In order to supply the necessary slaves Raamses II (1290–1224 B.C.E.), or perhaps his father before him, Seti I (1308–1290 B.C.E.), enslaved the entire group of Habiru. The total enslavement of the Hebrews continued for more than ten years until there arose a liberator by the name of Moses.

The sojourn of the Hebrews in Egypt may be traced by following the shift of the Egyptian capital city from north to south and back again with the rise and fall of the various dynasties: [2]

Period of favor: 1710–1550 B.C.E.	Hyksos Rule XV to XVII Dynasties	Capital at Avaris (North)
Period of disfavor: 1550–1308 B.C.E.	Egyptian Revival XVIII Dynasty	Capital moved to Thebes (South)
Period of the Exodus: Seti I (1308–1290 B.C.E.) Raamses II (1290–1224 B.C.E.) (Pharaoh of the Exodus)	Egyptian Revival XIX Dynasty	Capital at Avaris (North)

The precise identity of Moses and his family origins never may be known. In fact, there were those early modernists who would deny the historicity of Moses altogether. Contempo-

rary modern scholars, on the other hand, are inclined to acknowledge the reality of Moses. At the same time, they feel
that the Biblical narrative is more of a "biography of Israel
than a biography of Moses." [3] The present view can be summarized as follows: "Though we know nothing of his career
save what the Bible tells us, the details of which we have no
means of testing, there can be no doubt that he was, as the
Bible portrays him, the great founder of Israel's faith." [4]

The origin of the name Moses was Egyptian. The Bible tells
us, however, that the name Moses means "to draw out" (Exod.
2:10) and that the baby Moses was discovered floating in a
reed basket in the Nile River by the Egyptian princess. She
then "drew him out" of the water and named him Moses after
the Hebrew word *mashach* which means "to draw out."
Some scholars tell us, however, that the name Moses really
comes from an Egyptian verb, "to beget a child," and that even
the Pharaohs used this verb as a part of their names. For example, the name Raamses which belongs to the Pharaoh of the
Exodus means "the god Ra had a child." Raamses was the
child.

The biblical story associated with Moses' birth is legendary,
resembling in many ways the stories told about Sargon I of
Akkad and other ancient national heroes. It was customary for
people in early times to clothe real people, especially great
leaders, with fanciful legends of miraculous preservation. It is
also questionable whether Moses ever was descended from a
Levite family. Some scholars feel that this family lineage deliberately was assigned to him by later writers who wanted to
show that their own position and prestige were derived from
the ancient authority of none other than Moses. Regardless of
his origin, however, it is quite reasonable to assume that Moses
could have been educated as an Egyptian prince in an Egyptian environment. Archaeological evidence indicates that many
people besides the royal family lived in the palace. Hostages

from conquered countries as well as those whom Pharaoh chose to favor frequently were given Egyptian educations.

Contemporary scholarship is divided in its opinion concerning the reasons or even the motivations for Moses' connection with the Hebrews. One school of thought contends that Moses was inspired by the religious revolution of Akhenaten. According to this theory, if the Exodus took pace under Raamses II, around 1290 B.C.E., and "if we are to credit the biblical account that Moses was then already an old man, then his youth practically coincided with the Akhenaten reformation." [5] This theory further suggests, however, that Moses went far beyond Akhenaten when he recognized that the concerns of religion and the welfare of men were inseparable. For example, Akhenaten was not motivated by any desire to elevate the moral tone of the life of his people or to improve the wretched economic conditions of the dreadfully exploited Egyptian masses. Moses, on the other hand, recognizing the close kinship between ethics and monotheism, was drawn to the enslaved by human compassion.

The point of view most popular with scholars is the Kenite hypothesis. According to this theory, Moses, when he led the enslaved Hebrews out of Egypt, directed them to the Sinai desert wilderness region. This was a logical step for him to take because previously when he had killed the Egyptian and had fled from Egypt, he had gone to the desert wilderness regions associated with Mount Sinai. Here he met a group of people known as the Kenites. They were semi-nomadic smiths in the employ of the Egyptian government. They worked the copper mines to be found in the areas of Sinai and further to the east in the southern part of Canaan and Midian. Likewise, they had commercial contacts with Palestine and had borrowed the alphabet developed by the Canaanites. The Kenites also worshiped a god whom they called Yahweh and whose home was on the top of a mountain, believed to have been

Mount Sinai. The Kenites in the time of Moses were both more worldly and prosperous than the poor and ill-fed people living today in the Sinai peninsula.

It was here among the Kenites that Moses also had learned about the God Yahweh. It was this same God Yahweh who subsequently "appeared" to Moses, while he was pasturing his sheep in the Sinai region and who had inspired him to return to Egypt. Some scholars, however, believe that the God Yahweh had been known already to Moses through his mother, who may have been related to the Kenites. In either instance, what is of importance, according to the Kenite hypothesis, is Moses' belief that, if the former slaves were to be transformed into a free people, they had to enter into a covenant with this very same God Yahweh. Thus, it was inevitable that at the time of the exodus he should lead them to the very mountain region with which the God Yahweh was associated.

A third contemporary view is expressed by the Israeli scholar Yehezkel Kaufmann:

Did Moses know the speculations of the priests of Babylon and Egypt, or of the "solar monotheism" of Akhenaton? Was he an Egyptian? These matters are neither here nor there. Moses is the historical person who first envisioned the peculiar ideas of Israelite religion. His racial stock is of no consequence, the only significant fact being that his new idea was neither Egyptian nor Babylonian. His thought cannot be related to any "monotheistic tendencies" in Egypt or Babylon without distorting it. Those tendencies did indeed aspire to a sort of monism, but it is not a question of number that distinguishes the Israelite idea of God. Belief in "one Marduk" or "one Re" or "one Aton" is, for all that, no less pagan. It is not an arithmetical diminution of the number of gods, but a new religious category that is involved, the category of a God above nature, whose will is supreme, who is not subject to compulsion and fate, who is free of the bonds of myth and magic. This idea, which informs all of biblical creativity, is what paganism never knew. As Moses must be considered the initiator of a religious revolution, so he must be considered the creator of an original idea.

Why and how this idea arose in his mind we do not know. We should not know even if we possessed more than those remarkable legends relating the revelation made to Moses. It is possible, however, to delineate the social and historical background of that revelation.

The prophetic type of Moses belongs to the earliest stage of Israelite prophecy. Moses is an antique model of an apostolic prophet; he is a leader and judge having political authority ... he makes his appearance in time of trouble ... he "judges" Israel all his life ... he fights idolatry and personally works judgments on idols and their worshipers.

But there are also peculiar features about Moses. He is accompanied by two other prophetic figures, his brother Aaron (his "mouth" and "prophet" to Pharaoh), and his sister Miriam, a prophetess and poetess. ... Such a family of prophetic personages is never again found in Israel. But pagan prophecy—and this is particularly true of Arab kāhins (priests)—often manifested itself as the property of a family of seers.

Like the kāhins, Moses is not connected with an established temple or cult. Whether Moses was ever himself a kāhin or not, he seems to have grown up among a family of such seers, and this surely affected him. The ancient Hebrew kāhin-clairvoyant was the social type that served as the vehicle of his appearance as prophet and leader ... the new message of Moses clothed itself in a form familiar to the people of those times. That a divine spirit revealed itself to a lonely seer was not an incredible thing; that this man should become leader of his people was also not unheard of. And, since the ancient Hebrew seer was not bound by a specific cult or temple, Moses enjoyed the freedom necessary for the expression of a new idea. To this seer, however, there appeared not a familiar spirit but a supernal, omnipotent God. Moses returned to his people not a clairvoyant, but a messenger of God. ... He did not learn a priestly doctrine in Egypt, Midian, or elsewhere; he did not arrive at his insights through meditation, nor did he seek to communicate to a circle of disciples a new theological truth that had dawned upon him. He was sent; his God revealed himself to him and let him hear his voice. Intuitive insight took the shape of a prophetic vision. The legend of the burning bush is the necessary prelude to Moses' appearance as a messenger of God.[6]

Despite the plausibility of any one or all of these three modern theories, it is more probable that both the direct motivation and the exact sequence of events which led up to the exodus of the Hebrews may never be known. That Moses did emerge as the leader of the Hebrews and that there was an exodus of Hebrews from Egypt represent the only conclusions which can be ascertained with any degree of reasonable certainty.

A number of issues, in connection with the Exodus, still deserve our attention. They are: (1) the timing of the Exodus; (2) the ten plagues; (3) the crossing of the Red Sea; and (4) the location of Mount Sinai.

(1) *The timing of the Exodus*

Generally, when we think of slaves, we have a picture of an individual who is sold to a master. This definition of a slave is correct, but it does not include the type of slavery in which the Hebrews found themselves. The Hebrews were not personal slaves. Following the expulsion of the Hyksos, as scholars have pointed out, the government headed by the pharaoh replaced the nobility as the primary owner of slaves. The Hebrews, as a result, became in the course of time government slaves who, as a group, carried out the orders of Pharaoh. Consequently, they were permitted to live with their families in their own homes. They owned sheep and cattle which they were allowed to pasture on the shores of the lake areas surrounding the cities in which they lived.

In the springtime of the year, shepherd peoples generally

offered the sacrifice of a lamb. Apparently, it was the practice even in Egypt for the Hebrews to gather as a group and to conduct this ceremony in an outlying area three days' journey from the many different cities in which they worked. It is probable that Moses seized on one of these occasions as the time for the escape from Egypt. He undoubtedly knew that it was also Pharaoh's custom to send his slaves into the outlying areas in the springtime to assist with the planting of the wheat crop and to help with the calving and lambing of his herds and flocks. Likewise, Moses may have been aware of the fact that a series of calamities in recent years had befallen the Egyptians. All of these circumstances may have been interpreted by Moses as signs that the time was at hand for the exodus.

(2) *The Ten Plagues*

The calamities which Moses interpreted as signs for the escape of the Hebrews are known as the Ten Plagues. Various explanations of these events have been offered by modern scholars. Early modernists, for example, emphasized that there are three different accounts of the plagues, with no one version containing all ten catastrophes. Moreover, with each successive explanation having been composed as much as four, five, and eight centuries, respectively, after the actual events described, the early modernists felt that the later versions tended to emphasize, and also to magnify, the miraculous aspects. On the other hand, some contemporary modernist scholars, noting that catastrophes similar to the plagues still occur to this day in Egypt, have suggested that the plagues were real, having been connected to each other, like a chain reaction, with the first calamity bringing on the second, etc. (The discoloration of the Nile was due to the presence of tiny organisms; the waters became foul and brought on a plague of frogs, which, in turn, resulted in the presence of lice and flies, affecting the cattle, etc.) [7]

The consensus of modern scholarship, however, holds that attempts to explain the plagues, whether through literary analysis or through comparison with known natural phenomena is "intriguing but ill-advised. The minimum that must be said is this: natural disasters struck Egypt, disasters in which Moses and the people saw the power of Yahweh and which finally gave them occasion to flee from Pharaoh." [8]

(3) *The crossing of the Red Sea*

Modern scholars also have tried to explain the crossing of the Red Sea on the basis of literary analysis and of natural phenomena. As in the case of the plagues, early modernists recognized three separate sources for the crossing. The first, and also the earliest, account attributed the turning back of the waters to an east wind; however, in the third and latest version, Moses used his rod to part the waters so that the Hebrews could cross through the sea on dry land. While the natural explanation of the earlier account has continued to intrigue Bible students to this day, at the same time, certain logical difficulties continue to remain. For example, if a storm accompanied by a tidal wave is advanced to account for the crossing, how can one account for the fact that the Hebrews crossed over in the face of such a wind? Is it necessary to assume, moreover, that all the Egyptians drowned just because the wheels of their chariots became stuck in the mud? Could not Pharaoh's soldiers have escaped before the storm subsided and the waters rushed back to their normal levels? Therefore, while modern scholars still would like to know precisely what did happen, many acknowledge that the answer never may be known. Of three things they are convinced, however: (1) Most important of all is the fact that for those Hebrews who did live through the experience, the whole episode left an indelible impression. (2) The Hebrews did not cross the Red Sea which lies at the tip of the Sinai Peninsula where the Gulf of Suez and the Gulf of Aquabah come together. The Bible uses the term "Yam Suf" which literally means "a sea of reeds." When the Bible was translated into Greek in the second century B.C.E., the term "Yam Suf" was identified with the Red Sea. The Yam Suf was probably one of the lakes on the border between Goshen and the Sinai Peninsula where the shepherd people of Egypt often pastured their flocks. Some scholars try to identify the Yam Suf with Lake Timsah, which was incorporated into the Suez Canal. The exact location of the Exodus, however, in the eyes of contemporary scholars, is not a matter of great importance. (3) The number of Hebrews who escaped from Egypt could not have been "six hundred thousand men on foot, besides children. And a mixed multitude went up also with them; and flocks and herds, even very much cattle" (Exod. 12:37–38). First of all, Egyptian records are completely silent about the Exodus. From this fact, scholars conclude that while the exodus was a big event for the Hebrews, it could have been no more than a minor incident in Egyptian history. Second, neither the land of Goshen in northeastern Egypt nor the Sinai peninsula could have supported such a population. Finally, corroborating evidence is brought both from the Bible (Judges 5) and from archaeology. A series of letters discovered in the City of Amarna in Egypt describes how a group of Habiru invaded Canaan more than a hundred years prior to the Exodus. Contemporary scholars, therefore, have concluded that it is no longer necessary to believe that all the Habiru groups underwent the Egyptian experience. Some of the Habiru wandered directly into Canaan where they became identified later with the Hebrews of the Exodus.

(4) *The location of Mount Sinai*

Many different theories have been advanced about the exact location of Mount Sinai. Some scholars prefer to place the mountain in the southern tip of the Sinai peninsula, at a site which in Arabic is called Jebel Musa ("Mountain of Moses"). From the fifth century c.e. on, there has been an unbroken tradition that Jebel Musa is the Sinai of the Bible. Today, the Monastery of St. Catherine is located on top of the mountain. In 1956, when the Israeli army entered the Sinai peninsula, a team of archaeologists was told by the monks that, according to their tradition, the monastery had been built on the historic site of the giving of the commandments. Other scholars, influenced by the possible biblical allusion to volcanic eruptions, prefer a location east of the Gulf of Aquabah in Midian (the northwest corner of present-day Saudi Arabia). There is no agreement of opinion, however, that Sinai was necessarily an active volcano. The description in Exodus 19 could have been that of a violent mountain storm. Some scholars feel that the references to lightning and thunder and the quaking of the mountain may be similar to those found in other early religions whenever gods appeared, came to visit their people, or performed some act on a mountain.

A third group of scholars maintains that Mount Sinai was located about 140 miles due east of Goshen, 50 miles southwest of present-day Beersheba in Israel and about 80 miles northwest of ancient Midian. This area is known as the southern Arabah, or the broken highlands of Israel's southern or Negev region, and contains a number of water springs which could have supported several thousand people over a long period of time. It is also closer to Kadesh, where the Hebrews spent most of their sojourn in the desert-wilderness.

While scholars are inclined toward one or the other of these theories, the consensus of contemporary scholarship indicates "we must admit that we do not know. Nor is the problem of crucial importance for the history of Israel. . . . Though the location of Sinai is uncertain, it is as certain as anything can be that it was there that Israel received that law and covenant which made her a people." [9]

CHAPTER **IV**

The Covenant at Sinai

FOR MOST people the drama of Sinai is found in the supernatural revelation of the Commandments. The story of what actually may have happened at Mount Sinai, however, is found in a small but frequently overlooked passage in Exodus 24. This passage tells us that once the people had assembled at Mount Sinai Moses built an altar at the foot of the mountain. He also set up twelve pillars, supposedly to represent the people according to the twelve tribes. He then sacrificed animals, dashing half the blood against the altar. This act was a symbol of Yahweh's participation in the ritual. The other half of the blood he had poured into basins while he read to the people "the book of the covenant." As soon as the people pledged themselves to accept and obey Yahweh's demands, Moses took the basins of blood and sprinkled the blood upon the people. Then the leaders of the people went to the top of Mount Sinai where they ate together. Thus was the covenant between Yahweh and the people sealed (Exod. 24:1–11).

Modernists and traditionalists alike today agree that "the book of the covenant" consisted in a set of commandments and other laws now found in the Torah. They also agree that the purpose of these laws was to unite the nonorganized former slaves into a people. The traditionalists, however, assume that these laws were revealed supernaturally by God at Mount Sinai. The modernists, on the other hand, believe that the commands and laws were created by men over a period of time.

Among the modernists there are two different theories concerning the origin of the Ten Commandments. In order to present the first view, developed by Dr. Julian Morgenstern, President Emeritus of the Hebrew Union College-Jewish Institute of Religion, it is necessary for us to look many years ahead into Jewish history. Dr. Morgenstern believes that there is not one but five sets of Ten Commandments in the Torah.[1] Each of these sets of commandments represents for him, moreover, a constitution connected with a religious revolution. The Torah, he believes, does not preserve the Ten Commandments developed by Moses, which served as a constitution for the Hebrews in their desert wanderings. In fact, he feels that we may never know what the original set of commandments stated. All that remains is the tradition that at Mount Sinai a series of commandments was produced by Moses. Later generations, he believes, developed this tradition and authored different sets of commandments. Our present version, found both in Exodus 20 and in Deuteronomy 5, is a product of a religious revolution which took place nearly six hundred years after the time of Moses.

In the year 621 B.C.E., Dr. Morgenstern tells us, a young man by the name of Josiah sat upon the throne of the southern Kingdom of Judah. As a child, Josiah had been trained by the priests who had opposed the religious leanings of his father. Josiah's father had introduced many foreign religious practices into the country. Therefore, when Josiah came to the throne, the priests found the opportunity ripe to restore what they believed to be the pure worship of Yahweh. One day they let it be known that a newly discovered set of ancient writings, containing the laws of Moses and including the Ten

Commandments, had been discovered in the Temple. As soon as Josiah learned of this important discovery which explained the true worship of Yahweh, he ordered that the laws of the newly purified worship of Yahweh be observed throughout the land.

Dr. Morgenstern, who can be called an early modernist, believes that the so-called ancient writings did not come from Moses. He feels that these writings were the product of the priests themselves and that the Ten Commandments were their own version of the old Mosaic tradition needed to carry out their religious revolution. While the priests may have used some older materials, the newly discovered book was really a new book, the beginning of our present book of Deuteronomy. Thus, the religious revolution during the reign of King Josiah produced the version of the Ten Commandments found in Deuteronomy 5. A hundred years or so later, another change took place in ancient Jewish life, and the Ten Commandments took the form which is found in Exodus 20.

In keeping with the approach used by Dr. Morgenstern, many early modernist scholars feel that our present version of the Ten Commandments could not have come into existence before the time of the prophets who lived in the eighth and seventh centuries B.C.E. The prophets had a twofold message: (1) to urge the people to abandon their worship of foreign gods and to be faithful to the worship of the one God Yahweh; and (2) to emphasize to the people that the one God Yahweh wanted deeds of kindness and justice as well as animal sacrifices. These scholars feel that the Ten Commandments reflect these teachings of the prophets.

The seventh and eighth century B.C.E. prophets were interested primarily in social justice. In addition to challenging the people to be faithful to Yahweh, the God who had established a covenant with their ancestors, they reproved their generations for failing to carry out the terms of the covenant. From Amos, the first of the literary prophets, through Jeremiah, whose ministry extended through the fall of Jerusalem in 586 B.C.E., the seventh and eighth century prophets were concerned with man's treatment of his fellowman. Justice in all human relationships became their battle cry as they condemned injustice wherever they found it. The wealthy who trampled on the heads of the poor and the defenseless did not escape their wrath. Nor did the prophets overlook the leaders, as king, politician, and priest alike reveled in luxury and indulged in corruption. Even the people felt the fury of their anger because they, too, had succumbed to greed and selfishness. For example, Jeremiah, greatly disturbed by the worship of idols among the people and also by their lack of righteousness, spoke to them and said: "Will you steal, murder, commit adultery, swear falsely, burn incense to Baal [a god of the Canaanites], and go after other gods that you have not known, and then come and stand before me in this house which is called by my name and say: 'We are delivered' [i.e., we are safe because we have brought the sacrifices which God wants]" (Jer. 7:9–10).

It is immediately apparent that there is a striking similarity between this quotation from Jeremiah, whose period of prophecy covered the reign of King Josiah, and the set of Ten Commandments discovered during Josiah's rule. The following chart will illustrate further the similarities between the twofold message of the prophets and the Ten Commandments.

MESSAGE OF THE PROPHETS

1. The Jewish People should abandon their worship of foreign gods and should worship the One God.

2. The One God wanted deeds of kindness and justice as well as animal sacrifices.

TEN COMMANDMENTS

1. I am the Lord your God.
2. You shall have no other gods before me.
3. You shall not take the name of the Lord your God in vain.

4. Observe the Sabbath day to keep it holy.*

5. Honor your father and your mother.

6. You shall not murder.

7. You shall not commit adultery.

8. You shall not steal.

9. You shall not bear false witness.

10. You shall not covet.

Thus, many early modernist scholars concluded that our present version of the Ten Commandments could not have been written before the ethical ideas which they describe had been developed by the prophets who lived in the eighth and seventh centuries B.C.E. Once the prophets had spoken, however, it was quite natural, they add, for the Ten Commandments to have appeared shortly thereafter.

In recent years, because of new archaeological findings, some modernists, while still rejecting the supernatural view of the traditionalists, have claimed that the present set of Ten Commandments *do* go back to the time of Moses. These contemporary modernists cannot accept the views of Dr. Morgenstern and of other early modernists. They feel that many of the great ethical teachings were available to Moses and that the prophets many years later only emphasized and clarified

* The Deuteronomic version of the Ten Commandments attributes the observance of the Sabbath to a social reason, namely, the freeing of the Hebrews from slavery in Egypt. The implication is clear that only a slave works seven days a week.

the original teachings of the Ten Commandments. In the days of Moses, the Ten Commandments may very well have read: [2]

1. You shall have no other gods before me.
2. You shall not make unto you a graven image or any likeness.
3. You shall not take the name of Yahweh your God in vain.
4. Remember the Sabbath Day to keep it holy.
5. Honor your father and your mother.
6. You shall not murder.
7. You shall not commit adultery.
8. You shall not steal.
9. You shall not bear false witness against your neighbor.
10. You shall not covet your neighbor's house.

Among the documents which have been unearthed by archaeologists are copies of international treaties made in Western Asia during the period between Abraham and Moses. These treaties tell of the relationship between a king and his subjects. A careful study will show, claim these scholars, that Moses, by borrowing the form of these international treaties, developed the framework for the Ten Commandments and the covenant between Yahweh and the former slaves.

The following chart will illustrate the point: [3]

CHARACTERISTICS OF THE FRAMEWORK	TREATY	COMMANDMENTS
1. The giver of the treaty is identified:	"Thus says..., the Great King..."	"I am Yahweh, Your God..."
2. History of the relationship between the King and his subjects:	The treaties indicate that the subjects should be grateful to the King because of the good things which he has done for them.	In chapters preceding the commandments in Exodus and in Deuteronomy, Yahweh brings the people out of Egyptian slavery and is taking them to a promised land.
3. Terms of the treaty:	Among the terms is the requirement that the subject make no treaty with any other King.	"You shall have no other gods before Me."

CHARACTERISTICS OF THE FRAMEWORK	TREATY	COMMANDMENTS
4. What to do with the copies of the treaty:	The treaties should be deposited in the sanctuary of the subject and then should be read in public at different times. The exact times, however, were not specified.	The Torah tells how the commandments at Sinai were put into the Ark which was made for this purpose and which was kept in the Tent of Meeting. (Exod. 25:16,21)
5. Witnesses to the treaty:	The gods of both the King and his subjects are witnesses. There is also a summarizing sentence of all the gods who are the witnesses to the treaty.	Since there is only one God, the people themselves are the witnesses. (Josh. 24)
6. How the treaty is enforced:	Each treaty ends with a series of blessings and curses for those who keep or break the treaty.	While there are no such blessings and curses connected with the commandments, other groups of laws in the Torah do have them. (Book of Covenant— Exod. 21–23:19 Holiness Code—Lev. 26. Deuteronomic Law— Deut. 27–28 cf. Josh. 8:34)
7. How often are the treaties renewed:	A treaty is good only while both parties are alive. When one dies, the treaty must be remade.	Many times the covenant with Yahweh is renewed. For example, Moses tells the people that while the original agreement with Yahweh was made at Sinai (Horeb) by the fathers, the agreement now needs to be renewed with "all of us alive here this day." (Deut. 5:2–3)

In addition to shedding light upon the Ten Commandments, the discovery of the international treaties also revealed much information about the two kinds of covenants which were in existence in ancient times: (1) a parity covenant in which both parties bound themselves together as equals; and (2) a

suzerainty covenant in which one party was the giver of the
covenant and the other party was bound to obey the commands of the giver or the suzerain. This latter type of covenant was used very often among the Hittite peoples when their
kings made treaties or covenants with their vassals.

To his vassal, the suzerain "gives" a covenant, and within the
covenant the vassal finds protection and security. As the inferior
party, the vassal is under obligation to obey the commands issued
by the suzerain, for the suzerain's words are spoken with the
majesty and authority of the covenant author. To make a covenant in no way infringes upon the sovereignty of the great king.
And yet the covenant is not just an assertion of his power over his
inferior, as though the vassal were forced into obedience. The
most striking aspect of the suzerainty covenant is the great attention given to the king's deeds of benevolence on behalf of the
vassal. The vassal's motive for obligation is that of gratitude for
what has been done for him. Appropriately, the covenant is
couched in the dialogue form, "I and thou." Legal demands are
preceded by a preamble in the style, "thus saith the great king,"
and by a historical prologue that recounts the king's deeds of
benevolence.[4]

The nature of the suzerainty treaty probably was known
to Moses. In adopting it, however, he introduced two distinctive elements into the relationship between the freed-slaves and
their God Yahweh. Moses' first unique contribution was to
establish the covenant not with an individual nor even an entire
family but with a whole people. No other people of ancient
times, as far as anyone knows, tried to explain its life as a group
so completely in terms of an agreement with a one God as did
the former slaves of Egypt while they were at Sinai. Not even
the covenants which the Patriarchs had made with their one
God were so all-embracing. Abraham, Isaac, and Jacob made
their agreements between themselves as individuals or as members of a family and their respective one Gods. For Moses,

however, the covenant bound together an entire people and the one God Yahweh. This achievement was unique indeed and formed the basis upon which the religious life of ancient Israel developed. Through the covenant, various Hebrew slaves and their families became Israelites.

The Sinaitic covenant was a relationship that imposed upon the people certain requirements. Yahweh, on the other hand, was a sovereign king and was, therefore, not legally bound. Since he had entered willingly into the relationship for the welfare of the former slaves, Yahweh could bring the relationship to an end whenever He chose.

There was also a second unique feature of the covenant established by Moses. Whereas the Sinaitic covenant was based upon an already accomplished act of grace and issued in stringent stipulations, the patriarchal covenant rested only on the divine promise and demanded of his worshiper only his trust. For example, in the agreements established with the patriarchs (Gen. 15 and 17) it was Yahweh, not Abraham, who made certain promises which He would carry out in the future (that Abraham's descendants would inherit the land of Canaan). No obligations whatsoever were placed upon Abraham. Even the act of circumcision was merely to be a sign, and not an obligation as it later became, of the covenant. The circumcision served to indicate that a covenant existed. In a way it was Abraham's guarantee, or better perhaps, his proof that Yahweh had made a covenant with him. The covenant of Moses, on the other hand, was almost the exact opposite. It "imposes specific obligations upon the tribes or clans without binding Yahweh to specific obligations, though it goes without saying that the covenant relationship itself presupposes the protection and support of Yahweh to Israel." [5]

Yehezkel Kaufmann sees in the manner in which Moses established the covenant the third distinctive element of the Sinai experience:

The distinctively new element in the laws of the Sinaitic covenant was not their content. The cultures which the Israelite tribes had absorbed and out of which they had emerged had highly developed notions of law and morality.... The Bible itself recognizes the existence of a universal moral law from primeval times, to which all men are subject.... The Sinaitic covenant comes late in the history of man, even according to the biblical story. What point was there to YHWH's giving such ancient and elementary commands to Israel in an awful theophany at Sinai?

The novelty was in the very giving. For the first time morality was represented as a prophetic revelation, an expression of the supreme moral will of God. It was not the doctrine of sages, or the command of rulers, nor even the wisdom of a god who revealed laws along with other matters of art and science.... This law was the command of a God, his absolute will. The idea was expressed in an unparalleled legend: God revealed himself not to a visionary, a priest, or a sage, but to a whole people. Men heard the command from the mouth of God. Morality was thus transfered from the realm of wisdom to the realm of prophecy, the realm of the absolute divine command.

All the laws of the Torah are given to the nation, and the nation as a whole is answerable for their violation. This does not reflect a primitive moral sense, as yet bound to the conception of the collectivity of the tribe or the people. The cultural environment of Israel had long since passed the stage of collective morality. Babylonian, and especially Egyptian, wisdom deal constantly with the individual; this is the level of biblical wisdom as well. It is more ancient than the morality of Torah and prophets. The Sinaitic covenant superimposes upon the ancient individual obligation a new, national one. Morality ceases being a private matter. Because the covenant was accepted en masse, by all, all become responsible for its observance. When the Israelites stood together and heard the command "I am YHWH your God," a new moral subject was created; the community of persons that know YHWH. The religious-cultic distinction of Israel is complemented by a moral distinction. Both are equal in rank, according to the conception of the Torah, and fundamentally connected. YHWH did not elect

Israel to found a new magical cult for his benefit; he elected it to be his people, to realize in it his will. The religious covenant was, therefore, by its nature a moral-legal one as well, involving not only the cult but the structure and rules of society. Thus the foundation for the religion of the Torah was laid, including both cult and morality and conceiving both as expressions of the divine will.[6]

CHAPTER V

Entrance into Canaan

I T MUST not be assumed that the experience at Mount Sinai solved all of the problems which faced Moses. There was need for food and water. There was danger from enemies, both from within and from without. There was also the need to translate the covenant-idea into everyday experience.

After the covenant had been established, Moses and the people continued their wanderings. The Bible tells us that they were in the desert forty years. We now know, however, that forty was a round number used by many ancient people to refer either to "a generation" or to "a long period of time." Moreover, archaeological evidence has shown that during the thirteenth and fourteenth centuries the Sinai peninsula as well as the Negev as a whole were ignored and "uninhabited by strong, civilized, permanently settled populations, possessed of fortified towns and deeply rooted in the land." [1] The evidence of a "power vacuum" explains why Moses and the people were able to remain unmolested for a long period of time in this region in a semi-permanent settlement. Their headquarters area was Kadesh Barnea, a desert oasis. Here they not only provided as well as they could for their needs but also began to forge the unity which enabled them later to enter the land of Canaan. Gradually, family units became stronger, and in time many of the families began to merge with each other to form clans. Thus, the nucleus of the twelve tribes which were to form later the structure of government in Canaan began to appear.

The desert wanderings were not without their difficulties for Moses, however. For example, some of the people, when they realized the many dangers and difficulties still before them, began to yearn again for the "fleshpots of Egypt." Compared with the frugal desert-wilderness conditions, the hardships of their days in slavery seemed less burdensome. Many people, consequently, began to protest and to look for leaders who would lead a rebellion against Moses. They found such persons in Aaron and Miriam, the very brother and sister of Moses (Num. 12), and in Korah, Dathan, and Abiram (Num. 16). In fact, on one occasion, a group chose new leaders and tried unsuccessfully to invade the land of Canaan (Num. 13–14). In each instance, Moses was able to overcome the revolts and murmurings and to reassert his leadership.

One of the main sources for the continuing dissatisfaction was the shortage of food and water. The Bible tells us that Yahweh would come to the rescue of Moses in these instances by providing food miraculously, so to speak, in the form of manna and quail (Num. 11 and 16). Also, the Bible story relates how Moses was commanded to speak to the rock so that it might give water (Exod. 17 and Num. 20). Recent investigation has shed much light upon these two Bible episodes. Students of desert life have discovered certain insects which suck sap from desert plants, producing a sweet sticky substance. To this day, the natives of the desert call the sap "mun" and eat it as relish on their bread. Also, they have reported that in the fall of the year, large flocks of quail migrate regularly over the Sinai area, flying from Europe to winter in Arabia and Africa. These birds are exhausted from their long flights, and, as a result, are caught very easily when they stop at the Sinai peninsula to rest.

Again, it has been reported that the limestone formations found in certain parts of the Sinai area have been known to yield water. Once a British Camel Corps, which was policing the region, reported that it was digging for water in the rocky sides of a valley where a slow trickle was coming through the limestone rock. One of the men accidentally hit the rock with a heavy blow. The hard rock crumbled, and a great gush of clear water came from the soft rock which was underneath. It is possible that Moses, having lived for a considerable period of time in this same region, was familiar with this fact (Num. 21:1-13).

Gradually, as new family bonds were being forged and as the old generation which had lived in Egypt began to die out, the position of Moses became firmly established. The new generation, trained under the leadership of Moses, began to look with respect to the Ark of the Covenant, a wooden chest which was supposed to contain the two tablets of the Sinaitic Commandments. This Ark was kept in a Tent of Meeting, the second object which was sacred to Moses and his followers. The Tent was like a shrine which Moses entered so that he might be with Yahweh. Here, in the presence of his God, Moses would develop the laws of Sinai, it is believed, to meet the requirements of the new life which he and the children of the former slaves were entering. The Ark of the Covenant and the Tent of Meeting, borrowed originally from the Kenites, now became the unifying symbols of the covenant between Yahweh and the Israelites.

During their wanderings in the desert and their stay in Kadesh Barnea, many other roving tribes joined themselves to the followers of Moses. Soon it became apparent that the broader pasture lands, lying to the north in the fertile regions of Canaan, were needed for the enlarged herds. The time was at hand at last for Moses to plan the entrance into Canaan. As he weighed the different possibilities, Moses realized from the report of his spies that the direct route northward was guarded by strong Canaanite fortresses; moreover, failure of the rebel group successfully to invade Canaan through the south convinced him that a less direct route was necessary. The path, therefore, had to lead through the land of Jordan which lay to the east.

It is difficult to trace all the wanderings of the Israelites while in the desert-wilderness. The biblical accounts are quite confusing, and many scholars feel that the present Bible account represents the wanderings of many groups which have been combined into one tradition. At the same time archaeology does make it clear that the Israelites were donkey-using people. The camel, we now know, was not to be domesticated for several centuries. As a result, the Israelites could not travel far from the oases or the pasture lands of the Negev and Jordan. This evidence may account for the fact that Moses chose to follow the well-traveled trade route through the four kingdoms of Jordan, turning not "aside to the right hand nor to the left" (Num. 20:17), in his attempt to enter the land of Canaan from the east. While many biblical place names still remain unidentified, archaeological findings do tend to support the route outlined in Numbers 33. Diggings also have shown that in the thirteenth century B.C.E., Moab and Edom were ringed by a line of fortresses, which may explain why Moses led the people around these countries to the more vulnerable lands of Ammon and Bashan (Num. 21).

At one time, it was thought that the land of Canaan was inhabited by a group of people whose culture was rather primitive. Since the discovery of the Rash Shamra tablets in 1929, however, a new picture of the Canaanites has been drawn by archaeologists. The Canaanites had, indeed, a highly developed form of civilization which flourished under the protection of the Egyptian empire. In fact, one scholar has stated that the life of the Israelites "was crude in comparison to the highly sophisticated culture of Canaan." [2] For example, the Canaanite city of Beth-Shan has been excavated. The findings revealed a considerable degree of wealth. The houses were well built, and their contents indicated that an active trade was carried on with Syria and Cyprus. Occasionally, objects of art even from Egypt were found. In contrast, excavations from the Israelite towns established in the hill country during the period of 1200–1000 B.C.E. indicated the presence of poverty everywhere. House walls were crude and ill-planned. Art was exceedingly primitive, and there was no evidence of trade with foreign peoples other than with immediate neighbors. Even the fortifications were poorly built.

Canaanite civilization attained its greatest achievements between the thirteenth and seventeenth centuries B.C.E. From the excavations at Rash Shamra we know that in addition to inventing for business purposes two original alphabets that used consonants instead of pictures, the Canaanites possessed an extensive literature. For example, three mythological epics, as well as parts of other myths, rituals, and hymns have been discovered by the archaeologists. In their language and style many of these Canaanite literary finds showed striking similarities to Hebrew poetry, especially to such early poems as the Song of Miriam (Exod. 15), the Song of Deborah (Judges 5), the Blessings of Moses (Deut. 33), and the Twenty-ninth and Sixty-eighth Psalms.

The Canaanite influence also is found in later Hebrew passages which date in their present form from the period 650–350 B.C.E. (especially in Ezekiel, Habakkuk, the parts of the

Book of Isaiah written during the Babylonian Exile, Job, and
Song of Songs). It can be proved also that substantial parts of
Proverbs, for example, were direct borrowings from the
Canaanite literature.

Dr. Albright, the noted American archaeologist, writes that
"there can be no doubt whatever that Hebrew poetic literature was under immeasurable obligation to Canaanite poets . . .
who fashioned the vehicle and cultivated the style which have
given Biblical verse most of its formal appeal. . . . Through the
Bible the entire civilized world has fallen heir to Phoenician
(Canaanite) literary art." [3]

Canaanite civilization also was distinguished by its highly
formalized religion, which consisted of a pantheon or organization of gods. At the head of all the gods stood the king or
the father-god, El, and his wife, Asherah. He was, however, a
leader in name only, for the chief active deity was the great
storm-god, Baal, who ruled from a high mountain in the north
and who was regarded as the lord of all the gods and the creator of mankind. In order to carry out their highly organized
religious life, the Canaanites built many temples. They also
used sacred trees and special hills as places for their altars. To
assist the people, there was also an organized priesthood.

While the Canaanites looked upon their gods as universal
gods, the Canaanite religion, on the other hand, represented
"an extraordinarily debasing form of paganism, specifically of
the fertility cult." [4] Fundamental to their religion was the
myth of Baal, whose death and resurrection symbolized for
them the death and rebirth of the annual nature cycle. (A
fuller description of the Baal myth will be found in Chapter
12.) The Canaanites, therefore, developed a series of elaborate
rituals, many of which can be described as imitative magic, because they believed that by acting in a certain way they could
influence the gods to do the same. For example, in order to

induce the gods to bring rain, they would call out a "rain-maker," who would climb a tree and pour water upon the ground. For the same reason sacred prostitutes, both male and female, were maintained in the temples in order to reenact the Baal cycle. As the myth was reproduced through the ritual of prostitution, the forces of nature were thought to be reactivated and the desired fertility in soil, beast, and man guaranteed. These rituals led inevitably to certain debasing practices, including, in addition to sacred prostitution, homosexuality and other orgiastic rites. Even the three major female deities, Asherah, Astarte, and Anath, were portrayed as sacred prostitutes or pregnant mothers. Fortunately, the Hebrews borrowed primarily the literary rather than the spiritual achievements of the Canaanites. The ethical and moral heights reached in the Bible were not discovered in the writings unearthed at ancient Ugarit (Rash Shamra). In fact, many sections of the Bible must be understood precisely as reactions to and, consequently, as protests against the licentiousness of the Canaanite fertility cult.

Politically, the land of Canaan was part of the Egyptian empire. The Canaanites developed a system of city-states, each of which was ruled by a king. In the center of the city was the king's palace, while all about were the huts of the common people. Since he was able to control a certain amount of territory around his city, the city also became a city-state. Archaeologists tell us that the kings must have had access to large groups of laborers, because many of the cities were protected by tremendous fortifications. The Canaanite city-state in many ways resembled the feudal system of the Middle Ages, with its lords and peasants and walled cities. There was, however, no organized overall system of government which united all the Canaanite city-states into a strong political unit. Nor was Egyptian rule strong. As long as the kings paid their tribute to

Pharaoh, they were left free to rule their respective city-states as they chose.

The entrance of the Israelites into Canaan must be viewed against the backgrounds of both Canaanite civilization and international politics. Fortunately for Joshua, the international scene was favorable to the Israelites. There was an international vacuum, marked by chaos in Mesopotamia and Egyptian weakness. To the east, in the Mesopotamian river-valleys, there were no military powers which could interfere. The empires of the Tigris-Euphrates river valleys were to lie dormant for nearly six more centuries. To the west, Egypt was entering upon a period of military decline which was to last for nearly six hundred years. No longer could the armies of Pharaoh protect adequately their interests in Canaan.

The decline of Egypt, moreover, brought with it a group of corrupt Egyptian governors over the city-states. These men were exceedingly oppressive and greedy. Unrest was rife among the people, and often they rose in revolt against their kings and the Egyptian governors. Archaeological excavations point out that just prior to the invasion of the Israelites, Canaanite culture had entered upon a period of decline. Houses, tombs, fortifications, and standards of art became poorer. Some of the people even moved out of the city-states.

Favored by the international situation, the Israelites moved swiftly into Canaan, and in a series of surprise attacks gained a strong foothold. Their success became all the more remarkable when it is remembered that they had neither chariots to use in pitched battles on the flat plain country nor heavy equipment to lay siege to the fortified city-states. Joshua had to plan his strategy in such a way that the Israelites, with only bows, slings, staves, stones, and a few swords and spears as weapons, could triumph. Therefore, he sought out as his obvious targets those areas which were thinly populated and difficult even for the Canaanites to control. Then he planned a threefold attack.

First, he sought to gain a foothold in the sparsely settled hill country of Central Canaan (Joshua 6–9). His initial objective was the conquest of Jericho. For many years, people, in keeping with the Biblical description of the great walls of Jericho, have regarded this city as a mighty fortress which required nothing less than an act of God to accomplish its destruction. Early archaeological reports have supported this view, even to the extent of showing that an earthquake may have been the cause of the crumbling of the walls. Recent archaeological excavations, however, have shown that while at one time Jericho was a powerful military bastion, the Jericho of Joshua's time may have been little more than a fort. It is highly probable that the memory of the once-great city influenced the manner in which later generations told the event.

From Jericho, Joshua turned to the town of Ai, which the Bible says he destroyed. It is now widely believed that the story about Ai, which in Hebrew means "the ruin," has been blended with the tradition of the capture of the nearby city of Bethel. Archaeological excavations at Ai have shown that this city actually was destroyed many centuries before and that in Joshua's time it was still a heap of ruins. On the other hand, excavations at Bethel show that this city was destroyed during the time of Joshua. Thus, it may very well be, archaeologists tell us, that Joshua's conquest of Bethel was later combined with the story about "the ruin."

After establishing a foothold in the central hill country, Joshua undertook the second phase of his campaign. He turned his attention to the south. The Israelites carefully avoided the fortress of Jerusalem. The reputation of the Israelites, however, had gone before them, and four of the Canaanite cities sought to make a treaty with Joshua. The Gibeonites, who formed the strongest group among the four, were afraid of the Israelites. They sent a delegation to Joshua, stating falsely that they, like the Israelites, were strangers in the land and should not be destroyed like the other Canaanites. By this trick, the Gibeonites were able to gain a treaty and to save themselves and the people of the other three cities. Encouraged by their continuing successes, the Israelites moved swiftly to the defense of the Gibeonites when the other Canaanite kings threatened to punish the Gibeonites for their treaty with Joshua. The Bible tells us that Joshua prayed for the sun and moon to stand still in order to give the Israelites enough time to defeat the combined forces of the Canaanite kings. There have been many interpretations of this passage. Some have claimed that an eclipse of the sun took place. Another scholar has interpreted the prayer to mean that Joshua was hoping that the sun would not rise too soon nor the moon set too early so that the Israelites, in the misty hours of early dawn, could launch a surprise attack.

Emboldened by their victory over the Canaanite Alliance, the Israelites even ventured out into the coastal plains (Josh. 9–10). The result of the southern campaign was the addition of a considerable amount of territory, in which the tribe of Judah was to settle (Josh. 10).

The final phase of Joshua's campaign was carried out in the north, in the direction of Galilee. By a series of swift attacks, the Israelites were able not only to destroy the important city-state of Hazor but also to add much living space for many of their tribes (Josh. 11).

It must not be assumed that the land of Canaan was completely conquered by Joshua and that the Israelites, after Joshua died, lived in peace. One tends to gain this impression as he reads the twelfth chapter of the Book of Joshua. However, as one reads carefully the beginning of chapter thirteen of Joshua and also the Book of Judges and follows the evidence of archaeology, the conclusion is quickly drawn that the fighting between the Israelites and the Canaanites continued for several centuries more. While Joshua's campaign enabled the Israelites to settle in the hill country, it was still necessary for the next generations to deal with the remaining unfriendly and unconquered city-states. Also, some of the defeated city-states offered, from time to time, renewed resistance. Again, there were new invaders with whom the Israelites had to deal. Continued military action, therefore, was always necessary, and archaeological evidence indicates that every Canaanite city which has been explored was destroyed at least one to four times during the next two centuries.

We shall have to postpone, however, our discussion of the final conquest of Canaan. First, we need to bring the story of Israel's religious growth up to date. To this important chapter of the birth of the Torah we now turn.

CHAPTER VI

The Covenant Reaffirmed

ONE of the first acts of Joshua after his military victories was to bring the family-clans together. He selected as his meeting place the city of Shechem in northern Canaan. Shechem was chosen advisedly, for it was not only an important political and religious center but also a city in which he found people sympathetic to his cause. Apparently, some of the Habiru who had never gone to Egypt and had entered directly into Canaan had chosen Shechem as a site for settlement. Archaeology gives clear evidence of this fact.

In 1887, an Egyptian woman, living near Tell el-Amarna, about two hundred miles south of Cairo, found over three hundred clay tablets inscribed with strange characters. These tablets proved to be nothing less than a file of the Egyptian foreign office during the first part of the fifteenth century B.C.E. They represented corespondence between two pharaohs and their military commanders in Canaan. These letters revealed the intrigues, jealousies, and feuds between the local governors and also portrayed with a wealth of detail the politics, trade, and commerce, the mythology, and the warfare of the times. Since the first discovery, many other finds have been made at Tell el-Amarna. Of importance to us at this point, however, is the fact that one of the Amarna letters told that the king of Shechem had made a treaty with some of the Habiru. By this treaty, Egypt lost control of Shechem, for the King of Shechem, Lab'Ayu, gave the city over to the Habiru.

The ceremony which Joshua enacted with the people at Shechem is described in the Book of Joshua, Chapter 24. In the presence of the assembled family-clans and their leaders, Joshua reviewed their sacred history. He began with the period of the patriarchs. His emphasis, however, was upon the great events of the Exodus from Egypt and the conquest of the lands of Transjordan and the Canaanite hill country. Following this summary, Joshua put a challenge to the people. He asked them to decide whether they would serve Yahweh or would follow other gods. The gods to which Joshua referred were not only the gods of the Canaanites that the Habiru had found in Canaan but also the gods of the fathers that they had brought with them from the land of Mesopotamia. To this challenge, the people, both those who had been at Sinai and those who had never undergone the Egyptian experience, replied, ". . . but we will serve Yahweh" (Josh. 24: 21).

Once the people accepted Yahweh as God, the time was at hand to reaffirm the covenant with Yahweh. For those family-clans which had been in the Sinai desert, it was only a matter of renewing their allegiance to Yahweh. For those Habiru who had settled directly into Canaan, however, it was a service of initiation into the covenant with Yahweh. The Bible describes this twofold event in these words:

So Joshua made a covenant with the people that day, and set them a statute and ordinance in Shechem. And Joshua wrote these words in the book of the law of God; and he took a great stone, and set it up there under the oak that was by the sanctuary of the Lord. And Joshua said unto all the people: "Behold, this stone shall be a witness against us; for it has heard all the words of the Lord which He spoke unto us; it shall be therefore a witness against you, lest you deny your God." So Joshua sent the people away, every man unto his inheritance [Josh. 24:25–28].

In view of the fact that there is no reference to the Sinai experience in the story of Joshua's covenant renewal, the question has been raised by some scholars whether Joshua's covenant was identical with the one which Moses had established at Sinai. The prevailing opinion holds that although Joshua also chose to cast his covenant in the form of the international treaties, a practice which Moses himself had followed (Chapter 4), the covenant at Shechem was a new covenant. Four major reasons are advanced to support this thesis. (1) The biblical sources insist that only Joshua and Caleb survived the desert generation. Scholars see in this tradition evidence which suggests "a discontinuity between the generation of Moses and that of Joshua." [1] (2) Those who entered into the covenant included not only a new generation but also many groups already in Canaan which had known nothing about the Exodus and the Sinai experience. (3) The desert covenant, designed for a nomadic people, was not revelant to the new agricultural conditions of Canaan. (4) The only obligation which Joshua placed upon the people was the prohibition of foreign gods. There may have been other stipulations; however, if there were, they have been lost. The question has been summarized as follows:

The point which is to be made here, is the fact that the covenant form itself furnished at least the nucleus about which the historical traditions crystallized in early Israel. It was the source of the "feeling for history" which is such an enigma in Israelite literature. And perhaps even more important is the fact that what we now call "history" and "law" were bound up into an organic unit from the very beginnings of Israel itself. Since the cultus was at least connected with the covenant proclamation or renewal, we can see that in early Israel, history, cultus, and "law" were inseparable, and that the history of Israelite religion is not the history of the

gradual emergence of new theological concepts, but of the sep-
aration and re-combination of these three elements so characteristic of Israelite religion, over against the mythological religions of
their pagan neighbors.[2]

From now on, not only the former Hebrew slaves but also
the Habiru who entered into the covenant at Shechem were
to be called Israelites. The Bible explains the term "Israel" in
connection with the patriarch Jacob, who had settled many
centuries before in the area of Shechem (Gen. 32:19). One
night Jacob was awakened from a dream by a stranger who
engaged him in a wrestling match. This stranger was no stranger, the Bible tells us. He was a messenger of God. When the
morning sun broke over the horizon, Jacob and the messenger
still were wrestling with each other. Neither one could prevail
over the other. Thus, the Bible tells us that Jacob's name was
changed to Israel, for in Hebrew Israel means "he wrestled
with God." Whether the tradition of Jacob and the messenger
be true, it may be impossible ever to know. Some say, for example, that the name Israel means "may El or God rule."
What is important, however, is the fact that after the covenant at Shechem, where the people "wrestled with Yahweh,"
both the former Habiru slaves and the Habiru of Canaan became one people, called Israelites, and over whom Yahweh
ruled.

From year to year, there were three occasions on which the
people would gather together: Pesach, in the springtime;
Shavuot, in the early summer; and Sukkot, in the fall at the
harvest season. Of these three festivals, only Pesach had been
known to any of the Habiru prior to their entrance into
Canaan. Pesach was an ancient nomadic festival celebrated by
shepherd peoples in the spring of the year. Shavuot and Sukkot, on the other hand, were agricultural holidays celebrated
by the Canaanites. As the Israelites lived in Canaan and them-

selves became an agricultural people, they borrowed these two festivals. However, whatever they borrowed, they impressed with their own stamp of Yahwism. Each holiday became the celebration of an important event in the history of Israel with Yahweh. For example, the Canaanite Shavuot became the time of the giving of the commandments at Sinai, and the Canaanite Sukkot came to represent the long period of wandering in the desert-wilderness, where the Israelites had lived in temporary homes called "sukkot" or booths.

Even the Pesach celebration bore this new imprint. The lamb which shepherds sacrificed in the springtime now became identified with the lamb which the Hebrew slaves slew in Egypt so that they could paint their doorposts as a sign for the angel of death (Exod. 12:21–23). The whole Passover, moreover, became the occasion for the celebration of the Exodus from Egypt.

These three festival reunions were observed in a threefold pattern. First, the elders would review the great story of how Yahweh had saved his people from slavery in Egypt. Second, the people would pledge themselves anew to their covenant with Yahweh. Finally, they would listen to the reading of the regulations which the covenant placed upon them. An understanding of this last procedure is most important for us as we trace the history of the birth of the Torah.

In Chapter 4, it was indicated that in the Sinai desert-wilderness Moses not only established a covenant between Yahweh and his people but also developed with them a group of laws which represented the people's responsibilities to Yahweh. These laws were part of the Book of the Covenant. As the people underwent new experiences, so these laws of the covenant needed further enlargement and interpretation. This process was accomplished by Moses and the elders as they sat at the Tent of Meeting and judged the people (Exod. 18). Joshua, it will be recalled, also read from a Book of the

Covenant at Shechem when he initiated the Habiru into the covenant. These laws, therefore, were so important to the covenant with Yahweh that they were reread and reinterpreted each time the Israelites gathered at Shechem to celebrate a festival.

The Book of the Covenant is identified by many scholars with those laws found today in the book of Exodus, chapters 21 to 23:19. Two different kinds of law were developed by the Israelites. The first may be called Apodictic law. The Ten Commandments, in Chapter 20 of the book of Exodus, is a good example of Apodictic law. These laws state merely: "You shall..." or "You shall not..." Many scholars feel that this form of law, while not unique to Israel, is so characteristic of its laws as to be a distinctive contribution of the Israelites to civilization. Other examples of Apodictic law are found in the Book of the Covenant in Exodus 22:27–30.

The second kind of law is called Casuistic law and is found widely among many ancient peoples. This law states: "If a man do so and so, then..." For example, Exodus 21:37 states: "If a man steal an ox, or a sheep and kill it, or sell it, he shall pay five oxen for an ox, and four sheep for a sheep."

For many years, scholars believed that the Book of the Covenant came from a much later period. Today, however, it is known as a result of archaeological excavations that similar collections of law were in existence at an even earlier time. The most famous example is the Code of Hammurabi, the king of Babylonia who ruled in the eighteenth century B.C.E. The discovery of this code of law forms an exciting chapter in the history of archaeology.

In 1897, the French scholar Jacques de Morgan was excavating the city of Susa in what is today Iran. Susa is claimed to be the Shushan of the biblical books of Esther and Daniel. During the digging, three large pieces of stone were unearthed. When the pieces were put together, an impressive monument stood seven feet five inches tall. At the top was a scene of King Hammurabi standing before the god Shamash. Most important, however, were the many lines of cuneiform writing which were carved into the monument. When translated, these lines threw more light on life in ancient Babylonia than did any other single discovery. No less than 250 laws of Hammurabi were inscribed on this stela or monument.

Archaeologists have wondered why the stela of Hammurabi, who reigned in Sippar in ancient Babylonia, should have been discovered in Susa, some 230 miles distant. The best guess is that a king of Persia who is known to have raided Babylonia some five hundred years later carried off this impressive monument as booty.

Since the discovery of the Code of Hammurabi, five other codes of Cuneiform law have been unearthed. These finds have pushed back the evidence for the existence of codes of law to a time before 2000 B.C.E. As a result of the discovery in Susa and the finding of other codes used by the ancient Assyrians, Hittites, and others, scholars today are inclined to accept the following. By the time of Moses, the kinds of laws found in the Book of the Covenant were widely known and accepted by many peoples. Therefore, while it may never be known just how many laws Moses actually authored, it is no longer denied that Moses was a great lawgiver. It was he who set the pattern for all future laws which were to become part of the covenant relationship between Yahweh and his people Israel.

The laws of Moses and the laws which later were developed in the spirit of Moses became part of the great oral tradition upon which our present Torah was established. It is possible that some of these laws were preserved even in written form. Whatever the manner of their transmission, the Torah today contains many of these early laws. Some came from the pre-Mosaic period; others, from the time of Moses and Joshua and from the early years of Israel in Canaan. The present form of the Book of the Covenant (Exod. 21:1–23:19), however, is said to have come from the period of the Judges, because it reflects the new judicial procedures which were formulated as the Israelites exchanged their nomadic, shepherd existence for the settled, agricultural ways of Canaan.

CHAPTER VII

Years of Transition

AFTER Joshua died, the Israelites, unlike the Canaanites, did not choose to set up their own city-states. They preferred to establish a confederacy made up of their family-clans. As we have seen in Chapter 5, the nucleus for such an organization had been in existence during their wanderings in the Sinai desert-wilderness. At that time it was no more than an organization of smaller family units. Now it had expanded into a formidable organization. Not only had the family units grown into larger clans but also many other wandering groups had attached themselves to the Israelites. In Canaan, too, the clans had been joined both by the Habiru who had come directly into the land and by the local residents who had gone over to the Israelite standard after the victories of Joshua. Finally, the Confederacy had been formalized at Shechem where the tribes—as they now could be described—renewed or were initiated into the Covenant with Yahweh.

The Confederacy, however, was at the most a loosely knit organization. While the tribes had a common basis of worship and a sense of mutual responsibility which had been defined for them by the Covenant with Yahweh at Shechem, they tended to remain primarily localized groups. Only in great emergencies or when stirred by the call of an inspired leader did several of the groups co-operate. Nearly two centuries were to pass before the twelve tribes were to become a united political unit. The Bible tells us that during the nearly two hundred years of the Confederacy, twelve leaders, called judges, arose from time to time in certain trouble spots in order to help the people defend themselves against their "oppressors."

The word "judge" is not to be confused with its present-day meaning, which is restricted to legal functions. When the Israelites called a person a "judge," they looked upon him as a leader who protected the rights of the people both by judging legal disputes and by taking military action. A judge, therefore, was more like a ruler, and this interpretation has been confirmed by archaeologists. The Rash Shamra tablets contained passages in which the term "judge" was equated with "king" or "prince." The Israelite judges, therefore, were primarily military champions or "deliverers" (Judg. 2:16; 4:4–5; I Sam. 7:15–17), and, because their exploits gained for them recognition from the other tribes of the Confederacy, many people often came to them to seek legal advice. In this way, the laws of the Covenant were further interpreted. This enlargement by the judges of the laws or responsibilities of the Covenant with Yahweh represented another important phase in the story of the birth of the Torah.

The position of the judge in ancient Israel, however, also differed from that of a king. His was not an hereditary office. Instead of being passed on from father to son, the authority of a judge was invested by a special endowment of Yahweh. The judges, the people believed, were set apart from ordinary men. Unlike the others, the judges were believed to possess some special gift, some special outpouring of divine grace. The term "charisma" has come to be used as an explanation of this divine power. It is a Greek word, meaning "divine or spiritual power." Each judge became a charismatic leader because, in the words of the Bible, "The spirit of Yahweh came mightily upon him" (Judg. 14:6; 6:34–35; 4:4–5).

Although the Bible would have us believe that the judges followed each other in chronological order, it is difficult to outline the events exactly. If all the years in which the Bible says the judges reigned were added together, the total would reach 410 years. We know, however, that the events of the judges took place between the time of the death of Joshua (c. 1225–1200 B.C.E.) and that of the first king, Saul, who began to reign c. 1020 B.C.E., a period of less than two hundred years. These two dates would indicate that the authority of some of the judges had to overlap each other; therefore, while the author of the Book of Judges chose to present these personalities in chronological order, it would be more accurate to say that the book gives primarily an account of the conditions and crises of the twelfth and eleventh centuries, B.C.E. We turn now to those events which brought pressures upon the Confederacy and upon the judges who arose spontaneously to save their people from the "oppressors."

The "oppressors" were of three kinds. There were not only the local Canaanites who had resisted the initial conquests of Joshua but also the invaders who came both from the east and from the west.

The most strategic area which the Canaanites controlled was in the north. At Megiddo, they had erected a strong fortress city which guarded the main trade route from Egypt to Mesopotamia, running through the valley of Jezreel. Restricted to the hill country and prevented from sending their caravans to the important trading centers, the Israelites were unable to enter into the economic life of the country. Only by using the back roads where they could escape the watchful eye of the Canaanite sentries posted along the main routes were they able to preserve themselves (Judg. 5:6). Soon the situation became desperate. The Bible describes the circumstances in these words:

And the Lord gave them over into the hand of Jabin, king of Canaan, that reigned in Hazor; the captain of whose host was Sisera.... And the children of Israel cried unto the Lord; for he [Jabin] had nine hundred chariots of iron; and twenty years he mightily oppressed the children of Israel. (Judg. 4:2, 3)

The story of Deborah, the woman judge, who rose to lead the people to victory over the Canaanites is told twice in the Book of Judges. Chapter 4 is a prose account which describes how Deborah spurred the people into action. Under the command of Barak, whom Deborah had summoned to lead the troops, the Israelites met General Sisera's Canaanite army in the vicinity of Megiddo. Inspired by Deborah, upon whom the spirit of Yahweh rested, some of the tribes of the Confederacy answered the summons to duty. Just prior to the battle, a heavy rainstorm developed. Soon the waters of the Kishon River overflowed the banks and poured out onto the plains of Jezreel. The chariots, which ordinarily would have given the Canaanites their superiority in arms, became helplessly trapped in the miry clay. Favored by the elements, the Israelites swept on to victory until they had "destroyed Jabin, King of Canaan" (Judg. 4:24).

The second version of Deborah's charismatic leadership is portrayed in poetic form in Chapter 5. This poem is regarded by scholars as an eye-witness account of the battle and represents one of the oldest passages of poetry in the Bible. While some of the details differ from those of the prose account, the story essentially is the same. In the poem, however, Yahweh's presence as the leader and champion of his people is strongly emphasized. The storm which caused the brook Kishon to overflow is evidence of Yahweh's active concern for his people. No one can stand before Yahweh, sings the poet, for

He is the Lord of Heaven and earth. Even the stars in their heavenly courses join in the battle (Judg. 5:20).

The great victory of Deborah and Barak over Sisera's army marked the end of any united Canaanite resistance against the Israelites. Archaeological work at Megiddo has produced evidence for dating the battle approximately in the year 1125 B.C.E. As long as the fortress-city of Megiddo was strongly defended and continued to block the trade routes, scholars feel that Deborah and her forces would not have ventured into the Plain of Jezreel. It seems, however, that Megiddo was deserted for some unknown reason around 1125 B.C.E. Because of this circumstance and the ensuing victory, the Israelite caravans were able at last to ply the established trade routes.

The Song of Deborah also reveals interesting insights into the organization of the tribal confederacy. Like the several American states under the Articles of Confederation, the tribes recognized no overall authority. For example, only six tribes chose to fight against Sisera. These were the groups most directly affected because of their proximity to the Plain of Jezreel. Only one neighboring tribe refused to co-operate. Asher, because of its exposure to the Canaanite coastal cities, may have preferred at the moment to cast its lot with the Canaanites, whose culture it considered to be far superior to that of Deborah and her supporters. It is possible also that the tribes of Judah, Simeon, and Levi belonged to a southern group centered around Hebron and, therefore, felt themselves unconcerned with the problems of the northern tribes.

New troubles, however, soon were to come from other directions. In the eleventh century B.C.E., there was a striking difference in the political organization between the inhabitants of Canaan and those on the other side of the Jordan. In contrast to the loose tribal confederation of the Israelites were the highly organized states of Moab, Ammon, and Midian. Instead of depending upon a spontaneously arising leadership, these countries had kings who exercised strong control over their subjects. Aware of the declining power of the Canaanite city-state and recognizing that Egypt no longer could exercise strong military control over its empire, these three kingdoms began to look with jealousy upon Israel's holdings both in Jordan and in Canaan.

On one occasion, Eglon, the king of Moab, invaded Canaan and seized the city of Jericho. So devastating was his campaign that the tribe of Reuben, which had chosen to live on the eastern banks of the Jordan, practically was wiped out. But "the Lord raised them up a savior" in the form of a left-handed leader named Ehud (Judg. 3:15). The Bible describes in dramatic fashion his exploits. First of all, he had a sword made with two cutting edges which he sought to present as a gift of tribute to the victorious king of Moab. Instead of sending the sword to Eglon, however, Ehud requested a private audience so that he might present the gift in person. When they were alone, "Ehud put forth his left hand, and took the sword from his right thigh, and thrust it into [Eglon's] belly [for he was a very fat man]" (Judg. 3:21). Taking advantage of the confusion which followed, Ehud escaped to the hill country and summoned the people. In the ensuing battle, the Moabites were severely defeated and "the land had rest" (Judg. 3:30).

In the years that followed, a series of attacks by the Ammonites, both in Jordan and in the Canaanite hill-country, were met effectively by Jephthah, a judge from the city of Mizpah in the territory of the tribe of Benjamin. Jephthah has become immortalized not only in the Bible but also in world literature and song because of an oath which he swore as he led the Israelite tribes into battle.

If you will indeed deliver the children of Ammon into my hand, then it shall be that whatsoever comes forth of the doors of my house to meet me, when I return in peace from the children of Ammon, it shall be the Lord's, and I will offer it up for a burnt-offering. . . . So the children of Ammon were subdued. And Jephthah came to Mizpah unto his house, and behold, his daughter came out to meet him with timbrels and with dances; and she was his only child; besides her he had neither son nor daughter. . . . (Judg. 11:30–31, 33–34).

Still another oppressor group was the Midianites, or the Arabians, as they also are called. Their raids struck deep into the heart of the valley Jezreel and also swept almost to the shores of the Mediterranean Sea in the south. The Bible tells us that these attacks put such great fear into the hearts of the Israelites that they "made themselves the dens which are in the mountains, and the caves, and strongholds" (Judg. 6:2). They had to flee from the valleys into the hill country where they took refuge in mountain caves. Archaeology has cast considerable light on these terrifying events. The Midianites had learned how to domesticate the camel, and for the first time in history, as far as is known, they used these animals for warfare. No longer were the Midianites limited by their nomadic ways. With the camel, they could venture far away from home, capture their booty, and return once again within a reasonable period of time to their pasture lands.

The Book of Judges relates that "the spirit of the Lord clothed Gideon" (Judg. 6:34), a leader from the tribe of Manasseh, who with only three hundred men was able to overwhelm the Midianites. Dividing his men into three groups, he planned a surprise attack. Soon after the night watch changed, the three hundred Israelites filled the air with the noise of their own horns. Then they smashed pitchers upon the ground and held burning torches high in the air as they shouted, "The sword for the Lord and Gideon" (Judg. 7:20). The noise and the flaming fires brought fear into the hearts of the Midianites, and they hastily retreated with their camels from the valley of Jezreel to the other side of the Jordan. Strengthened now by additional reinforcements, Gideon followed after them and saved Israel "out of the hand of Midian."

The period of the judges marked an era of great development in the material civilization and social organization of the Israelites. These new features of Israelite life have been described by Dr. William F. Albright:

Most of the destroyed Canaanite towns had been reoccupied, and these towns became foci of agricultural clans grouped in patriarchally organized families. The average population of the major towns was much smaller than in Canaanite times, and open spaces were used for sheepfolds and grain pits. Characteristic of the age were large rustic houses, with numerous rooms on the ground floor around an open courtyard, and other rooms upstairs. Construction and character of furnishings prove conclusively that these large houses were not aristocratic mansions, like the Canaanite buildings whose place they sometimes take, but were occupied by several smaller families, grouped around a patriarchal head. Moreover, thanks to the extremely rapid diffusion of the art of building cisterns, introduced not long before the end of the Canaanite occupation, it had become possible to build new towns and villages on sites far from any spring or running stream. And so hundreds of new settlements had arisen where no Canaanite settlement had ever been. Considerable areas of woodland, both east and west of the Jordan, had been cleared; vast numbers of olive trees and vineyards had been planted.

Moreover, commerce was fast returning to the place it held under the Canaanites; in some respects it probably surpassed any previous record in Palestine. Camel caravans were already providing new means of transporting the wares of the desert into Palestine, not to mention the tremendous new possibilities which they provided for cheap transport over greater distances. The rapid growth of the little country of Ammon, on the very edge of the desert east of Gilead, after the time of the Conquest, in which it played no role, until it was able to threaten Israel repeatedly in the course of the eleventh century, illustrates what the camel trade already meant at this time. In the Mediterranean sea trade was rapidly expanding. The Song of Deborah mentions the active maritime part played by members of the tribes of Dan and Asher. By the middle of the eleventh century, pottery imported from Cyprus appears again in Israelite sites, after a long interruption during which exceedingly little imported ware (except Philistine) is found.[1]

This increase in wealth, coupled with the fact that a new enemy was about to invade Canaan from the west, was to have far-reaching implications. Many Israelites began to concern themselves with the organization of a more stable government. Two unsuccessful attempts subsequently were made to replace the tribal Confederation with strong leadership. In Shechem, Abimelech, one of Gideon's sons, had himself crowned as king (Judg. 9). Again, Samuel about whom we shall speak in greater detail later, tried to establish the succession of judges by appointing his own sons as his successors. Both ventures failed because the individuals proved themselves to be a tyrant and corrupt administrators respectively. Nonetheless, the forces unleashed by the growing prosperity of the Israelites continued unabated, opening the way for "a new step in the political evolution of Israel." [2]

The Israelites were not the only people to enter the land of Canaan during the twelfth century B.C.E. In 1187, just a few years after the death of Joshua, there was an invasion along the Mediterranean coast by a strange people, called the "People of the Sea." These invaders established themselves quickly on the coastal plains and fortified five city-states. The "People of the Sea" are known to us as the Philistines, and it is from them that the name Palestine is derived. Some scholars believe that originally they came from the islands in the Mediterranean Sea, and most particularly from the Island of Crete. A large group of the Philistines had tried to conquer Egypt, but they were defeated; however, later they were successful in their invasion of Canaan. The Canaanite city-states, under the Egyptian policy of "divide and conquer," had never learned to co-operate with each other, and, as a result, they were no match for the Philistines. For nearly 150 years, the Israelites, too, lived in constant fear of the "People of the Sea," whose chariots ruled the plains and whose fortified cities guarded the great trade routes of the ancient world.

The strangle hold which the Philistines were to have upon the Israelites becomes even more dramatic when it is realized that the Philistines had introduced the use of iron into the land. Until this time men had used much softer metals for their implements. First copper and then copper mixed with tin to form bronze were the metals used by ancient man. Now the Philistines had brought the secret of using the much harder and more durable iron. At first, the iron was used for weapons; later on, agricultural implements were made of this more efficient metal. However, the methods of producing iron were guarded very closely by the Philistines, so that all who wanted implements of iron had to deal with them. A picture of this strangle hold is given to us in the Bible where we learn that the Israelites had no smiths who could make swords and spears (of iron) and that the farmers had to go down to Philistine country to sharpen their agricultural implements (I Sam. 13:19–22). Thus, the Philistines were able to maintain not only a military but also an economic control of Canaan. It was not until the first kings of Israel, Saul and David, were to break the Philistine monopoly that metalworking was developed by the Israelites. The introduction of iron resulted inevitably in a higher standard of living for the people. The significance of these events, however, will be seen later in Chapter 8.

There was one judge, Samson, who did try to defend the Confederacy against the Philistines. He came from the tribe of Dan, and the Bible tells us many stories about his feats of strength. Samson was, without a doubt, a man of unusual strength; however, the incidents connected with his life were magnified, it appears, as they were handed down by word of mouth from generation to generation (Judg. 14:5–6; 15:3–20). Certainly, the overwhelming military and economic advantages which the Philistines held would tend to make almost any victory by the less-favored Israelites border on the miraculous.

Despite his unusual strength, however, Samson was unable to break the yoke which the Philistines had placed upon the Israelites. The Bible relates that he fell in love with a Philistine girl who betrayed him. Because he was considered to be a holy man, the Bible tells us "no razor shall come upon his head" (Judg. 13:5). The secret of his strength lay in his hair, and as long as his locks remained unshaven he was able to prevail against the Philistines. Once he revealed his secret to Delilah, the Philistine girl whom he loved, and his hair was cut from his head, his strength left him. He was then taken prisoner by the Philistines who praised their god, saying, "Our god has delivered into our hand our enemy, and the destroyer of our country, who has slain many of us" (Judg. 16:24). The Bible story relates that one day the Philistines brought Samson out to entertain them at a banquet. What they did not realize was that since his hair had begun to grow again his strength, too, had started to return. Moreover, they did not know that the entire building was supported by the very same two pillars between which they had placed Samson. Carefully, Samson leaned upon the pillars, "the one with his right hand,

and the other with his left. And Samson said: 'Let me die with
the Philistines.' . . . So the dead that he slew at his death were
more than they that he slew in his life" (Judg. 16:29–30).

The struggle between the Philistines and the Israelites soon
was to reach a climax. While Joshua had chosen to establish
the covenant of Yahweh at the city of Shechem, it seems that
in time the city of Shiloh became the central shrine of the
Confederacy. To Shiloh the tent of meeting, together with
the Ark containing the Tablets of the Covenant, had been
brought. Here, too, a priesthood had begun to develop to help
in the celebration of the three festivals (I Sam. 1:3). Archaeologists tell us that the city of Shiloh was destroyed, presumably by the Philistines, about the year 1050 B.C.E. This evidence tends to fit in with the account of the defeat of the
Israelites described in the Bible (I Sam. 4). In this battle, the
Ark of the Covenant, which had been brought into the Israelite camp to inspire the soldiers, was captured, and the priests
who had been in charge were slain (I Sam. 4:11). The Ark
itself later was brought to the fortified city of Ashdod on the
Mediterranean Coast, where it was placed in the temple of the
Philistine god, Dagon (I Sam. 5:1–2).

This humiliating defeat climaxed the Israelites' growing demand for a new kind of leadership. They sought a person who
could help them make the transition from their ineffective
tribal Confederacy to a more stable form of government. The
person who came forth to meet the new challenge was Samuel
who, as a child, had grown up at Shiloh under the training of
Eli the priest (I Sam. 1).

Samuel is known as a judge-prophet. He was the last of the
judges, and, at the same time, the first of a new line of leadership. He was a prophet. He could not only judge cases and
lead the people against their enemies but also speak and act
in the name of Yahweh (I Sam. 3:20). We shall have the op-

portunity to deal with the history and meaning of the prophetic movement in Chapter 13. Here we are concerned with
Samuel and the role he played in establishing the monarchy.
The Bible presents us with two contradictory traditions about
Samuel and the selection of Israel's first king. Both of these
traditions, however, are undoubtedly rooted in the facts of
this period. It seems that there were different points of view
in Israel about the necessity for choosing a king, and each side
sought to show that Samuel supported its cause. For example,
the monarchists claimed that Samuel, as Yahweh's prophetic
spokesman, took the initiative in selecting Saul.

The monarchist account describes Saul as a handsome young
man who "stood head and shoulders above any of the people."
One day Saul set out to find some livestock which had become
lost from his father's herd. He searched all day but found
nothing. About to give up the search, he decided on one last
effort. He would go to the seer Samuel and pay for his advice.
When Samuel saw the young man, he knew at once that Saul
was the one man who could save the Israelites from the Philistines. Samuel's choice of Saul, however, was not accidental.
Saul, as was already pointed out, was not only a person of
great stature and prowess but also a member of the weakest
and most central tribe of Benjamin. In a Confederacy where
tribal jealousy ran high, it was of great importance, Samuel
realized, that whoever became king should engender as little
friction as possible from the very beginning. Samuel, therefore, took the initiative and anointed Saul secretly (I Sam.
9:1-10; 16). Shortly afterwards, the opportunity came for
Saul to be crowned publicly. The Ammonites had attacked
the city of Jabesh-Gilead in Jordan. The Ammonites were
ruthless in their methods and promised to make a treaty if
every man in Jabesh-Gilead would permit his right eye to be
gouged out. The people of the beleaguered city sent out a
hasty appeal for help to the other tribes. Saul was among those

who heard the appeal, and he responded in the spirit of the judges. Symbolically, he took a yoke of oxen and cut the oxen into twelve pieces; then he sent a part to each tribe to invite them to join him in the liberation of Jabesh-Gilead. The tribes responded, and after the victory they offered to Saul the throne. He accepted and was crowned in Gilgal "before Yahweh" (I Sam. 11).

The antimonarchists charged, on the other hand, that Samuel yielded only with great reluctance to the people's desire for the selection of a king. For them only Yahweh could be king. They remembered how Gideon had refused the crown when it had been offered to him (Judg. 9:22). They also recalled the bitter experience with Abimelech, who had been crowned King of Shechem (Judg. 9:6). For the antimonarchists a human king could mean only tyranny and even slavery. The popular demand for a human king, however, was too overwhelming. Because of the pressure, Samuel at first sought to avoid the issue by appointing his own sons as judges. This act would have changed the role of judge, making it an hereditary office regardless of whether or not the divine charisma had descended upon the heir. This plan failed, however, because both of Samuel's sons were corrupt in their dealings with the people. The move, moreover, was unsuccessful because the people wanted nothing less than a king who was like the kings of the surrounding nations. Only by imitating the other peoples, they felt, could Israel set up a stable government and repel the enemies. Even though Samuel felt that the people had rejected Yahweh as their only true king, grudgingly he consented to go along with them. The antimonarchist account tells us, however, that Samuel himself did not choose the king. He had the king chosen by lot among all the tribes. The lot fell upon Saul, the son of Kish of the tribe of Benjamin, who was then acclaimed king in the city of Mizpah (I Sam. 10:17–27).

CHAPTER VIII

The Golden Age

SAUL was primarily a warrior. He was neither wealthy, learned, nor a statesman. While he had been anointed, he was more like a judge than a king, as we are accustomed to think of the term. While it was Saul's charismatic quality, seemingly, which had gained for him his authority, at the same time, he differed from the judges in the fact that he was a permanent leader. The other judges served only temporarily in order to meet particular crises.

During his reign, Saul did not try to reorganize the Confederacy. He did not attempt to impose even a system of taxation, preferring to depend upon voluntary contributions. His very army was composed of a group of volunteers whom he recruited from among his supporters. He continued to live unpretentiously, without the usual fanfare which surrounds a royal court. He had neither a harem nor a hierarchy of court officials. In fact, recent archaeological excavations which unearthed Saul's palace at Gibeah, three miles north of Jerusalem, showed that it was more like a fortress than a palace. It was far from magnificent, containing few quarters for servants and courtiers. Pottery fragments indicated that the household vessels were rather simple and practical, bearing little ornamentation, while the bronze arrowheads and stones for slingshots give evidence that the techniques and equipment used for war also were quite plain. No wonder that Saul has been called the "rustic king" of Israel.

The major crisis confronting Saul as King of Israel was the enemy from the west. The Philistines had become bolder, and their forces continued to attack the outlying Israelite settlements. At first Saul mobilized the tribes and stemmed the Philistine advance. He was able not only to break the Philistine monopoly on the production of iron but also to drive them out of the hill-country (I Sam. 13-15).

Saul's efforts to deal with the Philistines, however, soon became complicated by two factors. The first was Saul's own personality. Saul felt secure to pursue his responsibilities only when he was certain that the spirit of Yahweh was with him. Since he was basically a charismatic leader, he was very sensitive to any indication that Yahweh might not approve of what he had done. If there were a doubt in his mind, he would become very moody. At times, he would become insanely jealous of anyone whom it might be said Yahweh favored. Therefore, the second complication was the growing popularity and leadership of David, upon whom, the people claimed, the spirit of Yahweh rested.

The crisis arose when Samuel became angry with Saul and accused him of "rejecting the word of Yahweh." Because he had failed to destroy every living thing in the war against the Amalekites, who were regarded as the traditional enemies of the Israelites, Saul began to believe that he had lost the favor of Yahweh. The Amalekites had attacked Moses when he led the family-clans through the desert-wilderness; consequently, a feud unto death had been pledged between Israel and Amalek. Saul's campaign against the Amalekites, consequently, should have been nothing less than a holy war in which every possession and every person should have become *cherem*, should have been destroyed. Saul, however, had permitted a number of his soldiers to keep some of the enemy's cattle and also had brought back the Amalekite king alive. Therefore, Samuel accused Saul of rejecting Yahweh and added that Yahweh in turn had rejected Saul as King of Israel. In time, the breach between Saul and Samuel continued to widen. Soon Samuel would not let Saul visit him any more, contributing greatly thereby to Saul's growing feelings of rejection. To Saul the absence of Samuel meant nothing less than the absence of Yahweh (I Sam. 15).

In the meantime, David, a young man of considerable personal charm and gallantry, whose undertakings were marked with repeated success, appeared on the scene of Israelite history. There are two traditions in the Bible about David's appearance in the court of Saul. In one account David was brought in as a musician to cheer the depressed king (I Sam. 16:14–23). In the other, David first won Saul's attention when he defeated Goliath, the giant leader of the Philistines (I Sam. 17: 1–18:5). (It may be mentioned here that in II Samuel 21:19, the slayer of Goliath is said to have been Elhanan of the tribe of Benjamin. This reference may cast some doubt on the story of David as a giant-killer, and may give some idea of how legendary stories gathered around national heroes.) Although the manner in which David became part of the royal court may never be known, his rapid rise to fame cannot be denied. He became fast friends with Saul's son, Jonathan. He married Saul's daughter, Michal, and became the trusted champion of some of the priestly groups. To Saul these achievements appeared to be nothing less than stepping stones by which David himself one day would ascend the throne of Israel. With each new success by David, Saul could recognize only one thing: the spirit of Yahweh had turned away from him and had descended upon David.

Against this background, we can now understand why David had to flee from Israel, taking refuge even among the Philistines, the arch-enemies of the Israelites (I Sam. 27: 1–7).

We can also understand why Saul, in one last desperate effort to gain the favor of Yahweh, went to the witch of En-dor to summon Samuel's ghost (I Sam. 28:8-25). Against this same background we can understand the hopelessness which filled Saul's heart as the Philistines marched into the plains of Jezreel. There on Mount Gilboa the small band of Israelites met the invaders from the west. The outcome was decisive. Although the Israelites were routed, Saul and his son Jonathan fought the enemy to the very end. When all hope was gone, Saul fell upon his sword, and the next day his head was posted on the walls of the nearby Philistine fortress (I Sam. 31:1-13).

After their victory at Mount Gilboa, the Philistines were the undisputed masters of the Israelites; they were in control of Canaan from the Mediterranean Sea to the Jordan Valley. Within seven years, however, their power was to come to an end for all time. From the depths of defeat, the Israelites were to rise to new glories. Under the leadership of David and his son Solomon, Israel was to enter upon a golden age. The "golden age," it must be pointed out in all fairness, was to have brilliant as well as less sparkling—in fact, even dim—aspects. On the one hand, it was to be a period of unexampled prosperity attended by unheralded territorial growth and an amazing flowering of the peaceful arts; on the other hand, it was to represent an era in which, though wealth came to some and slavery to others, all paid the price of an increase in the powers of the state and a burden quite without precedent in Israel. First, we shall present the more glittering achievements of the age, followed in turn by its less lustrous shortcomings.

The architect of the golden age was David. As a young man he fled, as we have seen, from the jealous Saul. He took refuge in the wilds of Judah where his kinsmen, as well as persons of questionable reputation, joined him. For some time, he lived as a bandit chief, striking the Philistines as the opportunity offered (I Sam. 23:1–5), trying constantly to escape from the pursuing Saul (I Sam. 23:19–24:22; 26), and supporting himself by exacting "protection" from wealthy citizens (I Sam. 25:7). Finally, caught between the Philistines, the King of Israel, and a population which considered him a nuisance at times, David offered his services to the Philistine King of Gath. He was welcomed openly and even given a town as a feudal holding. The King hoped that he would continue to make trouble for Israel. Some would call David a quisling or a traitor; however, most scholars contend that he wanted to remain loyal to his people and chose to play instead a clever game. While pretending to be on an expedition to destroy Judean villages, David actually would protect his kinsmen by attacking their enemies. He would not only defend the outlying Judean settlements but also divide the spoils of battle with them. The King of Gath, however, never suspected David and continued to promise him great power and prestige for his faithfulness.

Even following Saul's death, when David was anointed by some of the Judeans as the new King of Israel, the Philistines continued to put their trust in him. He was regarded by them as a vassal. In fact, the Philistines were eager to support David in his dispute with Ish-Bosheth, the son of Saul, for the throne of Israel, because civil war was to the decided advantage of the Philistines. David, however, played a skillful game. Within seven years, he was able to win over, either because of his popularity or by his careful planning, the allegiance of the other tribes. The civil war itself collapsed when Ish-Bosheth's main supporter deserted and came over to David's camp. Shortly thereafter, Ish-Bosheth himself was taken into protective custody. To strengthen further his claim to the throne, David brought Saul's daughter Michal again into his harem (II Sam. 3:12–15).

Only when the Philistines realized that he had united all

Israel under his banner did they become aroused, but by this time it was too late for them to hold David back. The seven years had given David sufficient time to consolidate his forces and to mass his strength. In the ensuing battles, the Philistine forces were roundly defeated, and once and for all they were shut up in their cities in the coastal plain bordering on the Mediterranean Sea. The Philistine military power, and also their monopoly over the production and use of iron, was broken. At last the Israelites, nearly two hundred years after they had first come into the land under Joshua, were able to enter upon their golden age in the land of Canaan.

Once the Philistines were contained, David turned his attention to the neighboring kingdoms which had continued to harass the Israelites. In quick succession, he subdued the Moabites, the Ammonites, the Edomites, the Amalekites, and the Arameans (II Samuel 5:17–25; 21:15–22). He also made a treaty with the King of Phoenecia. So brilliant were his military achievements that David's empire stretched from the mountains of Lebanon in the north to the borders of Egypt in the south, from the Mediterranean Sea in the west to the Desert of Arabia in the east. Within the boundaries of Israel now lay the great trade routes from Egypt to Babylonia and from the islands of the Mediterranean to the lands of Arabia, Africa, and even to far-off India. Neither before nor since the time of David has the territory of Israel been greater or embodied such strategic positions (II Samuel 5:10).

David was not only a military genius but also a skilled statesman and organizer. One of his first steps was to choose a new capital city. Mindful of the jealousies and rivalries existing between the tribes in the north which had supported King Saul's heir and those in the south which had supported him, he sought a neutral site. David found his answer in the city of Jerusalem. From the time the Israelites first entered Canaan, they had carefully avoided this heavily defended city-state. Built on a mountain, Jerusalem's fortress-like appearance had defied the poorly armed Israelites. David wanted Jerusalem, however, for his capital city precisely because it had never been part of any Israelite territory and, in addition, lay right on the boundary between the northern and southern tribes. He laid siege to the mountain fortress, and, once Jerusalem was captured, he made it his royal court and established there the seat of his authority as king over all Israel.

David's next step was to reorganize the tribal Confederacy. Originally, leadership in the Confederacy had depended upon a person's status in his tribe or upon the divine charisma. David abolished this system by making all leadership dependent upon the authority of the king. He replaced, therefore, the "elders" who sat at the gates of their cities and had served as judges for the people. In their stead, he selected judges who recognized that their authority came from the crown. He also appointed many other officials. Archaeologists tell us that the organization of David's court resembled in many ways that of Egypt. For example, like the Pharoah of Egypt, he, too, had a scribe whose function it was to write the king's personal letters and all governmental correspondence. Again, there was a recorder who served as David's public relations officer. There was also a chief of the military staff. Beginning with David's son, Solomon, there was to be in Israel, as in Egypt, a prime minister. The Bible refers to this person as "the one who is over the house" (I Kings 4:6). David, however, had no prime minister. David himself preferred to pass judgment upon the affairs of the country. All important documents received his personal seal. The departments of justice, public works, finance, army, and others were under his direct orders.

To guarantee further that the people's primary loyalty would be to the king and not to the tribal unit, David reorganized the land into administrative districts which did not coincide with the old tribal boundaries. He then ordered a census of the people so that all Israelites as individuals could be taxed and drafted into the military service (I Sam. 24). Prior to this time, as we have seen in the case of the judges and even of King Saul, each leader had to rely for his resources upon his own tribe and upon a group of loyal followers. Thus, we find that David had, in addition to his personal followers, a national army loyal to the state and to him as king.

David realized, however, that if his authority were to be deeply rooted, it had to rest upon the religious foundations of the Covenant. One of his first acts, therefore, was to bring the Ark of the Covenant to Jerusalem. For many years the Ark had remained in Shiloh, where it had been cared for by the priests. Here Samuel, too, had been trained. Shortly thereafter, as we have seen, the Ark was captured by the Philistines and the city of Shiloh completely destroyed. This catastrophe had intensified the Israelites' demand for a king who could ward off their enemies. For some reason, however, the Ark had been returned by the Philistines to the Israelites. The Bible tells us that a plague had broken out among the Philistines when the Ark was brought into their territory (I Samuel 5). For the next thirty years, however, the Ark had remained in the hill country of southern Canaan, where it was guarded by a loyal Israelite family (I Samuel 7:1). Apparently, the Israelites, too, did not know what to do with it.

The time had now come, concluded David, for the Ark of the Covenant to receive a permanent home in the new capital city of Jerusalem. Therefore, David ordered that the Ark be placed upon a new wagon and brought amid great pomp and ceremony to its new home. Thus, the religious center of the Israelites was shifted from the confederate sanctuary at Shiloh to the royal shrine in Jerusalem. In religion, as well as in government, David succeeded in establishing the central authority of the king.

The golden age for Israel that had begun with David soon was to reach its zenith under the dazzling accomplishments of his son Solomon. The reign of Solomon was a period of great material prosperity. Unlike his father, Solomon was not a military man. Nonetheless, like his father before him, he was a skilled politician and an able diplomat in international dealings so that he was able to bring to fulfillment the policies and programs which David had begun. In all truth, it can be said that in the combined reigns of David and Solomon, a period of only fifty to sixty years, Israel rose "from political obscurity to the rank of a small empire that could command the political attention and economic envy of nations roundabout." [1]

The international flavor of Solomon's reign was reflected both in his emphasis upon an extensive nationwide building program and upon the development of great commercial ventures which reached to the very ends of the then-known world. Almost immediately after he came to the throne, Solomon undertook a twenty-year building program for Israel. Having renewed the treaty with Hiram, the King of Phoenecia, he imported the most skilled craftsmen and purchased the finest materials which Hiram could offer. Seven years the Phoenecians and the Israelites labored together. Out of their efforts came a new and permanent home for the Ark of the Covenant. The Ark, which his father David had brought into Jerusalem, still was being housed in a temporary tent of meeting. Now Solomon had erected for its safekeeping a new Temple. Compared to modern standards, the sanctuary was rather modest; however, for its day it was a great architectural achievement. The Temple was styled in the manner of a Phoenecian house of worship. Its doors were made of cypress. Its walls were paneled with cedar, and its vessels were cast in gold. Here amid this Phoenecian splendor, Yahweh was enthroned as God of Israel (I Kings 5–7).

But even more magnificent was the palace which Solomon built for himself. Thirteen years in all the workmen labored on this structure, for this was no ordinary palace. It was more like a city within city. In addition to a house for himself, Solomon ordered a palace built for his Egyptian queen, one of the many foreign women he had married for international reasons (I Kings 9:24). For his royal courtiers, there was also a series of government buildings.

Nor was Solomon's building program restricted to Jerusalem. He had a master plan for all Israel. For example, in a number of strategic locations he erected fortified cities (I Kings 9:15–19). Here he stabled the horses which he had purchased from the Hittites who lived to the north and housed the chariots which he had bought from Egypt (I Kings 10:26–29). From these "chariot-cities" the soldiers of Solomon controlled the trade routes of the ancient world (I Kings 4:26; 9:10; 10:26).

Secure militarily, Solomon undertook to expand commercially. Because of his treaty with Hiram, Solomon had gained the use of a seaport on the Mediterranean where the Israelites soon learned the art of shipping from the searfaring Phoenicians (I Kings 10:22). Turning southward to the very tip of Israel, he also built a port on the shores of the Gulf of Aquabah. Here he constructed a fleet of ships, and from the port of Ezion-Geber the Israelite merchants sailed out to the Red Sea and the Indian Ocean (I Kings 9:26-28). He also worked the copper mines which he found nearby, and at Ezion-Geber Solomon built a copper smelting plant and developed the largest refinery in the ancient world (I Kings 7:45).

A fuller understanding of the cosmopolitan, international tone of the golden age can be derived from the visit of the

Queen of Sheba to Solomon. Sheba was a small country at the southern tip of Arabia. The Bible would have us believe that the Queen's visit was prompted by the fame of Solomon's wisdom (I Kings 10:24). It is, perhaps, more realistic to assume that the real purpose of her journey was to make a commercial treaty with Israel. Because Solomon controlled the great trade routes, he was able to interfere with much of the camel-caravan trade of Arabia. The Queen's real purpose in coming to Solomon, therefore, was to protect her own commercial interests (I Kings 10:1–13).

The reigns of David and Solomon, however, were not without their shortcomings. Each ruler had his own personality defects. Both father and son loved to indulge themselves in the manner of oriental monarchs. At times, they were over-impressed with their royal position; and, as a result, they frequently permitted their authority to get out of hand. For example, David thought nothing of sending a man to his death because he wanted to marry the man's wife (II Sam. 11). Also Solomon, despite his loyalty to Yahweh, permitted altars to foreign gods to be built even within the royal palace whenever it suited the politics of his international plans. Since many of Solomon's alliances were sealed by marriage, numerous foreign noblewomen, together with their servants and gods, were brought into his harem. The Bible relates that "he had seven hundred wives, princesses and three hundred concubines" (I Kings 11:3). The plan to erect chapels to the gods of his foreign wives, moreover, fitted in with his plans for commercial expansion. He realized that the merchants who came from distant lands would appreciate the courtesy of worshiping their own gods even in Jerusalem. Soon altars were erected for Ashtoreth, the goddess of the Zidonians, for Milcom and Chemosh, the gods of the Ammonites and Moabites, respectively, and undoubtedly for the gods of the

especially favored Egyptian princess, as well as for the gods
of all of Solomon's foreign wives.

In addition to their self-centered attitudes, both David and
Solomon showed at times considerable lack of judgment in the
manner in which they governed their people. For example,
when it became evident to Solomon that taxes alone could
not support his elaborate building programs, he resorted to
drafting a labor force. The slave labor was drawn not only
from conquered peoples but also from the Israelites themselves. Specifically, in order to secure wood for his building
program, Solomon had to make a treaty with King Hiram
of Phoenecia, who controlled the great cypress forests in
Lebanon. The agreement provided that the trees would be
floated down the Mediterranean coast of Phoenecia to the
city of Jaffa in Israel. There the timber would be carried
across the hills of Israel to Jerusalem. Since this program
required the work of more people than he could afford to
hire, Solomon drafted thirty thousand Israelites. He divided
them into three groups of ten thousand men each, with each
contingent working in the cypress forests of Lebanon for a
month. The other two months the group labored in Israel.
In this way, Solomon was able to carry out of the terms of
his treaty with Hiram (I Kings 5: 13–18). On other occasions,
it is recorded, Solomon drafted eighty thousand Israelites to
work in the stone quarries and seventy thousand men to
serve as laborers.

Thus, the achievement of new material splendor and international prestige during ancient Israel's golden age under
David and Solomon was purchased at a very high cost—the
cost of the life and liberty of its people.

The inevitable consequence of David and Solomon's mis-
rule was not long in coming. It took the form of a revolution
and the division of the united kingdom into two separate

kingdoms. The break had made its first appearance during David's reign, when the ten northern tribes which orginally had been loyal to Saul's heir Ish-Bosheth had tried to set up their own kingdom. While David chose to put down the rebellion, Solomon paid little heed to these sectional differences between the north and the south. Moreover, his policy served to intensify further the existing differences. Consequently, as soon as Solomon died, the spark that lit the successful fire of revolution was kindled. The northern tribes, under the leadership of Jeroboam, came to Solomon's son, Rehoboam, and pleaded that the yoke be lightened. It seems that Solomon's forced labor policy and taxation measures had fallen most heavily upon the more prosperious northern tribes. Rehoboam, however, did not sense the seriousness of the situation and instead threatened to use even more stern measures than his father had to bring the rebels into line. The smouldering spark of discontent now exploded into a blazing inferno of rebellion. The northern tribes gathered in council and proclaimed Jeroboam as their king. Jeroboam then appealed to Egypt for help. The Egyptians were more than willing to come to his aid, for a new Pharoah who wanted to restore Egypt's once-great military empire had ascended the throne. When Rehoboam received news of the impending Egyptian invasion, he had to forget all about Jeroboam's rebellion and muster all his strength against Egypt. This Egyptian political maneuver gave to Jeroboam the opportunity he needed to secure his newly established kingdom.

Thus, in the year 922 B.C.E., ancient Israel at the time of her greatest material prosperity and international prestige was divided in two by rebellion. The northern ten tribes were henceforth to be known as Israel. Only Judah and Benjamin to the south remained loyal to the dynasty of David and were to be called Judah.

CHAPTER IX

The Covenant Is Challenged

THE GOLDEN AGE of David and Solomon was more than a period of prosperity and prestige for ancient Israel. It was also an age of great literary achievement. These were the years when the royal scribes began to write for the first time the biographies of their kings. We have a record of these chronicles. They now form the basis of the books of Samuel, Kings, and Chronicles in our Bible. There were many other literary creations, too. Some of our present psalms were composed at this time. The Bible also refers to a number of books which long since have been lost. But above all, the golden age was the time when the Torah received its present outline.

Although the terms Genesis, Exodus, and Numbers may not have been used as names for books by the ancient Israelites, it was in the golden age that the basic outline of these books came into written form. Not everything which is included in these books today, of course, was produced at that time. As we have noted in Chapter I, the Torah represents the work of four different schools of editors. The golden age produced the first written edition.

Some scholars hold that this first written outline did not come into existence until after the division of the united kingdom in 922 B.C.E. They prefer the date c.850 B.C.E. Because of this difference of opinion, the date generally is listed as c.950–850 B.C.E. While it is true that the exact date may never be pinpointed, at the same time there is universal consent that the first written edition of the Torah came into being as a result of forces unleashed during the golden age. To this exciting chapter in the story of the birth of the Torah let us now turn.

The emergence into the iron age had brought great changes into the life of the ancient Israelites. In possession of this superior raw material, the kings of Israel were able to effect an economic revolution. A new and higher standard of living was made possible for the people. In agriculture, iron pruning hooks and sickles displaced crude stone implements. Each farmer could now own iron axes, mattocks, and plow points with which to till the soil. The substitution of hard iron nails for the softer copper ones initiated improvements in construction techniques and made possible the previously undreamed-of building programs of David and Solomon. The people, too, were building and living in excellent homes. As the Israelites mastered the use of iron, they began to free themselves from the chores of eking out a meager existence. Their new-found leisure time enabled them to partake of the many refinements of civilization which their neighbors had developed. They imported objects from abroad and immersed themselves deeply in the international culture of their day. They also turned to their Canaanite neighbors and learned from them the ways of their religion.

Brewed in this ferment of increasing prosperity and the mixing of religious cultures, there was born in ancient Israel a religious crisis. This crisis threatened to destroy the religious foundations of Israel which had been laid by Moses and so carefully nurtured in the succeeding generations. The problem was: could the covenant of Yahweh, fashioned in a desert-wilderness and reaffirmed by Joshua in the primitive settings of Shechem, still serve a cosmopolitan, wealthy, and culturally sophisticated people? There lived in Judah at the time a group of people who believed that the answer to this challenge could be put in the affirmative. They, therefore, set themselves the task of making the covenant relationship with Yahweh as meaningful to the Israelites of their generation as it had been to their ancestors before them. Out of their labors came the first written edition of the Torah.

These champions of Yahweh have been called by scholars the writers of the J School. The use of the letter "J" arose in Germany at the end of the last century. Since the writers in the golden age emphasized the name Yahweh, which in German is spelled "Jahveh," scholars came to identify them as the J School. Their individual names, however, are lost to history, and nothing is known of their activities. Their contributions, on the other hand, have continued to live on through the ages.

Fortunately, the writers of the J School did not need to start from scratch. By the time of the golden age the traditions of ancient Israel were rich and full. What originally had begun as loosely knit oral memories had developed over the years into a unified body of familiar oral and written traditions. For example, each year during the celebration of the nature festivals of Pesach, Shavuot, and Sukkot, the stories of the exodus from Egypt and the memories of the patriarchs were recalled. In time, the fixed order in which these stories were told formed a standard part of the celebration. In the same manner, religious rituals became accepted customs and were repeated with each occasion. In addition, the J writers were heir to another significant oral and written source, which, as we shall see, stemmed from the surrounding cultures.

The writers of the J School, thus, had much material with

which to work. Their task was not to create something new but to make the accumulated traditions meaningful to the new generation.

Before we turn to the Torah version of the golden age, it is important to examine the materials which the J writers found in the literatures and traditions of the surrounding Mesopotamian and Canaanite cultures. The most famous of all is the Epic of Gilgamesh, discovered in 1872 by George Smith, a young British archaeologist.

One day Smith was busy sorting clay tablets which had been discovered in the library of King Ashurbanipal (669–633 B.C.E.) in Nineveh, located on the Tigris River in Mesopotamia. Slowly and laboriously George Smith divided the tablets of the Assyrian king into six groups for convenience: war, business, literature, mythology, and so on. On this day, as he picked up a fragment to see to what group it belonged, his hand suddenly stopped in midair. The little clay tablet described how a ship had rested on a mountain top. This was followed by a story of the sending out of a dove which found no resting place and returned to the boat. George Smith realized that he had discovered a parallel version to the Biblical story of Noah and the Flood. As he examined the tablets further during the course of the next few years, he concluded that they constituted a continuous series of legends giving the history of the world from the Creation to some period after the rebellion of man. There were stories of how the world was created, the role of the serpent, how death came into the world, how man discovered that he was naked and clothed himself, the rebelliousness of man and the destruction by a flood, the building of an ark, flights of the dove and the raven, and other incidents which paralleled the Bible accounts.

Since the time of George Smith, other ancient literary

documents describing these same events have been found not
only in Nineveh but also in other places as well. The Flood
story particularly is known from many sources. Scholars
believe today that these ancient legends, created to explain the
origins and early history of the world, were widely used by
many peoples throughout the Fertile Crescent area, stretch-
ing from Mesopotamia in the east to Canaan in the west. In
fact, archaeologists today can show that the discoveries in
Nineveh are themselves based on even older traditions going
back to the people of Sumer, who lived in the Tigris-
Euphrates river valley before 3000 B.C.E. The Sumerians are
believed to have been the inventors of writing, and they, too,
had stories dealing with the creation of the world and the
Flood.

The epic of Gilgamesh contained two famous stories, both
of which have their parallels in the Bible: (1) Gilgamesh's
attempt to find everlasting life, and (2) the destruction of
the world by a flood.

Gilgamesh, the central hero of the epic, was two-thirds god
and one-third man. Gilgamesh sought the immortality of the
gods by building for himself lasting monuments to his greatness in his home city of Uruk. He was, however, an arrogant
ruler, and he oppressed his fellow townsmen. When the
people of Uruk appealed to the gods of heaven for relief, the
same goddess who had created Gilgamesh pinched off a piece
of clay and made the second principal character of the epic.
His name was Enkidu, and he was Gilgamesh's double.

Enkidu was an uncivilized man. His body was covered with
shaggy hair, and he fed on grass and played at the watering
places with the animals, who were his friends and whom he
protected. One day, one of Enkidu's enemies tried to civilize
him by enticing him with a young girl. As soon as Enkidu
tasted of the young girl's love, he became tame and no longer

sought to run with the animals. He preferred now to lead his life among humans.

In time Enkidu and Gilgamesh became fast friends, because each respected the other for his great strength. Together they set out on a hazardous expedition against a monster who lived in Cedar Forest. Despite the warnings of the people that their journey might bring them disaster, they were successful in killing the monster. In a dream, however, Enkidu had a foreboding of his own death as punishment for slaying the monster, and shortly after he died.

The rest of the Epic dealt with Gilgamesh's long and fruitless quest for endless life. Enkidu's passing had brought home to him the reality of death. Fearing his own demise, Gilgamesh undertook a long and dangerous journey to the place where Utnapishtim, the hero of the flood, lived. Gilgamesh asked him about death and life, but he was advised only to accept the fact that life was not permanent. No house was built forever, and no contract was ever sealed, counseled Utnapishtim. Gilgamesh, still undeterred, asked Utnapishtim why he had been able to live endlessly. The reply was the story of the flood and how he had been saved through his obedience to the god Ea. When he had finished recounting the story of the flood, Utnapishtim set a test to try Gilgamesh's heroism. Gilgamesh was not to sleep for six days and seven nights. Gilgamesh, however, was all too mortal, and he failed the test. As he was about to return to Uruk, Utnapishtim's wife suggested that her husband reward Gilgamesh for his perilous journey. He consented and revealed to Gilgamesh that if he could grasp a certain thorny plant which lay at the bottom of the sea, he could have eternal life. Tying heavy stones to his feet, Gilgamesh descended to the bottom of the sea, where he obtained the plant and called it "Man Becomes Young in Old Age." Returning home, Gilgamesh stopped for the night. While he was bathing in a pool of water, however, a serpent stole the plant. Immediately the serpent shed its skin. Frustrated in his search, Gilgamesh returned to Uruk. He now knew that "when the gods created mankind, death for mankind they set apart."

The flood episode represented only one scene in the Epic of Gilgamesh. When the great gods of the city of Shuruppah had decided to destroy mankind by a flood, the god Ea disclosed the divine decree to Utnapishtim, who was to be the hero. Ea told him to build a ship and to take aboard "the seed of all living things." The ship, moreover, was to be so many cubits high, and so many wide, and to provide certain rooms for different needs. After the ship was completed, Utnapishtim brought aboard his possessions, the animals, the members of his family, and the necessary craftsmen. In dramatic poetic fashion, the ancient Babylonian author of the epic then described in detail the approaching storm. Six days and six nights the wind blew, and on the seventh the storm subsided. When Utnapishtim looked outside, he noticed that "stillness had set in," and that all of mankind "had returned to clay. The landscape was as level as a flat roof." Finally, the ship came to rest on Mount Niser. On the seventh day, Utnapishtim sent forth a dove, but it returned, having found no resting place. The same happened when he sent out a swallow. Finally, he let free a raven; it found food and did not come back to the ship. So Utnapishtim offered a sacrifice on the top of the mountain. As the gods smelled the sweet flavor of the offerings, they gathered about Utnapishtim. There they held a council and decided that henceforth Utnapishtim and his wife, who had been human, should be like unto the gods.

Because of their strong universal influence, it is not surprising to find that the stories of the Gilgamesh epic and other similar sources were used by the Israelites, too. Undoubtedly, even during the time of the patriarchs they were well known. These legends of the Creation and early man formed part of the oral and written traditions which were handed down from generation to generation, from father to son. There was to be one major difference, however, between the version used by the Israelites and those treasured by the other peoples. As we are about to see, the Israelites were not indiscriminate borrowers. While they made use of these traditions which were readily available, they changed them to present their own views about Yahweh and the meaning of life. The Israelites infused these accounts with their belief in a One God with whom they were bound in a covenant relationship. These stories were for them only vehicles for expressing their covenant faith.

At one time it was believed that the Israelites originated all the stories of the Torah; however, archaeological discoveries, as we have seen, have given us reason to revise this point of view. Today, we know that the ancient writers used materials already in existence. Perhaps the first to do so in formal written fashion were the writers of the J School.

For the J writers, there could be no doubt that the covenant with Yahweh was just as valid in the golden age as it had been in the days of Moses and Joshua; consequently, they set themselves to their task with a literary skill and success unparalleled, perhaps, in human history. To accomplish their goal of making the old Mosaic tradition meaningful to the sophisticated generation of the golden age, the writers of the J School presented a new interpretation of history. There were two steps in their program. First, they explained to the people that Yahweh was the God of all history, even from the beginning of the world. Despite the fact that Moses had introduced the name Yahweh to the Hebrews for the first time in the Sinai desert-wilderness, the writers of the J School undertook to show that in reality Yahweh was also the God of Abraham,

Isaac, and Jacob. The patriarchs may have called Him by different names, they pointed out, but it was no other God than Yahweh himself who had made the covenants with the fathers. Finally, the J writers reached back to the very beginnings of Creation and made Yahweh not only the God of the Exodus and the God of the Patriarchs but also the Creator of the world itself. Yahweh was, therefore, the God of all history.

Second, they pointed out that Yahweh was more than the God of all history. He was also a God who had a special relationship with the Israelites. They recalled the old promise which Yahweh had made to Abraham that his seed would both inherit the land of Canaan and become a great nation. Moreover, they remembered that this promise was repeatedly renewed (Gen. 15:5, 13–16, 18:18) and sealed by a covenant (Gen. 15:7–12; 17–21). It was given also to Isaac (Gen. 26:2–4) and to Jacob (Gen. 28:13–15), and renewed to Moses (Ex. 3:6–8). This promise began to find its fulfillment, though never a complete fulfillment, in the days of Abraham; in the golden age, however, the J writers firmly believed that the original promise was at last being fulfilled completely.

CHAPTER X

The J School:
The Primeval Tradition

THE Torah edition of the J School was organized in three parts:

(1) The primeval traditions contained the narratives from the creation of the world to the time of Abraham. These stories dealt not with Israel alone but with all mankind. They are found today in the book of Genesis, chapters 2–11.

(2) The patriarchal narratives covered the stories of Abraham, Isaac, and Jacob, concluding with the account of Joseph in Egypt. In these episodes, found in Genesis 12–50, a great emphasis was placed upon Yahweh's promise to Abraham that his descendants would inherit the land of Canaan. Moreover, the different accounts of Abraham, Isaac, and Jacob were unified by the J writers and made to fit into the main theme of Yahweh's promise to Abraham.

(3) The fulfillment of the Promise to Abraham, described primarily in the books of Exodus, Numbers, and Joshua, recounted the sojourn in Egypt, the wanderings in the Sinai desert-wilderness, the murmurings and rebellions of the people, and the conquest of the land of Canaan.

Since the episodes belonging to the third part of the J writers' edition of the Torah have been dealt with at great length in previous chapters, the emphasis in this chapter will be placed upon the interpretations given by the J school to the primeval history. The following chapter will deal with the narratives of the patriarchs.

The Primeval Tradition

In presenting their interpretation of the primeval tradition, the J writers wanted to provide their generation with the necessary background material which would indicate why Yahweh, in order to fulfill His plans for mankind, had to choose Israel for special training. They accomplished this goal by emphasizing two points: (1) Yahweh, as the Creator and Father of all mankind, was concerned in every generation with how his children lived; (2) despite Yahweh's concern, from the very beginning man has insisted upon rebelling against Yahweh. The J writers, therefore, were interested not so much in writing a detailed history or a scientific treatise of the Creation and early history of the world as they were in selecting illustrations to emphasize their purposes. From a present-day historical or scientific point of view, there are many gaps in the J writers' account; however, from the standpoint of the J writers, the narrative represented the complete story of man's continuous failure to obey Yahweh. The J writers had one motivating purpose, namely, to lead their contemporaries to the inevitable conclusions that Yahweh had to choose Abraham and his descendants if His plan were to be fulfilled and that they were the heirs to this tradition.

The J edition of the primeval history can be studied best under the following headings: (1) Creation and the nature of man; (2) The Flood story; and (3) Noah's drunkenness and the Tower of Babel.

Creation and the nature of man

There are two stories of Creation in the Torah. The first account begins with the opening verse of Genesis (1:1) and continues through Chapter 2, verse 4a. (The "a" means that only the first half of verse 4 belongs to this Creation story.) This interpretation of the creation of the world, however, belongs to the P School, which will be discussed in Chapter 18. The J version of the Creation story is found in Genesis 2:4b–25. The raising of two questions immediately will dramatize the obvious differences between the J and P creation stories: (1) On what day was man created? and (2) Was man created alone? A rapid review of the Bible text will indicate that in the P version both male and female alike were created on the sixth day (Gen. 1:27–31). In the J version, however, there is no listing of days; moreover, man is not the last act of creation. He is among the first things created (Gen. 2:7), and woman is, as it were, an afterthought (Gen. 2:18–25). Traditionalists, as pointed out in Chapter 1, will try to harmonize these obvious differences. Modernists, on the other hand, will accept these two separate accounts and will try to understand them in their respective historical settings.

Turning now directly to the J Creation story, it can be said that the J writers were not so much concerned with the specific details of the order of Creation as they were with the kind of life situation in which man found himself. For example, they did not describe the details of the creation of the heavens, the earth, the sun, the moon and the stars, etc.; instead, they began their account simply with the phrase "in the day that the Lord God made earth and heaven" (Gen. 2:4b). Interested primarily in man, they told that he was made of the dust of the earth and that he was to live out his life on the earth. Man was to be a tiller of the soil; therefore, they gave him the name "Adam" which in Hebrew is derived from the same root as *adamah*, meaning "earth." Man also needed to relate himself to other humans; he needed a "helpmeet." Marriage was to be a necessary part of his existence; consequently, they derived the Hebrew word for woman, *ishah*, from the Hebrew *ish*, meaning "man." It was proper, the J writers taught, that "a man should leave his father and mother, and should cleave unto his wife" (Gen. 2:24). Man, however, was a creature who lived not only with himself and with others; he could enter also into a relationship with Yahweh. Man could be given responsibilities; thus, Yahweh placed man in the Garden of Eden and entrusted him with the care of the Garden.

The J writers wished to point out that from the very beginning man's relationship with Yahweh was such that man could choose either to obey or to disobey Yahweh. As they developed the story, they explained that man preferred to abuse his relationship and, consequently, to disobey Yahweh. Adam, for example, ate the forbidden fruit. The J writers also wished to explain that death was a natural consequence of human existence. Adam and Eve realized not only that they were naked but also that all human life was mortal and that they, too, would die. Moreover, during their lifetime, man and woman would need to toil in the sweat of their brow for their sustenance. Life could not be lived, concluded the J writers, without effort, nor was it devoid of pain.

By telling this story, the writers of the J School, like the author of the Epic of Gilgamesh, gave their answers to the universal questions which undoubtedly circulated among the ancient storytellers: Why were man and woman attracted to each other? Why was it proper to wear clothes? Why must there be the pain of childbirth and the misery of hard work? Why was the serpent hated by men? To these, however, they added one more question. It was the deeper question of why man, from the very beginning, having been created by Yahweh, refused to obey his Creator.

In the story of the Garden of Eden, and also in the episode of Cain and Abel, the J writers illustrated the record of man's rebellion against Yahweh. The defiance was best expressed in Cain's protest, "Am I my brother's keeper?" Violence and corruption, they concluded, accompanied all human life, and they pointed out also that the first city to be built was by Cain, a murderer, and that the father of musicians and the forger of metals was a descendant of Cain (Gen. 4:17–26). The climax of the rebellion came, in the eyes of the J writers, in a story of unknown origin in which the sons of God, let alone man, proved themselves defiant by stealing girls from the earth (Gen. 6:1–4). Thus Yahweh, who was described by the J writers as having human feelings, was "sorry," "grieved to the heart" that he had ever created man. It now became necessary for Yahweh to choose one branch of the human family; subsequently, he selected Noah, who was the most righteous man in his generation, in order to carry out his plan for mankind.

The Flood

The Bible preserves for us two versions of the Flood story. Both of these are woven together so that only the skilled eye can differentiate them. Like the Creation story, one version came from the much later P School; the other was the product of the writers of the J School. Both schools, however, were familiar with the flood story of Utnapishtim and with the other ancient sources of the deluge and, without a doubt, borrowed heavily from them. At the same time, it must be repeated once again that both the J and the P writers used these traditions only as vehicles for presenting their own views about life.

The following table will illustrate briefly some of the obvious differences between the J and P interpretations of the Flood narrative:

	J ACCOUNT	P ACCOUNT
1. Name used for God	Yahweh	Elohim
2. Number of animals	Seven male and seven female of clean animals and two each of the unclean (7:2–3)	Two of each kind of animal whether clean or unclean (6:19)
3. Source of the Flood	"rain from heaven" (8:2b)	"The fountains of the great deep . . . and the windows of heaven . . ." (7:11)
4. Aftermath of the Flood	Noah built an altar and brought a sacrifice of every clean animal. Yahweh promised not to curse the ground again and established the seasons (8:20–22).	Yahweh established a covenant with Noah. Yahweh promised not to destroy the earth again and placed a rainbow in the sky (9:1–17).

The Flood story of the J writers may be summarized as follows: When Yahweh decided to destroy man, only Noah found favor with Yahweh (Gen. 6:5–8); therefore, Noah was commanded to go into the ark with his family (Gen. 7:1). He was to take with him seven pairs of all "clean" animals, and only a pair each of the unclean (Gen. 7:2–3). After everyone was gathered in the Ark (Gen. 7:7) Yahweh shut them in (Gen. 7:16b) and the rains began to fall for forty days and nights (Gen. 7:12). The Ark was lifted high above the earth (Gen. 7:17b), and all forms of life were blotted out from the face of the earth (Gen. 7:22–23), except those which were with Noah in the Ark. At last the rains from heaven stopped, and the waters began to recede (Gen. 8:2b–3a). After forty days, Noah sent forth a raven to see if it could find a dry place. A week later he released a dove, but both the raven and the dove returned to the Ark, for the waters still covered the earth. Noah waited another seven days. When the dove returned with an olive branch in its mouth, Noah knew that the land was beginning to dry (Gen. 8:6–11a). So Noah built an altar and brought sacrifices from every clean animal. Finally, the J writers related how Yahweh, delighted with the sweet smell of the sacrifices, promised never again to curse the ground. Yahweh, too, realized that man had been given the power to do evil even from the time of his youth, from the very moment when he was old enough to know the difference between good and evil. Once again, therefore, Yahweh had shown his concern for man's welfare. The seasons of the year and the regularity of night following day were to be the signs that Yahweh did not wish again to destroy his creatures (Gen. 8:20–22).

In the telling of the Flood story, the J writers reaffirmed for their generation the basic truth that it was Yahweh who had directed the destiny of mankind from the beginning. Man might choose not to follow the ways of Yahweh, but Yahweh still carried out his purposes. If need be, He might destroy even his creatures, leaving only those who, He believed, would be faithful to Him.

While the similarities between the adventures of Noah and Utnapishtim, his Babylonian counterpart, are many, two important differences should be noted. In the Babylonian account, there were many gods, as we have seen in the last chapter, who not only decided to destroy mankind but also held a council to declare that Utnapishtim was now to be like the gods. For the J writers, on the other hand, there was only one God, and this God was Yahweh. Moreover, in contrast to the caprice of the Babylonian gods, Yahweh acted in keeping with a purpose. For example, the Babylonian gods might make Utnapishtim important because they liked the sweet smell of his sacrifices. For Yahweh, however, the fragrance of the sacrifices was only a reminder to Yahweh that he had preserved a righteous man through whom the divine plan could be fulfilled. Again, Utnapishtim was saved because the god Ea betrayed the secret of the other gods to destroy mankind. Noah, on the other hand, was the human counterpart through whom Yahweh enacted his plan. The whole Flood story, beginning with Noah's entering the Ark together with his family and the animals, was part of Yahweh's plan to make a new beginning in history.

Mention should be made at this point of one of the most notable archaeological attempts to document the Flood. In 1922, the famous British archaeologist, Sir Leonard Wooley, decided to find actual physical proof of the Biblical Flood. For seven years he labored in Ur of the Chaldees, the traditional birthplace of Abraham. One day his men began to dig into a huge graveyard pit. As the soil was removed, large quantities of household rubbish were found: the gray ashes from hearth fires, black soot, half-burnt wood, gray mud bricks, masses of broken pottery, etc. For forty feet the workmen dug, and Sir Leonard was able to date roughly the various layers of each civilization. Finally, there was no more debris, and only clean clay was to be seen. Its texture was very uniform, indicating that it had been laid there by water. At first, Sir Leonard thought that he had reached the river clay which formed the delta in ancient times. Later, however, he decided that this could not be, and he ordered his men to dig further. After eight feet of clay, they came suddenly upon more stone implements, clay sickles, flints, and painted pottery. These were from a much earlier period than those found above the clay. Sir Leonard came to a conclusion: the uniform bed of water-laid clay could have resulted only from a mighty flood. Here was the evidence he needed. He dug another pit further away and found more support for his theory. He finally concluded that a flood must have covered the lower valley lying between the Tigris and Euphrates Rivers, some four hundred miles long and one hundred miles wide. To the inhabitants of the valley at that time, this area was the whole world.

Since Sir Leonard's discovery, many other similar clay deposits have been found in other parts of the ancient world. Undoubtedly, there were many such floods which the people of a particular area believed destroyed the whole world. Scholars, therefore, feel that there were many flood traditions and that, despite the importance of Sir Leonard's findings, there is no need to assume that the flood described in the Bible occurred in the vicinity of the city of Ur of the Chaldees.

Noah's drunkenness and the Tower of Babel

The inevitable selection of Abraham became necessary, according to the J writers, because of the events which followed the Flood. These were: (1) the drunkenness of Noah (Gen. 9:18–27), and (2) the construction of the Tower of Babel (Gen. 11:1–9).

Not even Noah, whose very rescue from the Flood was to have marked a new beginning in history, proved himself equal to his responsibilities. The J writers related how Noah's children found him naked and in a state of drunkenness. Thus, he was disqualified according to the requirements of Yahweh. Many centuries later, the Rabbis, commenting upon Noah's inadequacies, pointed out that Noah was only relatively righteous. In contrast to the wickedness of his generation, Noah appeared to be a righteous man; however, had he lived in the time of Abraham, he would not have been righteous at all, for Abraham, they emphasized, would have been righteous no matter in which generation he would have lived.

The J writers had a twofold purpose, however, in telling the story of Noah's drunkenness. They wished to show that Noah was inadequate and also to emphasize that the people of their own generation were like Noah. For example, the story of Noah's drunkenness reflected the J writers' concern with the overwhelming impact which the religion of Canaan had made upon the Israelites.

The cultural backgrounds of the Canaanites and the Israelites were quite different. The Canaanites were agriculturalists, and their gods were responsible for making the soil fertile. The Israelites, on the other hand, had a nomadic shepherd background, and their God Yahweh was the one God who controlled not only the destiny of man but also the forces of nature. When the Israelites settled in Canaan and began to be farmers, however, many of the Israelites believed that they had to worship the gods of the Canaanites. Otherwise, they argued, the land would remain barren. In time, many of the Canaanite rituals became familiar practices among the Israelites.

The story of Noah's drunkenness was the J writers' way of describing the struggle between the Canaanite fertility gods and the Israelite God Yahweh. Noah, who had been saved by Yahweh to fulfill Yahweh's plan, failed in his responsibility precisely because he, too, had succumbed to the ways of the Canaanites with their wine-drinking and sexual license. This story was the J writers' warning to their generation that if they as a people were to be true to their covenant responsibilities with Yahweh, they had to guard themselves against the enticements of the Canaanite religion. The dramatic significance of their argument was heightened when Noah, realizing what he had done, pronounced a curse upon his son who, symbolically, was called Canaan.

The record of man's rebellion against Yahweh also was the theme of the J writers' interpretation of the Tower of Babel story. Archaeology has shown that a particular type of tower raised in successive terraces high above the plain was the most characteristic form of architectural construction in ancient Mesopotamia. The tower was called a "ziggurat," which in the Akkadian language meant "to be high or raised up." Some of the towers had a shrine on top and were, accordingly, temple towers. So far archaeologists have made a list of thirty-three such structures in twenty-seven different cities. Two of the most famous ziggurats were discovered at Ur and at Babylon.

The building of such towers was certainly done as early as the Sumerian period. At Ur the oldest ziggurat may have been constructed by the founder of the First Dynasty. Then in the Third Dynasty, around 2000 B.C.E., a much larger ziggurat was built over the first one. This was done by King Ur-Nammu, whose name and title are still to be read on the bricks of the monument. In the sixth century B.C.E., Nabonidus of Babylon repaired the upper part of the structure but, in an inscription, gave credit to Ur-Nammu as the former builder. Nabonidus also said that Ur-Nammu did not complete the work, but that it was finished by his son Shulgi. This tower, although now in ruins, of course, is still the best preserved of all these monuments and gives a powerful impression to the visitor who sees it loom up above the Mesopotamian plain. The base was 200 feet by 150 feet, the core was of unbaked brick, and the facing, about 8 feet thick, was of baked brick set in bitumen.

As for the ziggurat at Babylon, most of its bricks have long since been carried away for other buildings, and where it once stood there is scarcely more than an enormous hole filled with water which has seeped in from the Euphrates. Nevertheless, the excavator of Babylon, Robert Koldeway, was able to obtain some architectural evidence of the existence, and there is also some information in cuneiform sources and in Herodotus. The name of the tower was E-temen-an-ki, meaning "house of the foundation of heaven and earth." It stood in a very large enclosure about fifteen hundred feet square. It was erected upon a square foundation, each side of which was about three hundred feet long. The interior was of dried brick and the outer shell, almost fifty feet thick, of baked brick. From a cuneiform tablet and from Herodotus it is gathered that the tower rose in seven stories to a height of almost three hundred feet, and thus it was second only to the great pyramids of Egypt in imposing mass. Under the later kings Nabopolassar and Nebuchadnezzar, the structure attained its greatest magnificence, and the temple on top was covered with blue enameled tile. How early the tower originated is not known, but in its very impressive character it must have represented to all who knew Mesopotamia the very high point of man's striving toward civilization.[1]

The J writers used the historically accurate allusions to the rise of civilization contained in the story of the Tower of Babel to illustrate their thesis of man's rebellion. While early man built the world's first great, flourishing civilization, characterized by a great city and especially by a great tower, this same man also became corrupt. In fact, it was necessary for Yahweh to scatter the peoples of Mesopotamia to all parts of the earth and to diversify their languages in order to overcome man's own efforts to deify himself and to worship his material possessions.

In this manner, the J writers brought the period of the primeval history to a close. Man, having failed to find the fullness of life, had rebelled against Yahweh. He had not learned to live in peace with his neighbor. This conclusion led the J writers to the next theme of their Torah edition. The time now had come for Yahweh to choose Abraham, and, through Abraham and his descendants, to carry out His purpose in the world.

CHAPTER XI

The J School:
The Patriarchal Tradition

WHEN the golden age of Israel began in the tenth century B.C.E., more than seven hundred years had elapsed since the Hebrews had entered Egypt, and a thousand years perhaps since Abraham had lived. During this long interlude, the many stories of the old patriarchal traditions had undergone slow but radical changes. Originally, as we have seen in Chapter 2, the patriarchs were tribal heroes, unrelated to each other. Each one worshiped a separate god. By the time of the golden age, the popular tradition had made Abraham, Isaac, and Jacob father, son, and grandson; moreover, they all worshiped now the same God Yahweh. From their descendants also came the twelve tribes who, as a group, descended into Egypt, where they were enslaved. Thus, when the J school began to write in the tenth century B.C.E., the old ancestor heroes had lost their individuality. They had become personifications of the people of Israel itself. The names Abraham, Isaac, and Jacob had become synonymous with the early history of the Hebrews. Into this revised patriarchal tradition the J writers wove their theme.

The patriarchal history begins in Genesis 12 with the story of Yahweh's threefold promise to Abraham: "[go] unto the land that I will show you. And I will make you a great nation, and I will bless you . . . and by you all the families of the earth will bless themselves" (Gen. 12:1–4a). Here is the keynote to the entire J history:

(1) To possess a land,

(2) To become a great nation, and

(3) To be a blessing through whom all the other nations would be blessed.

The first two of these three themes, it will be recalled, are part of the promise which had been made to Abraham. The third, some scholars feel, was original with the J writers. At the same time, it must not be presumed that the J writers took undue liberties with the traditions. Whereas the early modernists believed that the J writers created most of their materials, contemporary modernists are more inclined to give greater credence to the literary sources.

The Yahwist, in shaping the individual narrative, probably did not go beyond some trimming of the archaic profiles and making definite fine accents. He could naturally act much more freely when joining originally independent narratives. . . . And the important thing is this: . . . his basic theological conceptions, are much less apparent within the individual narratives than in the character of the composition as a whole. . . . [they are] essentially expressed in the way he has linked together the materials, connected and harmonized them with one another . . .[1]

The threefold promise, whether based entirely upon tradition or in part original, runs, nonetheless, like a thread throughout the entire work of the J writers. Their primary purpose in retelling the stories of the patriarchs was to show that whatever happened to Abraham, Isaac, and Jacob was in accordance with Yahweh's plan. The patriarchs did not seek a new land merely to find better pasture grounds or more profitable outlets for their cattle business. They went to Canaan because it was part of Yahweh's promise that Israel should possess the land.

On the other hand, the J writers pointed out that it was not easy for the patriarchs always to achieve the promise. Time and again, the patriarchs found themselves in embarrassing situations, even despairing that Yahweh would help them. Yahweh, however, never abandoned his people whom He had chosen. Each time, at the critical moment, the J writers told, Yahweh intervened to save the situation and to renew the promise. The thread of this theme can be seen as we examine the narratives connected with each patriarch.

Abraham

The J writers told three different stories about Abraham in which the promise of Yahweh was on the verge of being lost. The first story concerned Abraham's wife, Sarah (Gen. 12:1–13:4). During a famine, Abraham took his family to Egypt where food was available. In order to gain Pharaoh's favor, Abraham used Sarah, who was a beautiful woman, as a lure. When Pharaoh wanted to marry her, Abraham did not protest. He even lied, claiming that she was his sister. If the marriage had taken place, the promise of Israel's future through the seed of Abraham would have been impossible. At the very last moment, however, Yahweh intervened, and the J writers described how Abraham and Sarah were sent away from Egypt with great riches. Upon his return to Canaan, Abraham called once again upon the name of Yahweh.

The second incident occurred between Abraham and Lot (Gen. 13:5–18). Because of a quarrel between their shepherds, Abraham suggested that they divide the land between them. The future fulfillment of Yahweh's promise hung in delicate balance upon Lot's decision at that moment. If Lot were to choose the land of Canaan instead of the area of the Jordan Valley, Yahweh's promise to Abraham that he would possess the land would be lost. The J writers told, however, that Lot chose the area of the wicked cities of Sodom and Gomorrah. Once again all turned out well, and in the next verses they described how Yahweh renewed again his promise to Abraham.

The third threat to the fulfillment of Yahweh's promise was the fact that Abraham had no son (Gen. 15). For lack of an heir who could carry on the family line, the promise of Yahweh would remain forever barren. The barrier appeared even more unsurmountable because Eliezer, Abraham's slave, was destined to inherit the family fortune. In a moment of weakness, Sarah offered Hagar, her handmaid, to Abraham as a wife (Gen. 16:1–16). Little did she realize that her offer would not solve the problem. Although Yahweh was concerned with Ishmael, who was born to Abraham and Hagar, the fulfillment of Yahweh's promise, according to the J writers, could be accomplished only through Sarah, whose family was related to Abraham's. Nonetheless, Yahweh once again renewed his promise by sending three messengers to Abraham at Mamre as he sat in the door of his tent (Gen. 18:1–16). They told him that despite the fact that both he and Sarah were old, a son would be born to them. Sarah, however, was more skeptical, and she laughed at the very thought that even Yahweh could accomplish such a result. The J writers played upon this incident and told that the name "Isaac" was taken from the same Hebrew root as the word "laugh."

Shortly after, the cities of Sodom and Gomorrah were destroyed (Gen. 18:17–19:38). Because of Abraham's favorite role in Yahweh's plan, he was informed in advance of Yahweh's intentions. The J writers even permitted him to intervene in behalf of the doomed cities. The fact that not even ten righteous men were to be found in Sodom and Gomorrah was used by the J writers to emphasize further the wisdom of Yahweh's choice of Abraham as the instrument through whom His promise was to be fulfilled.

Isaac

The J writers did not emphasize the life of Isaac. Their story of his birth was very fragmentary, and what we do have of it contains much material from the later editors of the Torah, namely E and P. The three incidents which the J writers did emphasize, however, indicated clearly that Isaac, like his father Abraham, was to be the instrument of Yahweh's promise.

First, the very fact of Isaac's birth was in itself important. Despite the laughter of Sarah and the doubt of Abraham, a son was born to them in old age, as Yahweh had promised (Gen. 21:1–2a, 7, 33). The second episode in which the J writers advanced their interpretation of history was the manner in which a wife was selected for Isaac (Gen. 24). Just as Abraham's marriage to Hagar could provide no acceptable heir according to the terms of Yahweh's promise, so the promise would be voided if Isaac were to marry a local girl. A wife had to be sought for him in Mesopotamia where the family homestead was established. The J writers, in relating this story, took full advantage of its drama. Would the servant of Abraham be able to find a suitable partner for Isaac? If Eliezer did, would she be willing to return to Canaan? Everything, however, turned out according to plan. For the J writers, nothing happened by chance. Yahweh was concerned constantly with his chosen people.

Little else was told by the J writers about Isaac. He seemed to be more like a carbon copy of his father. Like Abraham, he, too, tried to escape a famine but went to the land of the

Philistines instead of Egypt. He also claimed that his wife Rebekkah was only his sister (Gen. 26). (The use of the term "Philistines" is a good example of an anachronism. As we have seen in Chapter 7, the Philistines did not enter Canaan until 1187 B.C.E. One of the cities which they took over was Gerar, the city identified with Isaac. It was only natural, therefore, for the J writers, who wrote after the Philistines came to Canaan, to say that Isaac went to the land of the Philistines.) Once again, however, Yahweh intervened at the crucial moment, and the promise was renewed (Gen. 26:1–33).

Jacob

In contrast to the life of Isaac, the story of Jacob was told in great detail by the J writers. Each episode, however, fitted carefully into the outline of history in which Yahweh guided the outcome. Nonetheless, Jacob's path to success also was strewn with many obstacles. In fact, in the very birth of Jacob, the fulfillment of the promise was put to a severe test. Like Sarah, Rebekkah, too, was barren and bore a son only after Yahweh had made her a special promise to this effect. When she finally gave birth, she bore twins. Jacob, however, was born last, and the family inheritance, including the fulfillment of the promise, belonged to the eldest (Gen. 25:2–34).

Since the tradition of Israel was continued through Jacob and not Esau, the J writers had to explain away the problem of the order of Jacob's birth. This goal they achieved by telling two stories. The problem of the birthright gave the J writers little trouble. Since Esau had meager understanding of the meaning of his inheritance, the J writers concluded that it must have been of small worth to him; consequently, he was most willing to sell his birthright to Jacob for no more than a mess of pottage (Gen. 25:27–34). The problem of securing his father's blessing as the first born, however, proved to be somewhat more difficult. The J writers, aware that an oath or a blessing even though pronounced in error was irrevocable, solved the problem by permitting Jacob to trick his father. With the help of his mother, Jacob covered his arms with hairy garments and appeared before the aged and almost blind Isaac. At first Isaac was not deceived, and he thought "the voice is the voice of Jacob, but the hands are the hands of Esau." Despite his doubt, he pronounced the blessing of the first-born over Jacob (Gen. 27). In this manner, Jacob gained both the birthright and the privileges which Yahweh would confer upon Abraham's descendants.

No sooner had the J writers resolved one problem than they were confronted with another. Because of the animosity between the two brothers, Jacob had to flee the land of Canaan. Once again, the promise that the patriarchs would inherit the land was jeopardized. The J writers were fully aware of their problem, and they explained away their dilemma by telling three stories about Jacob. The J writers wove into each of these incidents their theme of Yahweh's concern for the patriarchs so that his plan for all mankind could be fulfilled through Israel.

The first story, which in its present form contains some E material, dealt with Jacob's departure for Haran (Gen. 28:10–19). The J writers pictured Jacob in a very dejected mood. Despite all that he had done to outsmart his brother, it seemed as though Esau had won after all. Since Esau was a hunter, a man who knew how to handle the bow and arrow, there was no doubt in Rebekkah's mind that he would seek his revenge. Therefore, she persuaded Isaac to send Jacob to Haran in Mesopotamia to find for himself a wife among their kinsmen. Jacob, understanding his mother's intentions, obeyed his father's wishes to go to Haran. With heavy heart, he set out on the way, reaching Beth-El that same night. Taking one of the stones of the field as his pillow, he lay down to sleep, and dreamed a dream. There was a ladder reaching to the heavens, and angels were descending and ascending. Then Yahweh appeared beside him and renewed the threefold promise given originally to Abraham: (1) that he would give to Israel the land; (2) that he would make Israel a great and numerous people; and (3) that through Israel all the families of the earth would bless themselves. When Jacob awoke in the morning, he realized that Yahweh had spoken with him. Strengthened by this promise, Jacob made a vow to be faithful to Yahweh, providing, of course, he be successful on his mission to Haran (Gen. 28:10–22).

The second story which the J writers told combined a series of legends (Gen. 29–31). Originally, these legends were no more than entertaining adventures which had befallen Jacob. The J writers, however, retold these legends to emphasize that Yahweh did concern himself with Jacob's welfare. For example, the familiar story of the well was reinterpreted to teach that it was not coincidence alone that Jacob found Rachel, who was his mother's brother's daughter (Gen. 29:1–14). Again, the old legend that Jacob possessed great herds of cattle and many flocks of sheep had special significance for the J writers. To them it was not by mere chance that Laban's flocks gave birth to streaked, speckled, and spotted offspring, which then belonged to Jacob (Gen. 29:25–43). Jacob had to be a man of wealth because Yahweh was guiding his destiny. Later, Jacob would need to use this very wealth to win over his brother Esau with lavish gifts (Gen. 33:1–17).

The third story was the account of Jacob's wrestling with the angel when he was returning to Canaan. Yahweh had kept his promise, and Jacob had become prosperous. Now it was necessary for Jacob to reaffirm the vow which he had made as a dejected young man when he first went to Haran. This story, too, was based upon an older non-Israelite source in which the angel's role originally had been taken by a night demon. All through the night the angel wrestled with Jacob; neither could outmaneuver the other. Finally the angel blessed Jacob, even though Jacob came out of the contest limping. Strengthened now by the renewed promise of Yahweh, Jacob went on to meet his brother Esau, and a reconciliation took place. The J writers had carried the story full circle. Jacob, now a prosperous man, not only was back in the land of Canaan but also was married and had many sons through whom the line of inheritance could pass. There no longer remained any question that the promise of Yahweh could be fulfilled.

Joseph

The patriarchal narratives were brought to a close by the J writers with the introduction of a short story. The stories of Joseph formed a bridge between the account of the fathers, Abraham, Isaac, and Jacob, and the enslavement in Egypt. Although the J writers did not choose to mention the promise of Yahweh even once in their story of Joseph, it is quite obvious to the modern reader that the theme of Yahweh's concern and purpose in human affairs was woven into every incident. For example, even though Joseph was sold into slavery by his brothers, it was not the evil intention of his brothers which was responsible for Joseph's becoming governor of Egypt. The very actions of his brothers were only a part of Yahweh's plan. Again, it was not a question of economics which prompted Jacob to move with his family to Egypt. The Hebrews settled in the land of Goshen because it was Yahweh's intention that they be enslaved in Egypt. In this way, the J writers set the stage for the appearance of Moses, the Exodus, and, most important of all, the establishment of the covenant relationship in the Sinai desert-wilderness.

The origin of the Joseph story went back undoubtedly to popular folklore. Many years before the appearance of the J writers, Hebrew storytellers were very familiar with the exploits of Joseph. Archaeologists today feel that the core of these stories is historically valid, because the ancient storytellers colored their accounts with much authentic Egyptian material. A few examples will illustrate the point. Egyptian inscriptions have shown that the title which Potipher gave to Joseph, namely "overseer of his house," was in actual use in Egypt (Gen. 41:40). So were the titles "chief of the butlers," and "chief of the bakers" (Gen. 40:2). Again, the birthday of the Pharaoh was the occasion for the release of prisoners (Gen. 40:21). Even Joseph's life-span of 110 years was considered to be the traditional length of a happy and prosperous life in Egyptian inscriptions (Gen. 50:22). In this way the ancient Hebrew storytellers preserved the traditions of Joseph which were to play such an important part in the J writers' account of Yahweh's plan to let all mankind be blessed through Israel.

The version of the Joseph cycle of stories which the J writers used, however, was based not only upon authentic traditions but also upon popular stories which in their origin had nothing to do with Joseph. Because of their popularity the Joseph narratives had attracted to them many other popular stories. The account of Joseph and Potipher's wife is, perhaps, the best illustration of this process.

In the British Museum in London is an old Egyptian papyrus manuscript which has been dated to the year c. 1225 B.C.E. It tells the story of two brothers, Anubis and Bitis, and the circumstances of the plot are very similar to the biblical story of Joseph and Potipher's wife (Gen. 39:1–20). Bitis was the younger brother, who lived in the same house with Anubis. Just as Joseph was entrusted with all the affairs of Potipher, so Bitis was given the responsibility of caring for all his older brother's property. This warm relationship between the two brothers was disturbed, however, by the wife of Anubis. One day when Bitis went to the house to get some seed for planting in the field, the wife tried to seduce him. Angrily, Bitis resisted and rejected the offer of his brother's wife. When he saw Anubis, however, he told him nothing about the incident. The wife, in the meantime, was seized by a strong feeling of guilt. Later that same evening, she complained to her husband that she had been mistreated by Bitis. Anubis was greatly angered, and Bitis had to flee from the house for his life.

In the Egyptian account, Anubis finally learned the truth and killed his wife, throwing her body out to the dogs. The J writers, in their reinterpretation of the story, did not tell what happened to Potipher's wife. They were concerned more with the fact that Joseph was imprisoned. There he would be able to interpret dreams and come to the attention of Pharaoh. The story of Potipher's wife, for the J writers, provided another illustration of how Yahweh's purpose operated in human life.

The third part of the J writers' reinterpretation of history —the Exodus from Egypt, the establishment of the covenant in the Sinai desert-wilderness, and the experiences leading up to the conquest of the land of Canaan—is found today in the books of Exodus, Numbers, and Joshua. These events were reviewed fully in earlier chapters, so it is unnecessary to repeat them here. What is important to restate, however, is the historical setting within which the J writers wrote.

The J writers lived in a golden age. The Israelites were not only prosperous but also international-minded. They eagerly welcomed all kinds of ideas from the farthest corners of the earth. Encouraged by their new-found wealth and influenced by the thinking of their neighbors, the Israelites during the age of David and Solomon began to challenge the effectiveness of the old Mosaic religion. They were now cosmopolitan worldly people. The covenant relationship with Yahweh, however, had been established in a desert-wilderness when they were no more than newly freed slaves. Perhaps, they concluded, a new religion now was in order.

The answer to this religious challenge was given by the J writers. The old religion was still valid. It had only to be modernized, they argued, not rejected. They set themselves, therefore, to this task and wove a reinterpretation of history into the oral and written memories of Israel. Yahweh was not just the God of the Exodus; he was nothing less than the God of all mankind, the Creator of the world itself. Yahweh, moreover, had a special relationship with Israel. Israel was to be the instrument by which Yahweh was to carry out his purpose in the world—that man find the fullness of life by learning to live with Yahweh and with his fellow man. At first man rejected Yahweh; therefore, to accomplish his goal, Yahweh had to make a threefold promise to Abraham. By the terms of this promise, He would give the land of Canaan to Abraham's descendants; Israel would become a great nation; and all the nations of the world would bless themselves through Israel. Now, in the golden age, reasoned the J writers, the promise of Yahweh was being fulfilled. The very evidence of David's and Solomon's reigns proved the fact of fulfillment: was not the conquest of the land of Canaan complete? Was it not evident to all that Israel was a great nation, enjoying abundant material prosperity and international prestige? Were not the nations of the world turning to Israel for leadership? Indeed, the period of Israel's greatest influence was yet to be, believed the J writers. There can be no doubt, concluded the J writers, that the covenant-relationship with Yahweh was just as valid now, if not more so, than it had been in the days of Moses.

In the golden age, the Torah received its written outline. It remained now for the other schools of editors and writers to enlarge that outline. To this new phase in the story of the birth of the Torah we turn next.

CHAPTER XII

The E School

THE united kingdom of the golden age came to an
end in the year 922 B.C.E. Despite the brilliant
efforts of the writers of the J school to weld the people together through a modern interpretation of the covenant relationship with Yahweh, the rivalry between the northern and
the southern tribes was too deeply ingrained to be overcome.
Moreover, Solomon's forced labor policy and taxation measures had served only to intensify the existing differences. The
consequences were inevitable. In the next generation the leaders were unable to cope with the crisis. They had neither the
personal charm nor the political prestige with which to keep
the fighting factions from destroying the empire which David
and Solomon had built. As a result, the bitterness and the re-
sentment between the north and the south continued to grow,
until at last revolution broke asunder the kingdom. Never
again was Israel to attain such status as a political power as
she had during the golden age.

During the two hundred years of its existence, the northern
kingdom of Israel was to have twenty rulers. Of this number
seven did not die of natural causes. It was not unusual for a
king to be assassinated or even to commit suicide. The intrigue
between the rival factions in Israel was almost beyond description. While some of the kings ruled Israel for as much as

twenty years, and some even for forty, it was not uncommon for a king to be deposed after only a year or two of rule. In fact, one monarch had a reign of only seven days.

In this period of relative political instability, the territory of Israel was reduced constantly. To the north, the Syrians were beginning to be stirred by their national ambitions. Gradually they worked their way southward. War raged intermittently between Israel and Syria, with the result that the territories east of the Jordan, including the all-important trade routes, eventually were lost to the Syrians.

An interesting highlight in the continuing wars of Israel for control of the territory east of the Jordan has been furnished by archaeology. In 1868, a Christian missionary was traveling in the area just east of the Dead Sea. About halfway along the shoreline in the Arab village of Dhiban, he came across a monument made of black basalt stone. Shortly after his visit, some of the local Arabs, either out of fear that the stone would be removed from their town or out of a desire for greater profit through the sale of many pieces rather than one stone, broke the monument into many fragments. Fortunately a copy of the writing on the stone had been made first. A frieze, made by placing soggy paper over the inscription and letting the paper dry, had preserved the message of the wars and the building program of Mesha, the king of Moab. The pieces of this monument, known as the Mesha Stone or the Moabite Stone, have been collected and may be seen today in the Louvre in Paris.

The Moabite Stone contained a record of the war between Moab and Israel, and also the only mention of the name of Yahweh ever found outside Palestine proper. In only one other place outside the Bible itself is the name Yahweh mentioned. In 1935, Sir James Starkey, the British archaeologist, discovered twelve tablets of correspondence, written by a soldier in a military outpost in the north of Canaan to his commander in the city of Lachish. This correspondence is known as the Lachish Letters and has been discussed fully in Chapter 1.

In his monument, Mesha boasted of his triumphs over the house of Omri, a king of Israel (876–869 B.C.E.). "Israel has perished forever," wrote Mesha. The Bible, however, gives a different and contradictory interpretation. Piecing together the boast of Mesha and the biblical account in II Kings 3:4–27, scholars have come to the conclusion that both sides tended, generally and quite understandably, to ignore their own losses and setbacks. These scholars believe that the following probably happened.

Mesha, the king of Moab, had risen in revolt against Jehoram, a grandson of Omri (849–842 B.C.E.). Jehoram then asked the king of Judah to form an alliance against the rebellious Moabites. In battle after battle the Moabites were defeated, until at last Mesha and a small group of followers found themselves trapped in a walled city. According to his stone, Mesha, believing that the setbacks were due to the fact that his god Chemosh was angry with him, tried to appease Chemosh by sacrificing his eldest son upon the walls of the city. The Israelites, believing that a curse had been placed upon them when Mesha sacrified his son, decided to give up the siege and returned home. Mesha, on the other hand, saw in the departure of the Israelite and Judean forces the return of Chemosh's favor and believed, or at least led himself to believe, that he had destroyed the house of Israel forever. His armies crossed the Jordan and regained control of the important trade routes running from Arabia to Damascus, the capital of the Syrians.

The boast of Mesha was incorrect. Israel did not perish. In fact, toward the end of her existence as an independent kingdom, Israel experienced briefly a political and economic revival which recalled the prosperity and prestige of the golden age itself. Jeroboam II, a man of dynamic personality and strong ambition, ruled Israel for forty years (786–746 B.C.E.). He renewed the treaty with the Phoenicians, who were then at the peak of their commercial and colonial activity in the Mediterranean Sea. Once again the marketplace teemed with merchants, and the rich were able to build for themselves both luxurious summer and winter homes. Literally, the people of the northern kingdom during this period reveled in the comforts and luxuries of the ancient world.

The reign of Jeroboam II was not only a period of national revival but also an age of religious ferment which saw the production of the northern equivalent of the J writers' edition of the Torah. Ever since the division of the kingdom, Israel had begun to emphasize what it considered to be the true Mosaic tradition. It was in the north that the traditions of the old tribal confederacy, which David had minimized, were preserved most strongly. In fact, Israel's first capital city was Shechem, where originally Joshua had brought the Israelites to reaffirm their covenant with Yahweh. It was in the north, too, that the idea of leadership through "charisma," through the spirit of Yahweh rather than through heredity, remained strongest. Perhaps this may explain, in part at least, why the Israelites had so many political upheavals and were never able to establish one royal line, as happened with David in Judah. The spirit of the north, quite obviously, was different from that of the south. It was inevitable, therefore, that, in an age of restored nationalism and renewed material prosperity and international prestige, Israel, too, should want to bring together her sacred historic tradition. Out of this ferment came the writings of what scholars have called the E School because of the preference for the name Elohim instead of Yahweh for God.

In Israel, there was a strong force present which worked constantly to corrupt the pure worship of Yahweh. The northern kingdom, unlike its sister southern kingdom, was closer to the culture of the Fertile Crescent. Its territory was more accessible, and, as a result, the religious ideas of the surrounding nations were able to spread to Israel quickly and easily.

In 1929, with the discovery of the Rash Shamra tablets, there emerged a clear picture of the region of the western part of the Fertile Crescent. The peoples were polytheists, believing in the existence of many gods. There was one god, however, who stood out above all the others, and whose life and death was told in the famous Epic of Baal. Baal was the storm-god, the god of rain and fertility who was pictured in the form of a bull, an animal, which represented strength and birth. In the beginning Baal was one of many gods; however, after a victorious struggle with a water dragon, his new-won fame brought him prominence. In time Baal, together with his sister Anath, began to build a temple. Suddenly their plans were interrupted by Mot, the god of the summer drought, who killed Baal and carried his body into the underworld. All the gods, except Anath, mourned deeply the death of Baal, the lord of the earth. Anath, instead, was enraged and undertook a long and difficult search to find her brother. When she did, a furious struggle ensued. Mot was killed, and Baal was brought back to life and placed again on his throne. With Baal's resurrection, the gods in heaven rejoiced once again.

The Epic of Baal formed the basis of a very practical religion for the farmers of the western part of the Fertile Crescent. Baal's death and resurrection represented for them the conflict waged in nature, namely, the changing of the seasons. Spring paralleled his birth, and fall his death. By dramatizing in a religious ceremony the story of Baal's birth and death, these peoples believed that they could guarantee the fertility of the soil and their own well-being.

When the Israelites settled in Canaan, they turned, as was explained in previous chapters, to the gods of the land. They did not mean to turn away from Yahweh, but soon Baal and Yahweh stood side by side. Especially in the popular religion was there a tendency to confuse the two. Yahweh often was referred to as "Baal." The Israelites also worshiped Yahweh according to the rituals of Baal. They took over the sacred trees and special altars which were located on hilltops. The Israelites also began to name their children after Baal. Some of the people even carried around small figurines or statues of the Canaanite gods.

The stories about Elijah were used by the ancient writers to illustrate the basic conflict between the worshipers of Yahweh and the followers of Baal. While these narratives were based upon popular legends, the Biblical writers, attempting to restore the true Mosaic worship of Yahweh, wove them into the Books of Kings to prove that Yahweh and not Baal was the true God.

One of the famous episodes in the life of Elijah was the story of his encounter with the prophets of Baal on Mount Carmel (I Kings 17–18). Elijah lived a rough, nomadic-type life on the edge of the desert. He would appear suddenly, perform his tasks, and then just as mysteriously disappear. Apparently, he was a man of great strength, and he wore garments made of leather and animal hair. One day this strange-looking man announced, in the name of Yahweh, that a drought would destroy the crops of Israel. His declaration was a direct challenge to the Canaanite Baal religion. Was Baal the real god of fertility? Or was Yahweh the master of nature? A drought did occur, and, according to the story, a famine followed, bringing many hardships to the people. Elijah then went around and, in the name of Yahweh, provided food and water and even restored the dead to life. Each of these miracles are not to be understood by us today in a literal sense. They were part of the many legends which always gathered around ancient popular heroes. The Biblical writers used these legends, however, to prove that Yahweh and not Baal controlled nature and the lives of all men.

The climax to the Baal-Yahweh struggle was to come soon. One day Elijah met Ahab, the King of Israel (869–850 B.C.E.), who immediately accused him of being the big troublemaker in Israel. The drought and the famine were due to Elijah's strange actions, charged the King. Elijah immediately challenged Ahab and told him that the misfortunes of Israel were due to his support of the Baal worship. Yahweh, not Baal, controlled the fertility of the soil, proclaimed Elijah. He then challenged the 450 prophets of Baal to a contest on Mount Carmel to determine who was the true God. The meaning of this challenge can be understood best by recalling the words which Elijah used when he spoke to the people: "How long halt you between two opinions?" (I Kings 18:21). The Hebrew, however, is much richer. Elijah, actually, was saying to the people: "How long will you keep hopping from one leg to the other?" Perhaps Elijah, when he spoke to the people, had in mind the picture of a bird climbing on a limb. The Israelites were like a bird hopping along on a limb until it came to a fork. Then the bird wanted to go ahead by putting forth one foot on one branch, and the other on the second branch. In the same way, charged Elijah, the Israelites wanted to keep one foot in the traditional worship of Yahweh and the other in the practice of Baal. The objective of the contest on Mount Carmel, therefore, was to settle once and for all the question of whether Yahweh, who had been made known to Israel by Moses in the Sinai desert-wilderness, or Baal, the god of the Canaanites, was the real god.

How shall we understand the miracle of the flame of fire which the ancient writers claimed kindled the offering of Elijah but not that of the Baal-priests, thus giving the victory to Yahweh? A number of explanations have been offered. Some attribute the miracle to accidental causes. For example, it has been suggested that the water which Elijah poured over the offering actually contained naphtha, which is known to exist in deposits on the slopes of Carmel. Others imply collusion on Elijah's part. They suggest that he waited deliberately until an electric storm was approaching in the hope that the exposed summit of Carmel would draw a bolt. There are also those who say that Elijah intentionally drenched the offerings with naphtha and then secretly ignited it. The truth of the matter is that we shall never know what happened. "We may reserve the right to question the form and content of the legend, but the faith of Elijah and his converts that created the legend is too authentic to tamper with, even though we cannot hold their faith in the same way." [1]

The emphasis upon the miraculous in the Elijah stories becomes even more significant when placed within the historical context of the treaty between Israel and Tyre which was sealed by Ahab's marriage to Jezebel, a devotee of the gods of Tyre, namely, Baal-Melkart and Asherah. According to the terms of the alliance, Jezebel was permitted, together with her retainers and the merchants who followed her in the interest of trade, to continue the practice of her native religion on Israelite soil. Jezebel, however, was filled with an almost missionary zeal for her god and was undoubtedly quite contemptuous of the cultural backwardness and austere religion of her adopted land. Soon, the court and the ruling class were thoroughly paganized, and the prophets of Baal and Asherah were given official status (I Kings 18:19). While the majority of the people went "limping on two opinions," and escaped, thereby, the zeal of Jezebel, those who remained steadfastly loyal to Yahweh soon felt the full force of her wrath. The more the followers of Yahweh resisted, the more enraged she became, and the more she invoked reprisals. Violence became the order of the day. Within this context it becomes readily un-

derstandable why any follower of Yahweh who had the courage openly to oppose the Queen would be clothed in time,
at least in the popular imagination, with the mantle of miracle-
working. The books of Kings, which were edited by those
devoted to the cause of Yahweh, certainly retained this element of the miraculous. The contest on Mount Carmel, while
it ended seemingly in a victory for Elijah, did not resolve the
issue. If anything, it only served to embitter Jezebel, whose
yearning for revenge became insatiable. Not even the revolution of Jehu (842–815 B.C.E.), the defender of the pure tradition of Yahweh, who killed Jezebel and destroyed the pagan
altars, was able to stem the tide. The worship of Baal continued to grow in the northern kingdom. By the time Jeroboam II came to the throne in 786 B.C.E., the major holidays of
Baal were celebrated widely in all Israel. It was common
practice, too, for the people to bring their sacrifices regularly
to the pagan altars and to worship statues in the form of bulls,
the very image of Baal himself.

The reign of Jeroboam II was the ideal time for the appearance of the E version of the covenant tradition. First, it
was a period of national prosperity and international prestige.
It was only natural, therefore, for the writers of the E school
to wish to emulate their southern cousins, the writers of the
J School, and to produce a national epic of their own.

Second, the national prosperity was bringing the long struggle between Yahwism and Baalism to a new climax. The
people, secure in their material wealth, had begun to take their
covenant relationship with Yahweh for granted. There was a
smugness about their attitude toward Yahweh, in which it
appeared that the people could do no wrong. Had not Yahweh made them prosperous and given them a position of international importance? This smugness was mixed also with
a sense of complacency. Yahweh, no matter what the people

might do, would not abandon his people. What difference would it make, therefore, if the worship of Yahweh were colored by the practices of Baal. Against this twofold background of nationalism and religious smugness and complacency, the writers of the E School undertook to bring together the story of their national epic. In this manner, the E writers also sought to restore the true worship of Yahweh.

The work of the E writers, despite a number of differences, tells fundamentally the same story as do the writings of the J School. "It is probable that J and E go back to a common original. . . . It is . . . reasonable to regard them as parallel recessions of a common original transmitted in different parts of the land, though both contain material handed down independently." [2] The E writers, however, in contrast to the J writers, attempted neither to present a new interpretation of history nor to show that Yahweh was the creator of the world. Their goal was to develop a sense of national pride; consequently, their interest lay in describing the history of Israel's historic experiences. The E story began, therefore, with the call to Abraham in Genesis 12, and the other main themes which they pursued were: (1) the deliverance from Egypt; (2) the wandering in the wilderness; and (3) the conquest of the land of Canaan. These three elements are found in the books of Exodus and Numbers. A summary of the E history can be found in the book of Deuteronomy 26:5–10. Many scholars believe that these verses originally were recited by the Israelites under Joshua at the northern shrine of Shechem when they entered the land of Canaan.

And you shall speak and say before the Lord your God: "A wandering Aramean was my father, and he went down into Egypt, and sojourned there, few in number; and he became there a nation, great, mighty and populous. And the Egyptians dealt ill with us, and afflicted us, and laid upon us hard bondage. And we cried unto the Lord, the God of our fathers, and the Lord heard our voice, and saw our affliction, and our toil, and our oppression. And the Lord brought us forth out of Egypt with a mighty hand, and with an outstretched arm, and with great terribleness, and with signs, and with wonders. And He has brought us into this place, and has given us this land, a land flowing with milk and honey. And now, behold, I have brought the first of the fruit of the land, which you, O Lord, have given me." [Deut. 26:5–10]

The E writers, in relating their national epic, emphasized the importance of Moses. In this way also they hoped to bring about a return of the people of their generation to the pure Mosaic tradition. For example, they attached considerable significance to the fact that the name Yahweh was revealed for the first time in the days of Moses (Exod. 3). The J writers held that the name Yahweh was known from the beginning of the world. Again, whenever a miracle took place, the role which Moses played became more exaggerated in the E version. For example, the J writers recorded that a natural force, an east wind, had caused the waters of the Red Sea to be pushed back (Exod. 14:21b); for the E writers, on the other hand, the waters parted only after Moses had raised his rod (Exod. 14:16, 21a). According to the E writers, Moses was the most important person in the history of Israel. Only to Moses did Yahweh speak "mouth to mouth" (Num. 12:7–8), and appear "face to face" (Deut. 24:10–12). To all others, Yahweh no longer spoke directly as He did in the J writers' accounts. Yahweh now made His will known through dreams, as in the cases of Abimelech (Gen. 26:3, 6), Abraham (Gen. 15:1), Jacob (Gen. 28:12), and Joseph (Gen. 40–41), and through the sending of angels or messengers (Gen. 21:17; 22:11, 15).

The E writers also gave prominence to the Book of the Covenant found in Exodus 20:23–23:19. This earliest body of law was presented as the basis of the Sinaitic covenant, and its specific ordinances were regarded as those to which the Hebrews originally had agreed when they entered the covenant. Moses, therefore, was pictured writing the words of Yahweh "in the book of the covenant" (Ex. 24:4–6) which appears also to have included the "words" of the Decalogue or Ten Commandments (Exod. 20). This book, however, was to be distinguished from the "two tables of stone" inscribed by God with "law and commandment" (Exod. 24:12).

While some scholars are of the opinion that the E writers in their interpretation of the Book of the Covenant came closer than any of the other schools to the real words of Moses, it is doubtful whether the Book of the Covenant in its present form actually stems from the time of Moses. The Book of the Covenant, as we have seen, was not a fixed code of law. As the Israelites learned to live in Canaan, they met situations which were unknown in the days of Moses and even Joshua. These conditions called for a clearer understanding of the basic laws of the covenant with Yahweh. For nearly two hundred years these explanations and interpretations of the old laws as well as the enactment of new laws were directed by the various judges who arose in Israel and by the elders in the meetings of the various tribes. The present Book of the Covenant, therefore, reflects the settled, agricultural environment of Canaan rather than the semi-nomadic shepherd life of the Sinai desert-wilderness (see Chapter 6). Nonetheless, the E writers in all probability still chose to appropriate the Book of the Covenant in order to enhance the status of Moses in the eyes of the people of their own generation.

In the same spirit, the E writers sought to develop a sense of national pride by giving prominence to those persons and places connected with the northern kingdom. For example, wherever possible, they emphasized the importance of Joseph and particularly that of his sons Ephraim and Mannaseh, whose descendants, according to the tradition, became two of the

most important northern tribes (Gen. 48:20). Special emphasis was placed also upon the incidents connected with Beth-el
(Gen. 28:17–22) and Shechem (Gen. 33:18–20), two important northern shrines. Again, in keeping with northern traditions, the E writers preferred to use the term Horeb for Sinai
and Amorites for Canaanites. The words Sinai and Canaanites
were part of the southern or J tradition.

Within their outline of national history, the E writers championed the cause of Yahweh, whom they preferred to call
Elohim. It was Elohim, not Baal, who called Abraham to go
to the land of Canaan. Nor was it Baal who saved the Hebrews from the bondage of Egypt and guided them in their
wanderings through the desert-wilderness. It was Elohim who
not only had rescued them from the bondage of Pharaoh but
also had enabled the Israelites to settle in the land of Canaan.
Elohim had been the God of Israel from the very beginnings
of its history.

The use of the plural form "Elohim" for the name of the
one God has been the subject of considerable discussion in
scholarly circles. As was pointed out in Chapter 2, it is abun-
dantly clear that the Hebrew ancestors worshiped God under
the name "El." The name "El" was also applied, as we have
seen, to the father-god of the Canaanite pantheon. It is also
possible that "El" came to be a general word for "god" and
might have been used as a substitute for some other divine
name. While these facts are known by scholars, the use of the
plural "Elohim" by the E writers and others still eludes them.
It can be concluded only that "just as the Canaanites had
sometimes used the plural of 'el,' 'god' to indicate 'totality of
the gods' so the Israelites used 'Elohim' to stress the unity and
universality of God." [3]

Into this broad outline, covering the periods from the patriarchs to the entrance into the land of Canaan, the E writers

wove many incidents which indicated the evils of the Fertile Crescent religions and emphasized the positive aspects of the worship of Israel's God. The story of the sacrifice of Isaac was such an example (Gen. 22). Near the city of Jerusalem, the capital city of the southern kingdom of Judah, was the valley of Hinnom. Here for many generations the Canaanites had practiced child sacrifice. In order to gain the favor and to influence their gods they would bring their eldest sons and through an act of religious faith offer them as burnt offerings to the gods. This practice was widespread throughout the Fertile Crescent. Already we have seen how Mesha, the king of Moab, had offered his eldest son to the god Chemosh. Not even the Israelites, whether of the northern or the southern kingdom, escaped this practice. As they took over more and more of the Baal worship, they also began to participate in this ceremony. Even the kings were not exempt from this failing. For example, Ahaz, the king of Judah (735–715 B.C.E.), burned his own son as an offering in the Valley of Hinnom. Jerusalem was being besieged by an enemy, and the king, already terror-stricken, hoped by this pagan rite to win the favor of some god who would then save the city (II Kings 16:3).

The E writers were concerned about this trend in the northern kingdom. They recalled that their ancestors were different from their neighbors in this respect. While the patriarchs had offered animal sacrifices, they had never participated in the sacrifice of human beings. The E writers chose to emphasize this point, therefore, by telling the story of Abraham. Whether the narrative of the near-sacrifice of Isaac was created by the E writers or was part of an old tradition is not certain. Whatever the origin, the fact remains that in either instance the story of Abraham and Isaac was woven by the E writers into the national epic of the northern kingdom in order to counteract the growing Baal influence and to emphasize that Yahweh did not require the sacrifice of children. Yahweh, they em-

phasized, wanted the children of Israel to live and to fulfill
their responsibilities under the covenant.

Because of the homogeneity of outline between the J and
E narratives, it is necessary for illustrative purposes to present
in detail only one example of the writings of the E School.
The story of Joseph has been one of the most popular of all
the tales in the Bible. Its dependence upon authentic Egyptian
local color and its absorption of current legendary materials
have been examined already in Chapter 11. Here it is appropriate only to compare the manner in which this material has
been treated by the J, E, and P writers. All chapter references
are to the Book of Genesis.

In summary, it is noted that the J and E writers had a natural inclination to emphasize and, above all, to put in the most
favorable light Judah and Reuben, the two ancestors whose
descendants supposedly constituted the cores of the southern
kingdom, Judah, and the northern kingdom, Israel, respectively. Puzzling at first, however, is the E writer's emphasis
upon Simeon, whose descendants became one of the southern
tribes. Simeon, like Reuben and Levi, was one of the older
brothers, which, according to scholars, means that he had once
been a mighty clan associated with the northern tradition.
This fact is confirmed by the evidence that Simeon joined Levi
in a mighty assault to conquer the northern city of Shechem
(Gen. 34). This background explains the E writers' interest
in Simeon. It seems, however, that the tribe of Simeon finally
settled in the south, lost its independence quite early, and was
absorbed into Judah as a secondary influence in the southern
kingdom. The P writers, on the other hand, because they
wrote long after the northern and the southern kingdoms had
been destroyed, showed little concern for this problem. Their
interest lay primarily in introducing into the J and E narratives those elements which would preserve certain ritual tradi-

	J	E	P
1. Joseph and his brothers.	The brothers want to slay Joseph. Judah suggests that they sell Joseph to the Ishmaelites instead. After selling Joseph, they dip his coat in blood and tell Jacob that he had been killed by a beast. Joseph is brought to Egypt (37:12-18, 25-27, 28b, 31-35).	The brothers want to kill Joseph, put his body in a pit, and tell Jacob that an evil beast had eaten him. Reuben, however, intercedes and suggests that they not kill him but only throw him into the pit. The brothers follow Reuben's advice. Midianite merchants later pass by (37:1-11, 19-24, 28a, 29-30). The text is silent about the Midianites rescuing Joseph, but it does tell of their selling him to Potiphar, an officer of Pharaoh's, the captain of the guard (37:36).	No reference.
2. Purchase of Joseph.	Joseph is brought to Egypt by the Ishmaelites where he is bought by Potiphar, an officer of Pharaoh's, the captain of the guard, an Egyptian (39:1).	No reference.	No reference.
3. Joseph and Potiphar's wife.	The only reference to this incident is found in the J account (39:1-23).	No reference.	No reference.
4. Joseph interprets dreams of officials.	No reference.	The stories of the butler and baker are found only in the E account (40:1-23).	No reference.

	J	E	P
5. Joseph interprets Pharaoh's dream.	No reference.	The well-known story of the seven fat and lean cows and the seven full and lean ears of corn is found only in the E account (41:1–36).	No reference.
6. Joseph appointed administrator.	No reference.	This well-known story is found only in the E account (41:37–45, 45–57).	"Joseph was thirty years old when he stood before Pharaoh—and Joseph went out from the presence of Pharaoh, and went throughout all the land of Egypt" (41:46).
7. Joseph's brothers come the first time to Egypt.	A first trip to Egypt is assumed when Jacob asks his sons to go again (43:1–2).	The major reference to the famine in Canaan and the coming to Egypt to buy food is found in the E account. Reuben repeats his original plea not to do harm to Joseph. Simeon is held hostage (42:1–37).	No reference.
8. Joseph detains Benjamin.	Judah becomes surety for Benjamin before Jacob. Also he intercedes before Joseph for Benjamin (42:38–44:34).	No reference.	No reference.
9. Joseph reveals himself to his brothers and is reunited with Jacob.	There is no mention of Joseph's revealing himself; however, Judah goes ahead to Joseph to announce the arrival of Jacob (46:28–47:4).	The main story is told primarily in the E account (45:1–46:5).	Reference is made only to Jacob's meeting with Pharaoh (47:5–6a [...best of the land], 7–11, 27b–28).
10. Joseph's economic policies.	This passage reflects the economic revolution which the Hyksos may have initiated (see Chapter 3) (47:13–26).	No reference.	No reference.

	J	E	P
11. Jacob blesses Ephraim and Manasseh.	No reference.	This account contains the popular narrative of the crossing of the hands in the blessing of Ephraim the youngest before Manasseh the oldest (48:1–2, 8–22).	While the blessing is mentioned, the popular narrative is absent (48:3–7).
12. Joseph reiterates his forgiveness.	No reference.	After Jacob's death, Joseph reassures his brothers that he will not harm them. "You meant evil against me; but God meant it for good" (50:15–22).	No reference.
13. Jacob's deathbed blessing.	A poem about the "twelve tribes" in which Judah is exalted above all the other brothers (49:1–28a).	No reference.	No reference.
14. Jacob's death and burial in Canaan.	The narrative tells of Joseph's relationship with Pharaoh and the attitude of the Egyptians when Jacob dies. Jacob is embalmed and buried in Canaan (50:1–11, 14).	No reference.	The account concerns itself only with Jacob's wish to be buried in the cave of Machpelah, where the ancestors were buried in the land of Canaan, and with his sons fulfilling this request (49:29–33; 50:12–13).
15. Death and mummification of Joseph.	No reference.	Joseph requests that his bones be taken out of Egypt when his descendants will return to the land promised to the Patriarchs. He is embalmed and buried in Egypt in the meantime (50:23–26).	No reference.

tion (burial in the land of Canaan) and which would maintain the genealogical records.

Midway in the history of the northern kingdom (c. 850 B.C.E.) there was a reawakening among the peoples of Mesopotamia. After nearly six hundred years of military insignificance, a mighty political force arose in the Tigris-Euphrates river valley. A new Assyrian Empire was beginning to stir again, and within a hundred years they were to become the most important political and military power of the time. Both Israel to the north and Judah to the south were to feel the effect of Assyria's might, and archaeology has shed some interesting highlights on these events.

In 1846 the palace of King Shalmaneser III, King of Assyria, was discovered in the ancient city of Nimrod. Among the archaeological finds was a monument which has come to be known as the Black Obelisk. This is a four-sided pillar of black limestone, six and one-half feet in height, which contains five rows of roughly carved pictures of Shalmaneser's military campaigns. In between the rows of pictures are inscriptions, describing the significance of the carvings. They tell that Shalmaneser in the first thirty-one years of his reign had received tribute from people of five different regions of the ancient world. One of these tributary kingdoms was Israel.

On the front of the monument, in the second row of the carvings, there is a picture of Jehu, King of Israel, kneeling before the King of Assyria. This is the first picture ever discovered of the ancient Israelites. Jehu is shown with a short, rounded beard and wearing a soft cap on his head. He is clothed in a sleeveless jacket and long fringed skirt with girdle. Behind Jehu stand Israelites, wearing long robes and carrying precious metals and other tribute. The inscription describes the nature of the tribute and also tells that the event took place in the eighteenth year of Shalmaneser's reign. This event took place, therefore, in the year 841 B.C.E. Soon after Jehu paid his tribute, internal strife broke out in Assyria. Shalmaneser, who called himself "the king without a rival," died in a revolt. For the next hundred years the Assyrians were so occupied at home with their internal problems that Israel and the other nations to the west were able to maintain their independence and, as we have seen during the reign of Jeroboam II of Israel, even enjoy a brief period of military and economic prosperity.

The Assyrian military and political decline, however, was only temporary. By 721 B.C.E., the Assyrian power had been revived, and its armies attacked the kingdom of Israel. The Israelites, no match for the world's mightiest military force, were defeated. This marked the end of the northern kingdom. Never again was the kingdom of Israel to be restored.

The kingdom of Israel, as we know, was composed of ten out of the original twelve tribes. After the victory of the Assyrians, no more is heard of the northern tribes. A number of interesting theories have been put forth to explain this mystery of the "Ten Lost Tribes of Israel." For example, some say that the American Indians are the ancestors of the Israelites. In similar fashion, the ten tribes have been identified with a host of other peoples. The truth of the matter, scholars contend, is that the ten tribes were neither "lost" nor "preserved" in some distant part of the world. The Assyrians practiced a simple policy of forced migration with their defeated enemies. They would take the leaders and a substantial segment of the defeated population and move them into a different country. Then they would bring into the defeated country other peoples. In this way the Assyrians would keep their conquered lands populated, and, at the same time, would forestall any future rebellions. This same policy was applied to the northern tribes of Israel. The Assyrians forced a large group of the leaders and the people to migrate, presumably to the Tigris-Euphrates area. There the people assimilated. They married their neighbors and took over their practices so that they could not be identified any more as Israelites. Into Israel itself, in the meantime, the Assyrians brought other peoples. These, too, chose husbands and wives from among the remaining Israelites. Many of them became followers of Yahweh, and today a small group of their descendants still lives in Israel. They are known as the Samaritans. Interestingly enough, their Bible consists only of the Five Books of Moses and the Book of Joshua, preserving the main literary sources which formed the basic writings of the E school.

When the northern kingdom was destroyed, the E school came to an end. The E document, however, was preserved. A writer of the J school, living in the southern kingdom of Judah, either was familiar with the tradition of the north or had a copy of the E document. For him this literary record was no less sacred than his own J materials. Even though the kingdoms had separated, each shared a common historical tradition and was bound in a covenant relationship with the same God Yahweh. This J writer, therefore, took the E tradition and combined it with his own J version. Since this editor was himself a follower of the J school, he gave preference to the J materials. For example, wherever the two versions recorded the same event, it seems that he retained the J account and discarded presumably the E interpretation. On the other hand, wherever the two sources supplemented each other, he appears to have used both materials by combining them into one continuous narrative. This new document has come to be known as JE.

The attempts of the J editor to form JE were not always too skillful, however, and today the trained scholar can easily distinguish the two sources. One of the keys which unlocks this puzzle is the use of the names Yahweh (Lord) and Elohim (God). The J school, as we have noted, preferred the name

Yahweh, and the E School, Elohim. By tracing passages where these names appear, one can separate the two materials. The process, of course, is much more complicated, and many other factors also need to be considered. Not the least of the complications is the fact that the P School many years later also preferred the name Elohim.

Thus, the next stage in the birth of the Torah came to fulfillment. The following chart will illustrate the three formal steps through which we have carried the Torah birth story so far.

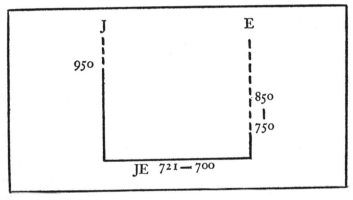

The broken lines signify the informal tradition in both oral and written forms; solid lines, the transmission of the formal tradition in written form.

CHAPTER XIII

The Prophets

IN SUPPORT of the J and E writers, there arose both in Israel and in Judah a group of men which has left an indelible imprint upon Israel's ancient religion and particularly upon the story of the birth of the Torah. These religious giants were the prophets of the eighth, seventh, and early sixth centuries B.C.E., who were not only the staunch defenders of the covenant but also the champions of social justice, which they considered to be the heart of the agreement between Israel and Yahweh.

The prophets, according to the time of their appearance, have been divided generally into three groups. The point in history around which these distinctions are made is the Babylonian exile which took place in 587/6 B.C.E. This was the year in which the Babylonians, who had succeeded the Assyrians as the world's most powerful empire, conquered the city of Jerusalem and destroyed the holy Temple. The Babylonians then transported many of the Jewish people to Babylonia, where they lived in exile for fifty years. Finally, in 536 B.C.E. the Persian king Cyrus, who had destroyed the Babylonian power, issued a decree permitting the people to return to the land of Judah.

The following groups of prophets now may be distinguished. Those prophets who lived before the Babylonian exile began in 587/6 B.C.E are known as the pre-exilic prophets. Those who delivered their messages from 587/6–536 B.C.E. are called the exilic prophets. The prophets who spoke in the name of Yahweh after the people had returned from Babylonia are referred to as the post-exilic prophets. Our concern in this chapter will be with the pre-exilic prophets.

Before turning to the historical development of the prophetic movement, it is necessary to note briefly several distinctions between the Christian and the Jewish listings of the prophets in the Bible. According to the Jewish tradition, the following books of the Bible belong under the heading of the prophets:

1. Early Prophets
   a) Joshua
   b) Judges
   c) First and Second Samuel
   d) First and Second Kings
2. Later Prophets
   a) Isaiah
   b) Jeremiah
   c) Ezekiel
   d) The Twelve: Hosea, Joel, Amos, Obadiah, Jonah, Micah, Nahum, Habakkuk, Zephaniah, Haggai, Zechariah, Malachi

The Early Prophets have come to be designated by scholars as the preliterary prophets. This title refers to the fact that none of the actual writings of these prophets has been preserved. The books listed under the heading of the Early Prophets, they note, contain only stories about the prophets and their activities. The Later Prophets, on the other hand, they prefer to call the literary prophets. The writings of these men, they point out, have been preserved in the books bearing their names.

Christianity makes a distinction among the Later Prophets which is not found in Judaism. In the Christian Bible, for example, the first three prophets are known as the Major Prophets and The Twelve are referred to as the Minor Prophets. No vital significance should be attached, however, to this difference in terminology. The terms "major" and "minor" do not imply that the Major Prophets are of greater importance than the Minor Prophets to Christians. The terms refer only to the number of chapters found in each of the books. For example, the Major Prophets have from forty-eight to sixty-six chapters, while the Minor Prophets include only one to fourteen chapters. In Judaism, on the other hand, these terms are absent, and all the books referred to in the Christian Bible as Major and Minor Prophets are listed simply as Later Prophets. The term "The Twelve" refers to the fact that originally all twelve of these books were written on one scroll.

One other distinction needs to be noted before turning to the history of the prophetic movement. In Judaism some books included in the section of the Prophets are listed in the Christian Bible under the books of history. For example, all the Early Prophets of Judaism belong in this category. In Judaism these books were included among the Prophets because their authors were believed to have been divinely inspired. The book of Joshua was written by the inspired Joshua; while the books of Judges and I and II Samuel were the products of the inspired authorship of Samuel. The prophet Jeremiah was the author of I and II Kings. This interpretation followed the traditionalist Jewish point of view. Jewish modernists today, whether of the early or contemporary schools, do not accept this explanation of the authorship of the books of the Early Prophets. When the Bible was canonized at the turn of the Common Era, however, the modernist point of view was unknown. All books, therefore, were either accepted or rejected for inclusion among the books of the Jewish Bible in accordance with the traditional point of view, namely, the extent to which their authors were believed to have been divinely inspired. On the other hand, it will be noted as well that in Christianity certain books included among the Prophets are listed in Judaism under the third section of the Jewish Bible, namely the Writings. The Book of Daniel is a case in point. The Jewish tradition holds that prophecy ceased with the prophet Malachi, around 400 B.C.E. Since the final editing of the Book of Daniel was completed after the time of Malachi, however, it was ineligible for inclusion among the Prophets. The fact that the setting of Daniel was in the Babylonia of the sixth century B.C.E. was inconsequential to the ancient authorities.

Let us now turn to the evidence which preserves for us the records of the pre-exilic prophets and seek to understand the historical settings for their messages.

The growth of the prophetic movement can be traced by noting the shift from the prophet as a member of a professional group to that of a lone individual who spoke in the name of Yahweh. In the beginning, the prophets moved about as a group. Although there are records of such activity as early as the time of Samuel (I Sam. 10: 1–12), we do not know who these prophets were. Their names are lost to us. We do know, however, that they were professional soothsayers who would make predictions for a fee. Some scholars today refer to them as mad enthusiasts. Employing musical instruments and ritual dances, the professional prophets frequently would work themselves up into an artificial state of emotional excitement before prophesying.

In contrast to the professional prophets stood the individual prophets. They went alone, and frequently were very lonely

people. They used neither music nor dance to work themselves up into a state of frenzy. Sometimes they would appear
suddenly out of nowhere, as it were, to announce their messages. At other times, they would dwell among the people,
prophesying as the occasion demanded. Some, like Amos,
prophesied for only a brief period of time. Others, like Elijah,
Isaiah, and Jeremiah, carried on their activities over extended
periods of history. They received no fees for their prophecies;
nor could they be summoned, as were the professional prophets, to deliver an oracle at the whim or wish of a king. These
prophets were the servants of Yahweh. They would speak
only that which their inner convictions compelled them to
prophesy. The great prophets were uncompromising individ-
ualists, and it mattered not to them whether the king approved
of their words or the people were flattered and pleased by
their messages. Since they spoke what they believed to be the
true words of Yahweh, their prophecies generally were introduced with the phrase, "Thus says Yahweh."

The role of the individual prophet was to explain to the
people of his day what was involved in the covenant relationship with Yahweh. It is improper, therefore, to look upon
them as fortunetellers, or even as wise men who foretold specific future events. Some Christian groups today, for example,
hold that the prophets were concerned more with developments in a later time than they were with the immediate problems of their own generation. The prophetic purpose, they
claim, was to point out to the people the qualities which a
Messiah would possess and the conditions under which he
would come in order to redeem Israel and mankind from its
sins. These prophecies, it is claimed further, were fulfilled in
Jesus, who was the Messiah, and were confirmed again by the
record of his life and teachings found in the Four Gospels of
the New Testament.

While it is true that the prophets spoke about the future,

they did so primarily in general terms. A careful check of the prophetic predictions will show that whenever they did try to predict specific events of the future, they were more often wrong than right. Their predictions went wild again and again. The prophets had no special occult or magical power. They were concerned with pointing out to the people of their respective generations that the will of Yahweh must prevail and not with foretelling specific, isolated events. Their message, simply stated, was: if Israel would contiuue to violate the terms of its covenant with Yahweh, then Israel would be punished; if, on the other hand, the people were faithful to Yahweh, they would receive Yahweh's blessings.

The prophets saw everything from the standpoint of the divine will. If they pointed to the future, it was only to give warning of the events of their own day. A more appropriate term for the prophets, therefore, than "foretellers" would be "forthtellers." The prophets told forth the status of Israel's covenant relationship with Yahweh and set before the people the inevitable consequences of their actions. The prophets were Yahweh's earthly spokesmen for the divine plan of reward and punishment.

Insofar as they did indicate the general directions of human progress, it was due to the fact that they were better qualified students of the present than others. They were in profounder sympathy with the eternal purpose, and by keen discernment of its workings in the past and present were able to forecast the main lines of operation in the immediate future.[1]

Although the kingdom of Israel was more accessible to the influences of the Fertile Crescent, the southern kingdom of Judah, too, was affected by the religions of the neighboring peoples. Baal worship made vast inroads in the south as well as the north, affecting not only the popular religion of the people but also the more formal practices of the priests and

kings. The prophets, therefore, prophesied both in the south
and in the north. Wherever the covenant with Yahweh was
challenged by the neighboring religions, there they championed the cause of Yahweh.

The covenant with Yahweh was threatened, however, not
only by forces from without but also by factors from within.
Like the writers of the J and E schools, the individual prophets had to contend with the deep-seated misconceptions of the
covenant relationship held by their own people. The age of
the prophets was marked by an attitude of general religious
complacency on the part of all segments of the population.
First of all, the people believed that Yahweh would never
abandon them. Once the covenant had been established, Israel
was Yahweh's people and Yahweh was their God forever.
Nothing could ever change this situation. As a result, the
people, both of the north and the south, began to take Yahweh
for granted. Since Yahweh would always take care of them,
they began to minimize the role of their own obligations.
Once they had brought the required offerings to the sanctuary, they felt that they had done their duty and automatically
deserved Yahweh's favor. In summary, the people of Israel
and Judah tried to make religion as easy as possible.

The individual prophets challenged these two popular misconceptions of religion: (1) the belief in an indulgent deity
who would always bless his people no matter what they did,
and (2) the assumption that all one needed to do to fulfill his
covenant relationship with Yahweh was to visit the holy sanctuary on specified occasions and bring certain required offerings.

While the professional prophets continued to encourage the
people in their misconceptions, the individual prophets challenged this one-sided interpretation of the covenant relationship. Yahweh was not an indulgent deity who would overlook

their shortcomings, nor was religion an easy matter which could be disposed of by a few quick visits and baskets full of savory offerings. If the people failed to fulfill their obligations to the covenant, then Yahweh would punish them. The prophets, therefore, exhorted the people to return to the true meaning of the covenant. First of all, they sought to remind Israel and Judah that the covenant was a two-way relationship. Although Yahweh had accepted the Israelites as His people, he never guaranteed that He would continue to do so unreservedly forever. Neither Israel nor Judah were automatically favored nations, proclaimed the prophets. Second, the prophets emphasized that ritual observance was no substitute for human rights. The individual prophets championed the cause of Yahweh by re-emphasizing the old covenant tradition of social justice. Yahweh also wanted righteousness, that men should learn how to live with each other in peace and in mutual helpfulness.

The early modernists believed that the prophets first introduced the concept of social justice into the covenant relationship. In the beginning, they claimed, Moses emphasized the unity of Yahweh, namely the concept of monotheism (the belief that God is one). The prophets then added the ethical aspect to the monotheism. By this evolutionary process the early modernists believed that Judaism's doctrine of ethical monotheism came into being. Contemporary modernists, on the other hand, contend that ethical monotheism goes back to the time of Moses, and perhaps even before. The concepts of justice and righteousness were to be found in the codes of many ancient peoples. The Code of Hammurabi, as we have seen, was one example. Many of these same ethical principles were incorporated by Moses and other Israelite leaders into the Book of the Covenant. Thus, the contemporary modernists hold that the individual prophets inherited the covenant tradition of ethical monotheism. The role of the prophets, therefore, was not to introduce to the people of their day a new interpretation of the covenant with Yahweh but to cause both Israel and Judah to return and to fulfill the original obligations of the old covenant relationship with Yahweh.

While the pre-exilic prophets were the champions of the traditional covenant relationship with Yahweh, at the same time there were occasions when they despaired of fulfilling their task. The misconceptions of the covenant relationship were too ingrained ever to be removed. The people had indulged themselves too long to be dissuaded by a few speeches and even threatening predictions. Beginning, therefore, with the prophet Amos in the eighth century B.C.E., the individual prophets can be called prophets of doom. Some, like Amos, held out no hope at all; others believed that while the people would be punished for their shortcomings, the covenant would be preserved by a "saving remnant," a small group which would remain steadfastly loyal to Yahweh.

The prophets, however, were not interested in being disloyal to their people. It was no light task for them to accuse their fellow countrymen of great social injustices and misunderstandings. On the contrary, they were devoted loyalists; nonetheless, they felt a higher calling, a calling which transcended a narrow, self-centered nationalism. Their first loyalty, the prophets felt, was to Yahweh, and for the fulfillment of their inner conviction they were willing to suffer much. Amos, for example, was banished from the northern kingdom while Jeremiah was accused of sedition, was spat upon, flogged, exposed in stocks, and barely escaped the death penalty. Despite their own personal difficulties, however, the prophets continued to exhort their contemporaries and to challenge the spiritual complacency of their generation with the words: "Thus says Yahweh."

Amos

Amos was the first of the literary prophets whose actual words and acts were preserved in written form. Unfortunately, we know very little about him. The Book of Amos tells us that in addition to pasturing his flock among the hills of his native Judah he would puncture the figlike fruit of the sycamore trees so that the insects which grew on the inside could come out. Concerning his private family life and his other activities, there is complete silence. We do not know even whether the writings of Amos were compiled by the prophet himself or by a circle of prophets who treasured them. He is identified merely as Amos who was among the herdsmen of Tekoa, a village a few miles south of Jerusalem, and who prophesied during the reign of King Jereboam II of Israel (786–746 B.C.E.). These events were supposed to have taken place two years before "the earthquake." While some scholars have tried to pinpoint the exact hour of Amos' prophecies, most biblical students conclude that the brief events of Amos' prophetic career occurred around 750 B.C.E.

The Book of Amos consists of a series of little "oracles" spoken by the prophet on different occasions, but all within a relatively short span of time. The main prophecy, however, is contained in the first two chapters and was spoken presumably at an important religious celebration when the people were gathered in the sanctuary at Beth-el in Israel. On this occasion, Amos' words were at first reassuring and comforting, and immediately found favor among the gathered Israelites. He was reproving Israel's strongest enemy, the Syrians of Damascus (Amos 1:3–5). For their many sins against Israel, Yahweh would punish them. Their king would be destroyed, and the Syrians would be exiled. How comforting was this thought to the people of Israel. Yahweh, the God of Israel, would continue to protect his people just as he had taken care of them since their exodus from Egypt. In fact, there would come a day to be known as the "Day of Yahweh" when Israel would be rewarded because she was the people of Yahweh. With growing satisfaction and even enthusiasm, perhaps, the people of Israel listened as Amos continued to pronounce words of doom upon their other traditional foes, the Philistines in Gaza, the Phoenecians in Tyre, and their old enemies the Edomites, the Ammonites, and the Moabites in the lands across the Jordan (Amos 1:6–2:3). Nor were they at all disturbed when their own sister-kingdom to the south, Judah, became the target for Amos' accusations (Amos 2:4–5). Apparently, they were quite pleased as they heard the impending destruction of their enemies.

Suddenly, however, the mood of the people was to change. Ominously, the voice of the prophet continued to challenge: "For the three transgressions of Israel, yea, for four, I will not reverse it" (Amos 2:6). Yahweh, proclaimed Amos, was angry even with his people Israel. Israel, too, had sinned. The other nations would be punished for crimes committed in time of war. Israel, however, like Judah, would suffer Yahweh's wrath for sins committed in time of peace and prosperity. Israel had forsaken its covenant relationship with Yahweh. No, the "Day of Yahweh" would not be a day of light and reward. It would be a day of darkness and utter calamity (Amos 5:18).

Hardly had Amos finished his message of Israel's doom, when Amaziah, the priest at Beth-el, sent word to King Jeroboam II that a prophet had spoken treason: "Jeroboam shall die by the sword, and Israel shall surely be led away captive out of his land" (Amos 7:11). Amos then was summoned before Amaziah and ordered to leave Israel, never to prophesy there again. Convinced to the end that the doom of Israel was at hand, Amos once again defied the priest. Amos was not a professional prophet. He took up the word of Yahweh neither for a fee nor to please the whim of king or priest. Again, he repeated Israel's impending punishment for its sins, and only then, can it be presumed, did he turn his back upon Amaziah and return to his native Judah (Amos 7:12–17).

Amos is known as the prophet of social justice. So strong was he in his denunciation of the social inequities of his time that he was accused, as we have seen, of treason. However, to view his pronouncement of doom merely as the inevitable consequence of Israel's social sins is to miss the main purpose of his prophecies. True, Israel was to be punished because of her guilt in social crimes, but, above all, Israel was to be punished because these social injustices comprised the very essence of her unfaithfulness to the covenant, to her calling as a people of Yahweh. The covenant called upon Israel to pursue a life of justice in all human relationships. Therefore, when Israel's wealthy merchants, lusting for power, trampled on the heads of the poor and defenseless, the terms of the covenant were being violated. In a similar vein, the covenant was being repudiated whenever the public leaders, reveling in luxury and corrupted by indulgence, remained unconcerned about the future of their country; when women urged their husbands on to greater greed and selfishness; when the law courts favored the business people over all others; and when the priests remained silent and offered no protest against the inhumanities which were being carried out within the very sight of the temples at Bethel, Gilgal, Dan, and Samaria.

Stirred by the insensitiveness of those who thought that Yahweh would protect his people no matter what they did to their fellowman as long as they brought their required sacrifices, Amos uttered his famous prophecy of social justice: "I hate, I despise your feasts," he spoke in the name of Yahweh (Amos 5:21). For Amos, the covenant called not just for sacrifices. During the forty years in the desert Israel never brought offerings, yet it was in the desert-wilderness of Sinai that the covenant was made. It was a covenant between Yahweh and his people Israel, true, but it was a covenant whose conditions demanded of its participants righteous action. Thus, Amos, like the J and E writers before him, summoned Israel to return to the covenant and to be faithful to its conditions.

> Seek you me and live (Amos 5:4).
> . . . let justice well up as waters and righteous-
> ness as a mighty stream (Amos 5:24).

Hosea

Unlike Amos, the prophet Hosea was a native of the northern kingdom of Israel. However, like Amos, he was no less disturbed by the great social injustices of his age. Having been raised in the spirit of the E writers, he was keenly aware of the covenant which Yahweh had made with his ancestors in the desert-wilderness of Sinai. As he looked about him, he was revolted by what he saw. Israel's social immorality knew no bounds.

> Because there is no truth, nor mercy,
> Nor knowledge of God in the land.
> Swearing and lying, and killing, and
> stealing, and committing adultery!
> They break all bounds, and blood
> touched blood (Hos. 4:1–2).

Not only the people of the street and the market place but also the rulers had betrayed the covenant. The kings of Israel had abandoned the purpose set forth in the covenant—to become a people of Yahweh. Instead, they sought to make the nation like all other nations. No longer were the energies of the people directed to the fulfillment of Yahweh's will; to the contrary, the nation's resources were being dissipated in the

building of fortified cities and in the support of alliances to
play off Egypt to the south and Assyria to the east against
each other. The consequences were inevitable, exhorted Hosea.
Israel's strength could only be consumed by such foolish policies. Already he saw that its kings were being murdered and
political intrigue had become the fashion of the day.

> They are all hot as an oven,
> And devour their judges;
> And their kings are fallen,
> There is none among them that calls
> unto Me (Hos. 7:7).

Not the least of all, the religious leaders, too, had become
corrupt. Priest and professional prophet alike had begun to
serve the whims of the people rather than the conditions of
the covenant. Like the fertility cult of Canaan, the worship
of Yahweh had degenerated into a means of obtaining the
good things of nature. The purpose of religion was "to get
something"—whether it be prosperity or security—rather than
to acknowledge one's dependence upon Yahweh, who had
brought the Hebrews out of Egypt and had made a covenant
with them.

Hosea understood that all of Israel's troubles—her internal
social, political, and religious decay, as well as her external
military danger from both Egypt and Assyria—stemmed directly from the fact that she had been unfaithful to the terms
of her covenant with Yahweh.

Hosea expressed Israel's unfaithfulness through the form of
parable. While some scholars may claim that the story of
Gomer is make-believe, it is generally held that the events
which Hosea described were taken directly from his personal
life. Most scholars conclude that Hosea used himself and his
marriage as a case-study in point.

Gomer was his wife, and she bore him three children. In

time, Gomer proved herself untrue to Hosea, and she left him
in order to keep company with other men who, she felt, would
give her greater riches. Instead, she met with disappointment
on every side. Hosea, however, was willing to forgive her
faithlessness, and he brought her back, paying off the indebt-
edness which she had incurred in the meantime. After a period
of discipline, he took her back again as his wife.

Gomer, for Hosea, was the symbol of unfaithful Israel. As
Gomer had played the harlot, so Israel had broken the covenant. In the beginning, Yahweh, the husband, so to speak, had
married Israel, the bride. It was a marriage to last for all time.
But Israel, the bride, had proved herself to be unfaithful by
becoming estranged from her husband: "For the spirit of harlotry is within them, and they know not Yahweh" (Hos. 5:4).

Like Gomer, Israel believed that she would receive greater
gain by pursuing a false and idolatrous religion and by placing
her trust in foreign powers. Little did she realize, however,
that she had sold herself too cheaply. All that she sought
from Baal had been provided, in reality, by her husband, Yahweh (Hos. 2:10).

Therefore, Yahweh rejected his beloved. The very names
which Hosea gave to his children symbolized Yahweh's rejection. The firstborn he called Jezreel (Hos. 1:4). It was in
the valley of Jezreel that one of the kings of Israel had been
murdered, and the prophet reminded the people that Yahweh
would punish the new royal house for its atrocities. The
daughter was named "Lo Ruchamah," meaning "not pitied" or
"the one who has not obtained compassion" (Hos. 1:6).
Through his daughter's name, Hosea conveyed the thought
that Yahweh's patience with Israel was exhausted. Finally, his
second son bore the name "Lo Ami" or "not my people," a
final sign that Yahweh had dissolved the covenant and had
rejected his people (Hos. 1:9). Just as Hosea at first had abandoned Gomer to her idolatries, so Yahweh now chose to cast

off faithless Israel: "She is not my wife, neither am I her husband" (Hos. 2:4).

Although Israel was disloyal, Yahweh's love, nonetheless, was steadfast. No matter how many "cakes of raisins" (Hos. 3:1) Israel might offer in the worship of the Baal fertility cult, Yahweh still loved his people. In his mercy, He, too, like the prophet, would redeem His faithless lover. Then, after a period of discipline, when Israel would be stripped of all her false securities—the kings, idols, fortified cities, and foreign alliances—a new covenant would be established. Unfaithful Israel would have repented and have returned to faithful Yahweh. Then, said Hosea:

> That you [Israel] shall call Me Ishi [my husband]
> And shall call Me no more Baali [my master]
> ... And I will betroth you unto Me
> in righteousness, and in justice,
> And in lovingkindness, and in compassion.
> And I will betroth you unto Me in faithfulness;
> And you shall know the Lord (Hos. 2:18, 21–22).

Yahweh's purpose, prophesied Hosea, was to reconcile his faithless people to Himself.

CHAPTER XIV

The Prophet Isaiah

ISAIAH was a prophet who came from the southern kingdom and prophesied primarily to the people of Judah.[1] His ministry can be divided into two periods. When he first took up his prophecies, the northern kingdom of Israel was still in existence. Israel together with Syria had formed an alliance to ward off the mighty Assyrian power to the east. This Syro-Israelite alliance proved futile, for in rapid succession, Tiglath Pileser III (745–727 B.C.E.), the King of Assyria, was able to defeat the Syrians and to let his armies invade Israel's northern province, the Galilee, and overrun the Plains of Shaaron to the west. The second phase of his ministry began with the fall of the Northern Kingdom in 721 B.C.E. and lasted for an additional twenty years, culminating in the famous siege of Jerusalem by King Sennacharib and the Assyrians in 701 B.C.E. Thus, the range of Isaiah's prophecies covers a period of nearly forty years, having begun in 742 B.C.E., the year when King Uzziah of Judah died. During all these critical times, his message was a consistent one. He tried to interpret what Yahweh was saying through the tense political events of his own life, and he firmly believed that any alliance against Assyria, the new world empire, was a "covenant of death."

While Isaiah, like Amos and Hosea, was dedicated to the cause of Yahweh, he was different from them in many respects. For example, he was undoubtedly a man of the city, having grown up, perhaps, among the privileged class. While not too much else is known about him, it is obvious that the city of Jerusalem held a place of great affection in his heart. It was a city filled with many memories. It was the seat of Yahweh's Temple and also the place of David's throne. Apparently, he was raised in circles which placed great emphasis upon the House of David and its special relationship with Yahweh. In one other respect he differed from both Amos and Hosea. Unlike both of them, Isaiah was silent about the Exodus and Israel's wilderness tradition. Certainly, he must have been aware of them, but they seem to have had little influence on his prophetic utterances.

The Book of Isaiah has preserved in considerable detail the events leading to Isaiah's call as a prophet. In words of vivid poetic imagery, Chapter 6 tells us that one day—it may have been a festival occasion, although this is not certain—Isaiah was standing just inside the main door of the Jerusalem Temple. At the other end stood a small altar with burning incense. Just beyond the altar, there was a series of steps leading to the dark interior of the Holy of Holies, the most sacred room in the Temple. Here King Solomon, many years before, had brought the Holy Ark, where it had remained mounted between two sphinxlike creatures—winged lions with human heads—known as cherubim. Here, in the Holy of Holies, it was believed that Yahweh was enthroned invisibly on the Ark.

Isaiah, pausing at the entrance to the Temple and with his eyes fixed on Yahweh's throne room, suddenly believed that he was standing not with mortals in Jerusalem but with the very hosts of angels in the heavenly council. Everything had become transformed. The priests of Jerusalem had become the seraphim of Yahweh and were now half human and half animal. Each seraph possessed three sets of wings. With one, they shielded their faces from Yahweh's blinding glory; with the second, they hid their nakedness; while with the third pair of wings they flew about, performing their appointed tasks. No longer did Isaiah hear the priests' singing; he was enraptured and heard only the response of the seraphim as Yahweh's radiance filled the entire earth.

"Holy, holy, holy is the Lord of Hosts. The whole earth is full of his glory" (Isa. 6:3). At first, Isaiah was taken aback with what he saw, for his eyes had beheld the King Himself. Reproving himself, he cried out that both as a man and as a member of Yahweh's people Israel he was unclean. His protest, however, was in vain. Suddenly a seraph took a red-hot stone from the altar and, flying down, touched Isaiah's lips with the glowing ember, cleansing him from all sins. Now he believed that he heard Yahweh's voice speaking to him, summoning him to speak Yahweh's word to His people.

"Whom shall I send, and who will go for us?" boomed out Yahweh's voice, and the now clean Isaiah volunteered. "Here am I; send me" (Isa. 6:8).

Almost immediately, however, Isaiah realized that he had undertaken a most frustrating task. While he had agreed to speak to the people, the biggest question was whether they would listen. Was not the heart of the people fat and, therefore, insensitive? Would they give heed to his admonitions, for were not their ears heavy and dull? How could they see the facts as he saw them, for they were indeed a people whose eyes were blind (Isa. 6:9–10). "Lord, how long?" inquired Isaiah. How long would this tremendous responsibility be with him? Yahweh then replied that Isaiah would need to be His messenger until the destruction would come.

> Until cities be waste without inhabitant,
> And houses without man (Isa. 6:11).

Isaiah, like his predecessors, spoke of the "Day of Yahweh." For him, too, it was not to be a day of light but a day of darkness. It was to be a time of judgment against the people of Judah because of their social injustices. Through a striking parable, known as the Song of the Vineyard (Isa. 5:1–7), Isaiah tried to counsel with his fellow Judeans. Posing, perhaps, as a singing farmer to attract their attention, he told of his disappointment. He had planted a vineyard, he sang, and had done everything possible to insure a good harvest, only to find that his vineyard had yielded wild grapes. He then asked his listeners what had gone wrong. What more could he have done? The question was a rhetorical one, for he then announced what he was going to do. He would tear down the vines and let the vineyard become a briar patch. Having sung his riddle in song, he then turned to its interpretation. It was Yahweh, and not the prophet, who was the true singer of the song, he announced, and the beloved keeper of the vineyard was none other than the house of Israel and the men of Judah. In a beautiful play of words Isaiah then interpreted that Yahweh had looked for justice but had beheld only bloodshed. He had sought for righteousness, but only the cry of the oppressed was to be heard (Isa. 5:7).

Although Isaiah's message was predominantly one of doom, at the same time he also held out a note of hope and encouragement to his people. In this respect, he followed in the tradition of the other early prophets. Amos, despite his message of doom, had summoned Israel first to return and then to be faithful to the conditions of the Covenant. Hosea, too, had urged the unfaithful people to repent and to renew the covenant with Yahweh.

Now Isaiah spoke of "a saving remnant." While it was Yahweh's purpose to enter into a controversy with his people, summoning them to stand trial before their Judge (Isa. 1:18–

20; 3:13–15), his intention, in reality, was to restore Israel as a holy people. Through their suffering they were to be purged of their sins in the same way that metal could be purified of its dross through fire (Isa. 1:24–26). Consequently, he named one of his children "Shear-jashub," meaning "a remnant would return." Isaiah believed that this remnant would be purified of its iniquities and would become again Yahweh's faithful people (Isa. 10:22–23).

The international crises of Isaiah's time may be understood best by examining two of the signs which the prophet used to interpret the events of the day. First, however, it is important to understand the meaning of the word "sign," as used by Isaiah. A "sign" is not to be confused with a "miracle," nor does it imply any form of magic. The prophets, as well as the J and E writers, used natural events to indicate that Yahweh was acting in human affairs. To them, these incidents were evidence that Yahweh was working through the lives of people and that He was not holding Himself aloof from the scene of history.

In the year 735 B.C.E., there came to the throne of Judah a young king, named Ahaz. He lived in troubled times, for all around him the nations had united to fight off the threat of the advancing Assyrians. Israel, the northern kingdom, had joined with its former enemy Syria in an alliance. The new-found allies invited Ahaz to join them. When he turned down their offer, the combined forces of Israel and Syria invaded Judah. Ahaz was beside himself. Not knowing what to do, he first offered his son as a human sacrifice in the Valley of Hinnom (II Kings 16:3). Finally, he concluded that his only hope was to make an alliance with Assyria.

Isaiah, however, was opposed to all human alliances which placed their trust in the strength of arms. Only reliance in the faithfulness of Yahweh could help Judah. "Trust in Yahweh;

be quiet and calm . . ." he counseled, for Israel and Syria are no more than "two tails of smoking firebrands" (Isa. 7:4). When Ahaz, however, refused to listen, Isaiah offered him a sign. "Behold," counsels Isaiah, "the young woman shall conceive and bear a son, and shall call his name Immanuel" (Isa. 7:14).

The word Immanuel means "God is with us." For many Christian people this sign of Immanuel has been taken as a prophetic foretelling of the birth of Jesus. As pointed out in Chapter 13, it was not the intention of the prophets to predict the distant future. Like the J and E writers before them, the prophets were concerned primarily with their contemporaries. It is within this same framework that one can best understand the sign of Isaiah.

Who the woman was is not known. Some scholars say that Isaiah was referring to Ahaz's own wife. The prophet's sign mentioned merely that "a young woman" was or soon would become pregnant and that the child who was to be born in the near future was to be called Immanuel. Before this child would be of age—and here lies the importance of Isaiah's sign—and would know how to choose between good and evil, the Syro-Israelite alliance would be broken and Judah would suffer at the hands of Assyria. There was no need, warned Isaiah, for Ahaz to become involved in an alliance with Assyria, for very soon the dangers which Judah faced at the moment would be at an end.

Archaeologists report that the "end of the conduit of the upper pool," to which the Bible refers as the meeting place between Ahaz and Isaiah, can be identified. This conduit or channel was part of the main water supply system of Jerusalem which came from a spring located in a nearby valley. Generally, the water was brought from the spring and collected into large open areas, known as the Upper and Lower Pools. These open areas were connected by a channel. It was at the point where the water flowed from the Upper Pool into the conduit, archaeologists believe, that Ahaz and Isaiah exchanged their remarks.

Despite Isaiah's warnings, Ahaz joined in an alliance with the Assyrians. However, as Isaiah had prophesied, the Syro-Israelite Alliance crumpled before the Assyrian onslaught. Instead of being confronted by two relatively weak neighbors, Judah had opened herself to the advances of a powerful foe. Tiglath Pileser, the Assyrian king, was delighted to oblige Ahaz, but not before he had extracted a huge tribute from him. Confronted with two distasteful alternatives, Ahaz yielded to the Assyrian request. He emptied the treasuries of both his palace and the Temple in Jerusalem and brought the tribute to Tiglath Pileser. Judah had now become the vassal of Assyria.

Thus, the first phase of Isaiah's prophetic career came to a close. Little more is heard from him until a number of years later. Apparently, he withdrew within his own prophetic circle and awaited a new generation which would be more favorable to his message.

Twenty years passed before Isaiah was to emerge from his voluntary retirement. In 715 B.C.E., Hezekiah, a wise and vigorous leader, had come to the throne of Judah. Religiously, he was a reformer. He not only put an end to worship at the high places which had become local shrines but also cleaned the Temple of all foreign objects. He wanted to concentrate all of Judah's worship in the Temple at Jerusalem. Politically, too, he wanted to be independent of Assyria; consequently, when Hezekiah removed the Assyrian altar from the Temple, it was regarded by all not merely as an act of religious reform but also as a sign of national defiance. Fortunately, the Assyrians were too occupied in northern Mesopotamia to give much consideration to Judah's new nationalism.

Hezekiah's initial success, however, proved to be too tempting, and he did not remain neutral for long. Gradually, he began to become involved in anti-Assyrian activities. In the year 711 B.C.E., when the Philistine cities along the coast of the Mediterranean revolted under the influence of a restless Egypt, Hezekiah was accused by the Assyrian King Sargon of complicity. The only thing which saved Jerusalem from the wrath of the Assyrian army was the fact that Hezekiah had not implicated himself too deeply.

New temptations still lay ahead for Hezekiah. In 705 B.C.E., the death of Sargon set off a series of revolutions in the Assyrian Empire. The leaders of the revolts were the King of Babylonia and the Pharaoh of Egypt. Each sent an embassy to Hezekiah, seeking his participation. Finally, he acquiesced, and the Judean armies joined in a successful attack upon the cities of Philistia which had preferred to remain loyal to the new Assyrian king, Sennacharib. We now know from the archaeological discovery of Sennacharib's records that Hezekiah even took Padi, the King of Ekron, back to Jerusalem as his prisoner.

The revolts were short-lived, however. Once he had established himself securely in his capital city of Nineveh, Sennacharib began a systematic conquest of his rebellious subjects. First, he moved eastward and crushed the revolting Babylonians. Then he marched with his army triumphantly westward. On the plains of Philistia he overwhelmed the Egyptian army. Finally, he invaded Judah. One section of his army advanced from the coastal plains; another group approached Jerusalem from the north. One after the other, the fortified cities of Judah fell before the advancing Assyrians. At last, the city of Jerusalem itself was besieged. Poised on the threshold of complete victory, Sennacharib wrote into his annals: "[Hezekiah] like a caged bird, I shut up in Jerusalem, his royal city."

During all these events, Isaiah was not silent. He had always opposed alliances against the Assyrians, and he still was steadfast in this belief. As early as 711 B.C.E., when Egypt first approached Hezekiah to revolt against Sargon, Isaiah walked naked and barefoot through the streets of Jerusalem. His actions were a sign that an alliance would be futile and, if Hezekiah insisted in joining the revolt, that Jerusalem would be stripped naked.

With Sennacharib's armies besieging Jerusalem, Isaiah performed what may first appear to be a surprise turnabout-face. Instead of urging Hezekiah to capitulate and to re-establish his allegiance to Assyria, he counseled against surrender. Assyria would be defeated, prophesied Isaiah (Isa. 31:4–9). What appeared to be a turnabout really was not. Isaiah still believed firmly that only Yahweh could check or take away Assyria's power. Neither Judah nor any of the other nations could destroy the Assyrians; therefore, it was important that Hezekiah continue to resist so that Yahweh's purpose could be made known. Yahweh was judging his people, and He would spare Zion (Isa. 37:33–35) so that a faithful and righteous remnant could remain to build a new Jerusalem (Isa. 10:20–21).

When Sennacharib sent a delegation to demand Judah's surrender, Isaiah delivered an oracle against the arrogance of the Assyrian king (II Kings 19:20–28). He also added a sign to signify that a remnant would be saved and that after three years the land would return to normal.

The first year, he indicated, the Judeans would eat food which had grown of itself in the field; the second year, they would eat food grown from the uncultivated seeds dropped from the plants of the first year. In the third year, however, the Judeans would "sow and reap, and plant vineyards, and eat the fruit thereof" (II Kings 19:29).

Suddenly, the Assyrians raised the siege and withdrew their

armies. The annals of Sennacharib make no mention of the event. This is not unusual, for it was not customary in ancient times for kings to record their defeats. The Bible offers only a legend which attributes the cause to the fact that "the angel of the Lord went forth, and smote in the camp of the Assyrians a hundred and four score and five thousand; and when men arose early in the morning, behold, they were all dead corpses" (II Kings 19:32–37). Perhaps this reference is an allusion to a plague which may have broken out in the Assyrian camp. A more probable explanation of the Assyrian withdrawal is that Sennacharib may have heard a rumor of a new uprising in Babylonia which prompted him to return in haste to Assyria (II Kings 19:7). Even though Jerusalem had not been conquered, he had accomplished his major objectives in the west. Egypt had suffered a staggering defeat, and the anti-Assyrian coalition which it had nurtured had been broken up. Hezekiah, too, had paid tribute (II Kings 18:14–16) and now was a prisoner in his own city. Sennacharib, it can be presumed, felt that he could well afford at last to turn his attention to the more pressing problems back home.

While the position of Isaiah was vindicated, the people did not realize the full implications of his prophetic utterances. The withdrawal of Assyria served only to reinforce the people's complacency and to fortify them in their smug assumption that Yahweh would never permit Jerusalem to be destroyed.

After the events of 701 B.C.E., the prophet Isaiah dropped from view and nothing more is known about him. Tradition holds that he was martyred many years later during the reign of King Manasseh (687–642 B.C.E.), who once again encouraged the building of Assyrian altars in the Temple at Jerusalem.

The memory of Isaiah, however, continued on as an in-

spiration to the people. Undoubtedly his prophecies were preserved by his disciples in the prophetic circles and then handed
down to succeeding generations. In time, the writings of many
unknown prophets were added to those of Isaiah. His original
prophecies are believed to be contained today in the following chapters of the Book of Isaiah: 1 to 11, which reflect his
early period, and 28 to 32, which deal with the later period of
his life. All the remaining chapters are regarded by scholars as
additions of later hands.

CHAPTER XV

The D School

THE E TRADITION was incorporated into the J version to form what we have called JE, presumably during the last years of the reign of King Hezekiah (715–687 B.C.E.). Nearly a half century was to pass before another significant step was to be taken in the birth of the Torah. During these decades Judah was to go through a dark age because the new king Manasseh, a true vassal to Assyria, used his long reign (687–642 B.C.E.) to prove his loyalty. He began by reintroducing the same foreign religious practices which his father had tried so hard to root out. For example, he brought into the Temple the worship of the sun, moon, and stars which the Assyrians regarded as deities, and he also erected altars so that they could be worshiped.

Since the Assyrians sanctioned astrology, magic, and divination in their religion, Manasseh also revived the old cult of necromancy. Ever since the time when King Saul, nearly three centuries before, had gone to the witch of En-dor so that the revived ghost of Samuel might advise him how to deal with the Philistines (I Sam. 28), such practices had been prohibited in Judah. Manasseh also restored human sacrifices, even offering his own son, because this, too, was an accepted way in Assyrian circles to court divine favor. Once Manasseh began introducing pagan practices to please his Assyrian overlords, however, he opened the gates wide to a whole host of influences. His actions also gave encouragement to the Baal worshipers among the people. Soon the high places which Hezekiah had destroyed were rebuilt, and the local shrines outside of Jerusalem which had been closed were reopened. Even sacred prostitution was practiced openly once again in Judah. Under Manasseh, therefore, conditions were not favorable for significant developments in the birth of the Torah.

During Manasseh's long reign, however, the supporters of Yahweh were not completely inactive nor silent. Unknown prophetic voices would rise from time to time to remind the people of their unfaithfulness to Yahweh. Perhaps the most famous of these utterances was attached to the words of the prophet Micah, who had lived in the previous century (Mic. 4:1–6). Apparently, these prophetic lines became quite popular, assuming the form of a floating oracle, for they are found also, though in a slightly abridged manner, in the Book of Isaiah (Isa. 2:2–4).

But in the end of days it shall come to pass,
That the mountain of the Lord's house shall be established
as the top of the mountains,
And it shall be exalted above the hills;
And peoples shall flow unto it.
And many nations shall go and say:
"Come ye, and let us go up to the mountain of the Lord,
And to the house of the God of Jacob;
And He will teach us of His ways,
And we will walk in His paths";
For out of Zion shall go forth the law,
And the word of the Lord from Jerusalem.
And He shall judge between many peoples,
And shall decide concerning mighty nations afar off;

And they shall beat their swords into plowshares,
And their spears into pruning-hooks;
Nation shall not lift up sword against nation,
Neither shall they learn war any more.

There were also those whose prophecies were preserved in their own names. Zephaniah, for example, denounced the pagan practices which during Manasseh's reign had defiled the people of Judah and their capital city of Jerusalem. He accused not only the king but also the entire leadership of the nation of abandoning the covenant. The great "Day of Yahweh" was approaching, warned Zephaniah, and he urged repentance upon the king and people alike. Like Isaiah, he, too, was particularly concerned that at least a remnant should repent and seek refuge in Yahweh (Zeph. 2:3).

With the death of Manasseh in 642 B.C.E. and the assassination of his son Amon two years later, and with the coming to the throne of the youthful Josiah who had been trained carefully by the priests, a new chapter in the development of the Torah was to unfold. The turning point came in the year 621 B.C.E., the eighteenth year of King Josiah's reign (640–609 B.C.E.).

One day, while workmen were repairing the Temple in Jerusalem, an old scroll entitled the "Book of the Covenant" was discovered. The finding of the manuscript was reported to Josiah, and he had its contents read to him. As he listened, Josiah realized that the scroll was a very ancient document, reporting what seemed to him to be the very words which Moses had used when the Israelites were about to enter the land of Canaan. Immediately, Josiah began to tear his garments. Having been trained by the priests, he realized at once that the words of Moses urging the Israelites to keep the covenant really were being directed at him, for neither he

nor his father had been loyal to the covenant with Yahweh.
Deeply stirred, Josiah ordered that the people of Judah be
summoned to the Temple for a ceremony of covenant renewal. When they were assembled, he read to them the contents of the newly discovered "Book of the Covenant," and
together they renewed their covenant with Yahweh (II Kings
22–23).

Having reaffirmed the covenant, Josiah undertook to carry
out a thoroughgoing religious reformation. His first step was
to eliminate all pagan practices from the Temple. The worship
of Baal and of the Assyrian gods was abolished. Child sacrifice
was forbidden, and the practice of sacred prostitution prohibited. He then proclaimed that the Temple was to be the
central sanctuary for all Judah. Here the true worship of
Yahweh would be watched over carefully by the official
priests. To insure the centrality of the Jerusalem Temple, he
ordered that all high places wherever sacrifices could be
brought to the gods should be torn down. He closed the
Temple at Beth-el as well as other shrines dedicated to Yahweh, and he disqualified their priests from performing any
religious functions. Finally, Josiah climaxed his reformation
by ordering that the long-neglected feast of Passover, which
commemorated the heroic struggle of Moses and the Hebrews
to free themselves from their Egyptian masters, be celebrated
once again in its full and proper manner. Thus, Josiah sought
to re-establish the covenant with Yahweh which had been
neglected and even violated by his father, the priests, and the
people of the land of Judah.

Scholars tell us that the idea of calling people together to
a central religious center to renew a covenant was a very old
one, even in the time of Josiah. It goes back, they say, to the
time of Joshua, as we have seen in Chapter 6, when he, too,
summoned the people to the central sanctuary of Shechem to
renew the covenant which first had been established in the

time of Moses. This tradition of covenant renewal was continued at the old central sanctuary at Shiloh during the tribal Confederacy and, it seems, was known also to the priests in Jerusalem. The tradition of covenant renewal provided the priests of the seventh century B.C.E. with the perfect means of restoring the true worship of Yahweh. It was quite apparent to them, however, that they could do nothing during the long reign of Manasseh. Patiently biding their time, they waited until Josiah came to the throne. Having trained him from early childhood, they had every reason to believe that he would be responsive to the idea of publicly renewing the covenant. Even during the dark days of Manasseh, therefore, new hope welled up within the small but faithful priestly group.

The reformation under Josiah marked a turning point in the story of the birth of the Torah. For the first time a book of the laws of Yahweh was established as the basis of national life. When Josiah ordered that the "Book of the Covenant" be read before the people, he was establishing a "constitution," as it were, which was to be the guiding rule for all the people. It was a book to be studied and to be followed by all the people. The significance of Josiah's reformation can be summarized in this quotation from the writings of the Israeli biblical scholar Yahezkel Kaufmann:

The books of earlier tradition were testimonies and memorials (Ex. 17:14) rather than books of study. The book of the covenant * was read to the people (Ex. 24:4-7); the stone tablets are a "testimony" (Ex. 31:18) and are stored away in the ark (Ex. 25:16). The priestly laws were "handled" and known only by the

* The Book of the Covenant in Exod. 21–23:19, referred to in this quotation, is not to be confused with the book of the covenant "discovered" in the days of Josiah. For a discussion of the Book of the Covenant see chapter 6.

priests. Prophets attempted to influence the people through speech and deed. Deuteronomy is the first to conceive of a Torah book, the possession of the people, to be studied, taught by fathers to sons, its precepts to be bound on the hand and written on the doorposts and gates (Deut. 6:7 ff; 11:18 ff). Israel's king is to write a copy of the Torah and read in it all his life (Deut. 17:18 f). It is to be inscribed publicly on stones (Deut. 27:3, 8); the priests are to read it to all Israel every sabbatical year (31:10 ff). The very style of Deuteronomy, repetitive and hortatory, is inspired by this purpose.[1]

The principle of a Torah book, in contrast to a Torah literature, thus began to take shape in the minds of the people. This step was most important for the future of Jewish life, for it laid the foundation stone upon which later generations erected the superstructure of Judaism. The events in the time of Josiah, in effect, foreshadowed the importance of the reading of "the book of the Law" by Ezra some two centuries later when the Torah in its completed form became the constitution of Jewish life (Neh. 8–9).

The "Book of the Covenant" which the workmen had allegedly "discovered" in the Temple forms today the nucleus of the Book of Deuteronomy, and its priest-editors are known as the D School. Their influence is said to have extended from around 700–650 B.C.E., when the composition of the "Book of the Covenant" may have begun, until sometime during the Babylonian Exile (586–536 B.C.E.) when the Book of Deuteronomy attained its present form. Some scholars contend that the Book of Deuteronomy was completed before the Exile. The same division of opinion exists about the Deuteronomic History. The D writers are responsible not only for the Book of Deuteronomy but also the present form of the books of Joshua, Judges, I and II Samuel, and I and II Kings. They had reworked the existing records from the time of Joshua to Josiah and preserved them for mankind.

When the Bible was translated into Greek in the second century B.C.E., the translators gave to many of the biblical books Greek names which have passed over into English. For example, noting that the intent of the Book of Deuteronomy was to review the events and laws of the time of Moses, they gave to the book the Greek name *Deuteronomion touto*, which means "the second law," i.e., the law which was being reviewed for a second time. In Hebrew the book is called simply *D'varim*, or "these are the words," the opening phrase of the book (Deut. 1:1).

Like the authors of the J and E schools, the D writers remain anonymous; however, they did develop a style and philosophy all their own. The D writers wanted not only to preserve a tradition but also to teach and to inspire the people to carry out the terms of Yahweh's covenant. They chose, as a result, a style completely different from that of the J and E writers. Instead of being storytellers, they were more like rabbis or ministers who give sermons, or even like debaters who try to convince people of the truth of what they are saying. The style of the D writers, therefore, was hortatory or didactic, for they felt that they had to teach the people of Judah how to be faithful to the covenant. Consequently, the D writers used certain phrases which they kept emphasizing over and over again. They warned the people not "to go after or to serve other gods," nor "to do that which is evil in the eyes of Yahweh," but "to hearken unto the voice of Yahweh." Moreover, the people are to be faithful to Yahweh, they taught, so that "it may be well with you" and that "you may prolong your days in the land." The language and style of the D writers was also a reflection of their formula of reward and punishment: obedience to Yahweh's commands would bring victory and prosperity; disobedience would bring Yahweh's judgment of suffering and failure.

The D writings, although composed by priests in Jerusalem, the capital of the southern kingdom, are regarded by scholars as part of a northern tradition. This conclusion is derived from the tradition of Joshua's renewal of the covenant at Shechem, a northern shrine, and also from a similarity in proper names used by both the D and E writers. For example, the D writers, like the E writers, used the same terms Mount Horeb and Amorites for Mount Sinai and Canaanites.

At the time of its "discovery," the "Book of the Covenant" probably consisted only of the material now found in chapters 12 to 26 of Deuteronomy. With time, however, this material was enlarged upon until it came to have its present form. The Book of Deuteronomy reports a series of three addresses which Moses gave to the people. The following outline of the Book of Deuteronomy has been accepted by Bible scholars:

The First Address: Chapters 1–4

1. Introduction, 1:1–5

2. Moses summarizes the events since the departure from Mount Horeb, 1:6–3:29

3. Moses advises Israel, 4:1–40

4. Appendix, 4:41–43

The Second Address: Chapters 5–26 and 28

1. Introduction, 4:44–49

2. Moses advises Israel, 5–11

3. Moses explains the laws, 12–26

4. Conclusion, 28

The Third Address: Chapters 29–30
Supplements:

1. The Shechem covenant ceremony, 27

2. Moses gives his last instructions, 31

3. Two old poems

   a. The Song of Moses, 32

   b. The Blessing by Moses, 33

4. The story of Moses' death, 34

The Second Address, because it includes the "Book of the Covenant" and touches upon the heart of the D writers' point of view, will form the basis of our analysis of the contents of the Book of Deuteronomy.

The D writers, like the J and E writers before them, were concerned with the fact that the people regarded the covenant with Yahweh as an ancient ceremony with little practical value for their own times. Therefore, almost from the outset they, too, dwelled upon the idea that the law of Moses was binding for all generations. While projecting themselves backward to the time of Moses, the D writers really were speaking to the people of their own generation. Thus, they speak through Moses to the people: "The Lord made not this covenant with our fathers, but with us, even us, who are all of us here alive this day" (Deut. 5:3).

Once they sounded the obligation for covenant renewal, the D writers began to review the laws of Moses, i.e., the contemporary laws which for the sake of effectiveness were being presented as the words of Moses. They began with the Ten Commandments, known in Hebrew as The Ten Words, which represented for them a summary of their religious reformation. Taking the commandments which scholars say could very well have come from the time of Moses (Chapter

4), they added to this shorter form those phrases which re-flected their own religious point of view. The result was the Ten Commandments as we know them today in Deuteronomy 5:6–18.†

    1. *I am the Lord ‡ your God,* who brought you out of the land of Egypt, out of the house of bondage.

    2. *You shall have no other gods before Me.* You shall not make for yourself a graven image, even any manner of likeness, of anything that is in heaven above, or that is in the earth beneath, or that is in the water under the earth. You shall not bow down unto them, nor serve them; for I the Lord your God am a jealous God, visiting the iniquity of the fathers upon the children, and upon the third and upon the fourth generation of them that hate Me, and showing mercy unto the thousandth gen-eration of them that love Me and keep My command-ments.

    3. *You shall not take the name of the Lord your God in vain;* for the Lord will not hold him guiltless that takes His name in vain.

† The order of the commandments in Judaism and in Christianity differ slightly. In Judaism, the superscription of the ancient treaties, discussed in Chapter 4, became the first commandment. The two commandments con-cerning "other gods" and "graven images" became the second commandment. By this procedure, Judaism emphasized the centrality of the Exodus expe-rience which made Israel a self-conscious historical community. The Exodus was "the crucial event" by which all previous and future events were judged. Protestant Christianity, on the other hand, omits Judaism's first command-ment and considers the commandments concerning "other gods" and "graven images" as the first two commandments. It should be mentioned, however, that Lutherans and Roman Catholics regard the commandments concerning "other gods" and "graven images" as the first commandment. Instead, they divide Judaism's tenth commandment into two parts. Their ninth command-ment refers to the coveting of a man's house, while the tenth deals with coveting a wife, servants, or animals.

‡ Wherever the word "Lord" appears, it is presumed that originally the name Yahweh had been written.

4. *Observe the sabbath day, to keep it holy,* as the Lord your God commanded you. Six days shall you labor, and do all your work; but the seventh day is a sabbath day unto the Lord your God, in it you shall not do any manner of work, you, nor your son, nor your daughter, nor your man-servant, nor your maid-servant, nor your ox, nor your ass, nor any of your cattle, nor your stranger that is within your gates; that your man-servant and your maid-servant may rest as well as you. And you shall remember that you were a servant in the land of Egypt, and the Lord your God brought you out by a mighty hand by an outstretched arm; therefore the Lord your God commanded you to keep the sabbath day.

5. *Honor your father and your mother,* as the Lord your God commanded you; that your days may be long, and that it may go well with you, upon the land which the Lord your God gives you.

6. *You shall not murder.*

7. *Neither shall you commit adultery.*

8. *Neither shall you steal.*

9. *Neither shall you bear false witness.*

10. *Neither shall you covet your neighbor's wife;* neither shall you desire your neighbor's house, his field, or his man-servant, or his maid-servant, his ox, or his ass, or anything that is your neighbor's.

The Deuteronomic version of the commandments is similar to that found in Exodus 20:2–14, differing basically only in the fourth commandment. The commandments found in Exodus reflect the philosophy of the later P School. The D writers were more concerned with identifying the observance

of the Sabbath with the Egyptian experience while the later
P writers were more interested in showing that the Sabbath
was ordained from the time of creation. The other differences
in the commandments are due to the stylistic differences between the D and P writers. It is the P version of the Ten
Commandments that is in general usage today.

After explaining the significance of the Sinai experience,
the D writers introduced a second summary which sought in
positive terms to convey to the people their responsibilities.
This passage has taken on unusual significance for both
Judaism and Christianity. Deuteronomy 6:4 is known as the
Shma from the first Hebrew word, meaning "hear." For
Jewish people, the first line, "Hear, O Israel, the Lord our
God, the Lord is One," has become its watchword, and together with the remaining verses has formed an essential part
of the prayerbook. For Jesus, too, this passage was of great
importance. As a Jew he was familiar with the Shma, and
when asked what the greatest commandment was, he replied
in the words of the Deuteronomist: "And you shall love the
Lord your God with all your heart, and with all your soul,
and with all your might" (Deut. 6:5–9).

After presenting these two famous summaries, the D writers
turned their attention to their interpretation of the meaning
of Israel's history. They explained to the people that Israel
stood in a unique relationship with Yahweh. It was not because their ancestors were more numerous than other peoples
that a covenant had been made with them. Yahweh had re-
deemed Israel from Egypt and established the covenant because of His love for Israel. Yahweh knew that Israel was
numerically the smallest of the nations; nonetheless, he chose
to be faithful to Israel and to keep His covenant with them
throughout all generations. It is important, therefore, reasoned
the D writers, that Israel now should remain faithful to Yahweh and keep the commandments, statutes, and ordinances

of the covenant. The very knowledge of Yahweh's choice of
Israel should itself lead the people to consecrated service.

Nor did Yahweh choose Israel because of any special righteousness on its part. Israel should remember, cautioned the
D writers, that the entire experience in the Sinai desert-wilderness was to teach the people that it was the wickedness of
the peoples of Canaan, the Amorites, coupled with Yahweh's
faithfulness to the promise made to Abraham that his seed
would inherit the land, which resulted in their entry and conquest of the land (Deut. 9: 1–6). Therefore, neither smug complacency nor self-sufficient righteousness should become the
people now, for it was still because of Yahweh's and not necessarily the people's faithfulness that the covenant remained
in effect. Lest the people deny this, the D writers reviewed
the story of Israel's own rebelliousness in the desert-wilderness, where time after time they sought to reject Yahweh
(Deut. 9–10).

Israel, in the view of the D writers, was a holy people. Yahweh had chosen them to be "His own treasure, out of all the
peoples that are upon the face of the earth" (Deut. 7:6).
Therefore, it was important for Israel to avoid all temptations
from the surrounding cultures. Just as Moses had warned the
people against intermarrying with the Amorites and adopting
their culture, so the D writers believed that the people now
should remove all foreign influences from the land and should
return to their true state as a holy people. Israel should abolish
everything which defiled the community, and not the least
of these were the idolatrous practices (Deut. 13: 1–18; 17:2–7),
and the sexual abuses (Deut. 23:13–25).

Israel's task as Yahweh's treasure, however, was not just
to separate itself from the influences of pagan culture. It was
also to dedicate itself to special service in behalf of Yahweh.
Israel was to be a loyal worshiper of Yahweh and a true
champion of Yahweh's justice. Thus, the D writers incor-

porated in the "Book of the Covenant" detailed elaborations
of the many ritual and ethical responsibilities which the
people should pursue (Deut. 12–26).

The introduction to the "Book of the Covenant" opened
with an exhortation which is reminiscent of the famous floating oracle found in the Book of Micah (6:8).

> And now, Israel, what does the Lord your God require
> of you, but to fear the Lord your God, to walk in all
> His ways, and to love Him, and to serve the Lord your
> God with all your heart and with all your soul; to keep
> for your good the commandments of the Lord, and His
> statutes, which I command you this day (Deut. 10:12–
> 13).

Then with great sermonic eloquence the D writers added:

> Behold, unto the Lord your God belongs the heaven, and
> the heaven of heavens, the earth, with all that is therein.
> Only the Lord had a delight in your fathers to love them,
> and He chose their seed after them, even you, above all
> peoples, as it is this day (Deut. 10:14–15).

Thereafter follows a long list of Israel's responsibilities as
a holy people. There were the ritual obligations of appearing
three times yearly at the Temple in Jerusalem—on the Feast
of Unleavened Bread (Passover), the Feast of Weeks (Pente-
cost), and on the Feast of Tabernacles (Tabernacles)—and of
bringing the required and free-will offerings. There were the
social or ethical responsibilities as well. Israel was to plead the
cause of the legally weak or helpless: the orphan, the widow,
and even the stranger who comes to dwell in the land. All
members of the community, whether rich or poor, free or
slave, of high or low esteem, were to be equal before the law
(Deut. 16:18–20). No Israelite was to exploit another through
murder, adultery, theft, dishonesty, false witness, or the taking

of interest. Injustice in any form destroyed Israel's holiness as a people.§ As a capstone to their demand for social justice, the D writers reminded their generation that many years ago their ancestors, too, had once been slaves in Egypt (Deut. 15:1–18).

In keeping with their formula of reward and punishment, the D writers placed both immediately before and after the "Book of the Covenant" two passages of curses and blessings (Deut. 11,28). It is their final warning to the people that if they obey faithfully, they will be blessed with good harvests and a high level of general social welfare; if not, then all kinds of disasters will befall them and they will be destroyed.

§ For a discussion of the influence of the prophets on the Ten Commandments, see Chapter 4.

CHAPTER XVI

The Prophet Jeremiah

THE Deuteronomic Reformation was short-lived. Although it was born out of a sincere effort of the priests and Josiah to return to the covenant established by Moses, the "Book of the Covenant" was "discovered" in an era of intense nationalism. Josiah was as much concerned with national revival as he was with religious reform. He dreamed of restoring the united kingdom with a single religious and political capital in Jerusalem.

The international political scene, moreover, was ripe for such a move. The once-mighty Assyrians were showing signs of severe stress and strain. To the east, new powers were rising. The future empires of Babylonia and Persia were beginning to assert their independence, and in 612 B.C.E. the Babylonians captured the Assyrian capital of Nineveh. While Judah was undergoing a religious revival under Josiah, Assyria was struggling in the last death-throes as a crumbling empire.

The international political situation, therefore, served only to embolden both Josiah and the Judeans. The very cleansing of the Temple of the Assyrian cult practices soon was regarded as an act not only of religious reform but also of national rebellion. When the Egyptians in 609 B.C.E. finally rallied to the defense of the Assyrians, Josiah cast his lot with the Babylonians. This decision proved to be fateful for the Deuteronomic Reformation.

At the battle of Megiddo, the Judeans were roundly defeated. Josiah was captured, and for his act of rebellion he was executed. Judah became an Egyptian province, and the Deuteronomic Reformation was brought to an inglorious end. With the defeat of the Egyptians by the Babylonians at Carchemish in 605 B.C.E., Judah, in turn, became a Babylonian province. The spirit of nationalism had served only to substitute one foreign master for another. Disillusionment set in among the people, and soon the covenant with Yahweh was compromised once again with pagan ways.

Events moved very swiftly after the death of Josiah. The details have been preserved for us by two sources: (1) archaeology, and (2) the Bible.

It was the practice of the Babylonian kings to record the chief events of each year in an official document or chronicle. In 1956, D. J. Wiseman of the British Museum discovered, while digging in the ruins of Babylon, four new tablets of the Chronicle. These give us for the first time outside the Bible the details of the fall of Judah to the Babylonians. Significantly, the new archaelogical evidence also confirms the account reported in the Bible. The Biblical story of the fall of Judah and the destruction of the Temple in Jerusalem in 587/6 B.C.E. have been detailed in the life and writings of the Prophet Jeremiah.*

Although Jeremiah lived and prophecied during the crucial years of King Josiah, there is no direct evidence that he was an active participant in the Deuteronomic Reformation. Some scholars say that Chapter 11 of the book of Jeremiah evidences the prophet's support of the Reformation; however, the matter is open for discussion.

* It is also found in II Kings 24:18–25:30 and II Chronicles 36.

We first learn of Jeremiah in the year 626 B.C.E., some five years before the "Book of the Covenant" was to be "discovered" in the Temple. He was then a young man of twenty-five, having been born and raised in a priestly family in the small village of Anatoth, three miles northeast of Jerusalem. In that year Jeremiah felt that he was called to be "a prophet unto the nations" (Jer. 1:4–10). Unlike Amos, who did not hesitate to go to Beth-el, and Isaiah, who responded "Here am I, send me," Jeremiah was fearful to heed the voice within him and received his call with great reluctance. No matter how he tried to fight off this imposing responsibility, in the end he succumbed, announcing simply that he felt himself predestined to be a prophet of Yahweh. Once he accepted the challenge, however, he sought to follow through with a holy zeal, and he began to take his stand against priest and prophet, against ruler and ruled alike. He tried to become as indomitable as "a fortified city, and an iron pillar, and brazen walls [walls of brass]" (Jer. 1:18).

Jeremiah's early prophecies (Jer. 2:1–4:4) are reminiscent of those of Hosea. For Jeremiah, too, Israel was like a faithless wife who had abandoned her husband (Jer. 3:19–20). She was like a harlot, driven by lust (Jer. 2:20–25), and throughout the land, the prophet saw the sinfulness of the people. The covenant with Yahweh had been defiled, for "upon every high hill and every green tree" Baal was being worshiped. Thus, a divorce must take place (Jer. 3:1–15), for Judah had understood even less than her now-destroyed sister kingdom Israel the significance of her unfaithfulness to Yahweh (Jer. 3:6–14). Jeremiah also recognized, however, that Yahweh wanted the people to turn from their harlotry and to return to Him. It was not Yahweh's purpose to destroy but to heal the broken relationship (Jer. 4-12). Jeremiah, therefore, called for "a circumcision of the heart" (Jer. 4:4). The "uncircumcised heart" represented for Jeremiah a person whose heart was hardened in stubborn rebellion. Through the use of this metaphor, the prophet asked the people humbly to submit themselves to Yahweh. By "circumcising the heart," the people could restore the covenant relationship, and the ancient promise to Abraham (Gen. 18:18) would come into effect: nations then would bless themselves in the name of Yahweh.

> If you will return, O Israel,
> Says the Lord,
> Yea, return unto Me;
> And if you will put away your
>   detestable things out of My sight,
> And will not waver;
> And will swear: "As the Lord lives"
> In truth, in justice, and in righteousness;
> Then shall the nations bless themselves by Him,
> And in Him shall they glory (Jer. 4:1-2).

Soon after the death of Josiah, an event of major importance occurred which proved to be a turning point in Jeremiah's life. Jehoahaz, one of Josiah's sons, had been made king (609 B.C.E.), but after a reign of only three months, the victorious Egyptians replaced him with a second son, Jehoiakim, who was as unlike his father as a son could be. Jehoiakim (609–598 B.C.E.) not only curried Egypt's favor to preserve his power but also indulged himself by enslaving his own people to build his magnificent palaces. He feared no one, and, instead of pursuing justice by fulfilling the teachings of the "Book of the Covenant," he shed much innocent blood. He also revived the old paganism which his father had tried so hard to eliminate. Idols appeared once more in the Temple, and soon child sacrifice was practiced again in the Valley of Hinnom, just outside the walls of Jerusalem. These tendencies

apparently found considerable favor among the people, for
with the death of Josiah they, too, apparently had become disillusioned with the Deuteronomic Reformation. Once again
the smug complacency and the self-sufficient righteousness
which the Deuteronomic priests and the prophets alike had
condemned came to the fore. The people returned quickly to
their old belief that they could get away with whatever they
chose to do or not to do, as long as they went through the
formalities of worship.

It was at this point in the history of Judah that Jeremiah
entered upon his greatest prophetic undertaking. Watching
the people entering and leaving the Temple, Jeremiah's zeal
for the covenant burned fiercely within him. Finally, he
could contain himself no longer, and he broke forth into a
prophetic utterance which has become known as the Temple
Sermon (Jer. 7).

It is futile to believe, thundered Jeremiah, that "The
Temple of Yahweh, The Temple of Yahweh, The Temple of
Yahweh" will protect Judah from all evil. Let the people
rather "amend your ways and your doings, and I, Yahweh,
will cause you to dwell in this place." Then in rapid order
Jeremiah listed some of the shortcomings of the people:

> . . . If you thoroughly execute justice between a man and
> his neighbor; if you oppress not the stranger, the father-
> less, and the widow, and shed not innocent blood in this
> place, neither walk after other gods to your hurt. . . .
>
> Behold, you trust in lying words, that cannot profit.
> Will you steal, murder, and commit adultery, and swear
> falsely, and offer unto Baal, and walk after other gods
> whom you have not known, and come and stand before
> Me in this house, whereupon My name is called, and
> say: "We are delivered," that you may do all these
> abominations?

The consequences are inevitable, proclaimed Jeremiah. Since the people had abandoned their covenant relationship with Yahweh, the Temple of Jerusalem would be destroyed just as Shiloh had been laid waste many years before in the days of Samuel.

Shortly after his Temple Sermon, Jeremiah was arrested and court martialed (Jer. 26). The priests, the false prophets, and the people alike charged him with treason. He was tried, convicted, and sentenced to death. Only the intercession of the princes who had served as judges saved him. Jeremiah was a prophet, a man who spoke in the name of Yahweh. It was an old tradition among the Israelites, prevailing even among the kings, that a prophet may not be put to death.

Jeremiah, while speaking to the people of Judah, also kept an eye on the international arena. After the battle of Megiddo in 609 B.C.E. where Josiah was killed, Jeremiah felt that the course of empires had changed. Babylonia now was destined to become the dominant world power. As a result, he undertook a series of "signs," which foreboded the tragic consequences of Judah's continued unfaithfulness. Scholars differ as to the exact dating of these signs. Most, however, prefer a date preceding the battle of Carchemish in 605 B.C.E.

The first sign took the form of a potter's wheel (Jer. 18). Jeremiah saw a potter seated in his pit, his feet spinning the wheel and his hands moulding the clay. Suddenly Jeremiah realized that the people of Judah were like clay in a potter's hand. For example, if the vessel were to be spoiled, owing to some imperfection in the material, it could be reworked into another vessel as the potter saw fit. The same was true of Judah. If the nation refused to be moulded in the divine design and insisted upon following its own paths, then Yahweh could repent of the good He had intended and could remould it by bringing upon it destruction. Drawing his analogy to a close, Jeremiah concluded that there was still time for Judah to return to Yahweh's favor. "Return you now every one from his evil ways, and amend your ways and your doings [Jer. 18:11] before it is too late," counseled the prophet.

On another occasion, Jeremiah brought a linen waistcloth and wore it, supposedly, to the Euphrates, where he hid it among the rocks. When the cloth became spoiled, he interpreted this sign to mean that Yahweh would spoil the pride of the people of Judah even though they had clung to him as closely as a garment (Jer. 13:1–11).

Another time, Jeremiah brought a clay bottle and broke it in the Valley of Hinnom, where human sacrifice was being practiced. This was his way of saying to the people that the destruction which would take place would be so great that the Valley itself would have to be used as a burial ground (Jer. 19).

After these signs, Jeremiah went to the Court of theTemple and repeated his message of doom. The treasures of the king would be seized, he announced, and together with the people they would be deported to Babylon. Also, Pashur, the chief officer in the Temple, would be exiled to Babylonia where ultimately he would die. The moment Jeremiah finished his message, he was seized by Pashur and the other priests, beaten and put in the stocks for the night (Jer. 20:1–6).

It was inevitable that sooner or later the prophet and the king, too, should clash. After the battle of Carchemish, it was important, Jeremiah felt, to restate his message. In order to prepare himself adequately, he retired in order to put his prophetic utterances into written form (Jer. 36). Patiently he reworked his earlier statements, which he had preserved by memory, combined them with his more recent prophecies, and dictated them to his faithful scribe, Baruch. Since Jeremiah was not permitted to enter the Temple grounds, Baruch took the completed manuscript to the Temple where he read it before the people. Soon a report of Baruch's reading was brought to the attention of the king, who ordered that the scroll be read to him. Jehoiakim's reaction was quick in coming. Prior to the battle of Carchemish, the realization of who the foe from the north might be remained vague and perhaps even meaningless. Now the enemy could be identified clearly. The foe from the north was Babylonia, and the threat, moreover, was imminent and real. Jeremiah's words, therefore, were no longer idle talk, the babbling of a mad prophet intoxicated with the spirit of a desert God. As can well be imagined, Jehoiakim was furious, and, with a few bold slashes of his knife, he cut the scrolls into pieces and threw them into the fire. He then ordered Baruch and Jeremiah arrested, but they were not to be found anywhere.

Once again, Jeremiah went into hiding. This time he was not to emerge for seven years, until Jerusalem itself was besieged by the Babylonians in 598 B.C.E. During this time, he redictated his prophetic utterances (Jer. 1–25) to his scribe Baruch, who also added a biographical narrative (Jer. 26–45) of the prophet. It is this edition of Jeremiah's life and prophecies which forms our present book of Jeremiah.

It was during this same period that he wrote his famous "Confessions." Altogether there are seven† which have been preserved, and they represent the prophet's personal diary, an intimate glimpse into his life-long struggle between rebellion and reaffirmation. Perhaps one of the most famous of these confessions is found in Jeremiah 20:14–18. In his seclusion, Jeremiah could look back upon his many years of prophetic ministry. While Yahweh had called him in the beginning to be a prophet, he had become instead a fugitive and a

† Jer. 11:18–23; 12:1–2, 4–5; 15:10–11, 15–21; 17:14–18; 18:18–23; 20:7–11; 20:14–18.

laughing-stock. Little wonder that the prophet believed he had been deceived by Yahweh. On the other hand, Jeremiah also realized that he could not escape his assigned task, for, if he were to remain silent, there was "in his heart as it were a burning fire" (Jer. 20:9).

Torn from within and hunted from without, Jeremiah poured into the Confessions his long years of prophetic frustration. He cursed the day "wherein I was born" (Jer. 20:14). On another occasion, he even sought vengeance upon his enemies (Jer. 18:20–21).‡ For these thoughts, however, Jeremiah rebuked himself. He, too, he concluded, needed inner purification, the opening anew of the heart.

> Therefore thus says the Lord:
> If you return, and I bring you back,
> You shall stand before Me;
> And if you bring forth the precious out of the vile,
> You shall be as My mouth . . . (Jer. 15:19).

After a silence of seven years, Jeremiah emerged strengthened and reassured. In the year 597 B.C.E., he entered upon the most difficult, and, surely for him, the most painful part of his prophetic work.

While Jeremiah was in hiding, the Babylonians had suffered a military defeat (601 B.C.E.). Jehoiakim seized this opportunity to make a desperate bid for independence by withholding tribute payment to Nebuchadnezzar, the King of Babylon. Jehoiakim died in 598 B.C.E., and he was succeeded to the throne by his eighteen-year-old son, Jehoiachin (598–597 B.C.E.). Soon the Babylonian armies descended upon Judah; Jerusalem was besieged and conquered. The Temple and the royal treasuries were confiscated, and within three months

‡ See also Jer. 11:20; 12:1–3; 17:17–18; 20:11–12.

after coming to the throne, young king Jehoiachin, together with his mother and the leading people of Judah, was taken away into exile. Upon the throne, Nebuchadnezzar placed Josiah's youngest son, Zedekiah (597–587 B.C.E.), who was weak and easily swayed by the advice of those around him.

One can imagine Jeremiah's despair when the Babylonian soldiers breached the walls of Jerusalem and captured the city. Like all his prophetic predecessors, Jeremiah, too, had brought a message of doom; however, he was deeply grieved when the calamity actually befell his people. While critics of their nations, the prophets still were patriots. So deeply troubled was Jeremiah by the exile of Judah's leadership that he felt compelled to emerge from his seclusion. No longer could he keep silent, for his people now needed encouragement. The doom that he had foretold had been visited upon them, and the situation called for a different emphasis. It called for a message of hope.

The hope which Jeremiah envisaged lay with the exiles in Babylonia, not with those who remained in Judah. In a famous vision, Jeremiah saw two baskets of figs placed in the Temple. The basket containing the good, ripe, and freshly picked figs symbolized for him the exiles. The future lay, according to Jeremiah, with the deportees, for Yahweh would restore them in time to Judah and make them his covenant people. The basket of bad figs, on the other hand, represented Zedekiah, his nobles, and the remnant of the people in Judah (Jer. 24).

Jeremiah had good reason to put his trust in the exiles and to suspect the weak and vacillating Zedekiah. The popular prophets of Judah and the leaders alike left no stone unturned to overthrow the burdening Babylonian yoke. When an anti-Babylonian coalition was formed under the leadership of a revived Egypt, they put pressure upon Zedekiah to cast his lot with the rebels. Jeremiah condemned the conspiracy, and he put the bars of a yoke upon his neck as a sign that Judah should submit only to the yoke of Yahweh (Jer. 27). The popular prophets were infuriated with Jeremiah's act of opposition. Finally, the prophet Hananiah, together with his followers, confronted Jeremiah. They broke the yoke from his shoulders and declared that within two years the exiles would be returned. Not to be outdone, Jeremiah made a new yoke of iron. This time he pointed out that yoke would not be broken, even as no human could break the yoke of Babylon. Jeremiah firmly believed that Nebuchadnezzar was the instrument of Yahweh's purpose (Jer. 28).

Zedekiah did not join the coalition, but his loyalty to Babylonia was not to be trusted. When a second alliance was formed subsequently in 588 B.C.E. under a new Egyptian Pharaoh, Zedekiah no longer could resist the temptation and joined the coalition. Nebuchadnezzar moved swiftly to put down the rebellion, and, before the year was out, his armies laid siege to Jerusalem. The situation of the besieged within the city quickly deteriorated. Zedekiah became frantic, and, in an attempt to gain the favor of Yahweh, sought to restore some of the Deuteronomic laws. All Hebrew slaves were freed. However, when the siege was lifted temporarily because of the advance of the Egyptian troops, the freed slaves were re-enslaved (Jer. 34; 37:5).

During this time, Jeremiah remained steadfast in his belief that the only course of action was surrender to Babylonia. In recommending this path, he was not a collaborationist who wanted to see his country controlled by a foreign power; nor was he a pacifist who was opposed to war on principle. Jeremiah saw the crisis as part of the design of God, which could not be changed by joining any alliance, whether pro-Egyptian or pro-Babylonian. When the Babylonians withdrew temporarily, Zedekiah asked Jeremiah to pray to Yahweh on behalf of a Judean victory. Jeremiah refused and counseled instead that the Babylonians would return and Jerusalem would be conquered. The king and the princes were indignant at the prophet's reply.

During this same period, Jeremiah, when he sought to leave Jerusalem for his home village of Anatoth (Jer. 37:11–15), was arrested and charged with deserting to the Babylonians. When the leaders of the people demanded Jeremiah's death, the weak vacillating Zedekiah wavered. Even though he regarded the prophet as nothing less than a traitor, at the same time he was afraid that Jeremiah might be right (Jer. 37:16–21). Finally, he gave in. Jeremiah was lowered into a cistern used to catch water in the rainy season where he was left to die. Again, Zedekiah's indecision proved to be decisive. He ordered one of his Ethiopian slaves to rescue Jeremiah. Secretly Zedekiah came to Jeremiah for another conference; however, the results were the same. Jeremiah remained steadfast in his opinion that Zedekiah should not oppose Nebuchadnezzar and his Babylonian armies (Jer. 38:14–28).

This meeting was probably the last between these two men. Shortly after, the Babylonians besieged Jerusalem again. The Judeans fought bravely but were no match for the mighty military strength of Nebuchadnezzar. Within a few months the walls were breached; within a year, the city and the Temple were destroyed. In 587/6 B.C.E. a second and final exile of Judeans was carried out. Zedekiah was captured as he tried to escape the city; his two sons were executed in his presence, and then he himself was blinded, placed in chains, and carried off as a pathetic prisoner to Babylon (Jer. 39).

The destruction of the nation had been accomplished. The dire doom of the prophetic message had been fulfilled, and the period of the Babylonian Exile was about to begin. With the Babylonian Exile, however, a new chapter in the story of the birth of the Torah was to commence.

CHAPTER XVII

The Babylonian Exile

THE period between the conquest of Jerusalem by Nebuchadnezzar (587/6 B.C.E.) and the edict of the Persian King Cyrus permitting the deported people to return to Judah (536 B.C.E.) is known as the Babylonian Exile. Despite their tragic military defeat, the exiles were to undergo during these years a period of great spiritual ferment. During the Exile and the events immediately following, the Torah was to receive the form in which we have it today and to become, as it were, the constitution for the development of Judaism in the future.

Three important trends can be traced during the period of the Babylonian Exile: (1) the emergence of the Synagogue in contrast to the Temple in Jerusalem; (2) the preservation and development of the prophetic traditions of Jeremiah and Ezekiel; and (3) the completion of the Torah. The first two of these trends will be discussed in this chapter, and the third will be treated in the following chapter.

The Synagogue

Although the Deuteronomic Reformation had suffered a severe setback with the untimely death of King Josiah, the Deuteronomic teachings concerning the centrality of the

Temple continued. The D writers had taught that three pilgrimages were to be made yearly to the Temple. These occasions were the ancient festivals of Passover, Shavuot, and Sukkot (Deut. 16:16–17).* After the destruction of the Temple by Nebuchadnezzar, the people who had remained in Judah still could make the pilgrimages to Jerusalem, although they could not carry out the sacrifices in the prescribed order. Many, therefore, offered their sacrifices on private altars.

The exiles, however, were confronted with a more critical situation. The D writers had linked Yahweh so closely with the Temple at Jerusalem that, in the popular mind, Yahweh had become identified with one specific geographic location. Consequently, the exiles felt, since they were unable to make the required pilgrimages to Jerusalem, that they were without Yahweh. The full impact of their dilemma is told in Psalm 137:1–5:

> By the rivers of Babylon,
> There we sat down, yea, we wept,
> When we remembered Zion. . . .
> How shall we sing the Lord's song
> In a foreign land? . . .
> Let my tongue cleave to the roof of my mouth,
> If I remember you not;
> If I set not Jerusalem
> Above my chiefest joy.

This dilemma had been foreshadowed when Nebuchadnezzar had exiled Judah's leaders the first time in 597 B.C.E. and had confronted them with a similar religious crisis. Distraught, the exiles had turned to the prophet Jeremiah and sought his counsel. They wanted to know whether they should regard the exile as a temporary or long-range situation, whether to es-

* See Chapter 6.

tablish themselves as permanent residents or to seek only make-shift employment to tide them over, and whether to build a new Temple or to provide another form of worshiping Yah-weh. These were real and pressing situations. Jeremiah's an-swer has been preserved by his scribe Baruch and is found in Jeremiah 29:4-7.

In his reply, Jeremiah freed Yahweh from all limitations of geography. Yahweh could and should be worshiped every-where, he advised, whether in Jerusalem or in Babylon. If sac-rifices were not possible, then prayers should be offered. More-over, counseled Jeremiah, the exiles were to live normal lives. They were to build homes, establish businesses, seek marriage partners for their children, and concern themselves with the welfare of the community in which they resided.

When the exiles of 587/6 B.C.E. reached Babylonia, they found that the advice of Jeremiah had been accepted by many of the original deportees. This example heartened them and gave them courage to normalize their own lives "in a strange land." In time, they, too, began to gather together and to reread the words of Jeremiah as well as those of the other prophets. They also remembered the collected traditions of what we have called JE as well as those of the D School. These traditions became very dear to them, and now they treasured them as they had the Temple before. In addition, the exiles would, from time to time, recite prayers to Yahweh. Out of these in-formal meetings a new institution soon came into existence.

Although the exiles did not know the term "synagogue," the Synagogue in contrast to the Temple gradually made its appearance in Babylonia. The word "synagogue" comes from the Greek word meaning "assembly," and it was applied later to the place where the people would assemble to pray and to study the traditions. In Babylonia, however, the Synagogue, though it was to become very popular and vital to the lives of the people, remained an informal institution. It was still secondary to the Temple in Jerusalem, for the exiles dreamed also of the day when the Temple in Jerusalem would be rebuilt to the glory of Yahweh.

Jeremiah's Message of Hope

In addition to Jeremiah's letter which freed Yahweh from the limitations of geography and cleared the way for the emergence of the Synagogue, two other prophetic emphases were to have a far-reaching impact upon the exiles in Babylonia. These were (1) the final prophetic utterances of Jeremiah and (2) the message of the Prophet Ezekiel.

The prophets were patriots. Even though their messages decreed "doom" for their people, they always pleaded with their people to turn from the evil of their ways before it was too late. When this failed and destruction seemed imminent, they still spoke of a "remnant" that would survive. It grieved them deeply to see their people suffer. This was true especially of Jeremiah. Once the Babylonians had conquered and the Temple lay in ruins, he knew that the time had come for him to strengthen his people, to give them encouragement in their greatest hour of despair. The burning question no longer was whether Yahweh would or would not punish the people because of their national pride and resultant complacency. The punishment had come. The "Day of Yahweh," as the prophets had spoken, was indeed a "day of darkness and not light." The people had recognized at last their sinfulness. The new concern, therefore, was: how can the people live? Thus, Jeremiah recognized immediately that his message could no longer be one of doom. Just as he had given hope to the exiles of 597 B.C.E., he realized now that he had to comfort those who remained in Jerusalem. He had to show his people how to live. The times called for a prophecy of encouragement, a prophecy

which spoke of hope for the remnant in Judah. Jeremiah's response was immediate and direct. His prophetic mission was
not only "to root out and to pull down and to destroy and to
overthrow" but also "to build, and to plant" (Jer. 1:10).

In the very hour when Nebuchadnezzar's armies were
pounding at the city gates and the downfall of Jerusalem
seemed imminent, Jeremiah chose to buy a piece of property.
As next of kin, he had inherited suddenly the right to buy his
cousin's field in his home village of Anatoth. To the people of
Jerusalem the purchase of the field seemed like an act of sheer
madness. Jeremiah, however, thought differently. Though imprisoned by his own king, he viewed this opportunity as nothing less than a sign from Yahweh that "houses and fields and
vineyards shall yet again be bought in this land" (Jer. 32:15).

Jeremiah sincerely believed that not only Judah but also
Israel, which had been destroyed more than two centuries
before, would be restored. This was the message of hope which
Jeremiah now announced, as he wept over the fallen of his
people and saw how "death stalked the streets and came in at
the windows" (Jer. 9:21). The restoration, however, was not
to be an ordinary event, nor was it to be simply a national
revival. It was to be marked by the establishment of a "new
covenant" to replace the original covenant which had been
broken. The goals originally set forth at Sinai were still valid:
"At that time . . . will I be the God of all the families of Israel,
and they shall be My people" (Jer. 31:1). Only now the
methods would change. The "new covenant" would be written in the heart and in the inward parts and not upon the out-
ward flesh, as was the old, by a rite of circumcision. The "new
covenant" would be an enduring agreement between the
people and Yahweh. Jeremiah thus envisaged a restored people,
both in Judah and in Israel as well as in Babylonia, a people,
moreover, strengthened by the "everlasting love of Yahweh."

> ... and I will be their God, and they
> shall be My people ... (Jer. 31:33b–34)

While Jeremiah sought now to give encouragement to his people, his own last days were filled with trouble and despair (Jer. 40–44). Although he was given an opportunity to go into exile with the leaders of Jerusalem, Jeremiah chose to remain in the city. By this act he was able to indicate clearly to his accusers that he was not a deserter. The taint of disloyalty clung to him nonetheless.

Soon after, when Gedaliah, the Babylonian appointed governor, was assassinated, the Judean leaders fled to Egypt. Fearful that he might betray them, they took the unwilling Jeremiah and his scribe, Baruch, with them to Egypt. The last reports of the prophet's activities concern themselves with a group of exiles in Egypt who had begun to worship Ishtar, the Queen of Heaven. His final preserved prophecy contained once again words of doom. Nothing more is known of his life, though it is believed that he died in Egypt.

The Prophet Ezekiel

The prophet Ezekiel was Jeremiah's younger contemporary. Exiled with the first deportees in 597 B.C.E., he settled by the banks of the river Chebar, just a short distance southeast of Babylon. Presumably he belonged to the Jerusalem aristocracy, and some believe that he was also a member of the powerful priesthood which claimed descent from Zadok, the High Priest originally installed by King Solomon. His call to prophecy came in the year 593 B.C.E. while he was in Tel-Aviv, a small village on the edge of the river. His prophetic ministry was to cover a period of twenty years (593–573 B.C.E.), and during this time he was to minister to the exiles both of the first and second deportations.

There is an interesting problem connected with Ezekiel's prophetic ministry about which scholars differ greatly. The question is: did Ezekiel spend his entire ministry in Babylonia or did he return to Jerusalem? The problem is presented in the opening three chapters, in which Ezekiel is commanded to go to Jerusalem, and again in Chapter 11, where he is lifted up "and brought . . . unto the east gate of the Lord's house [Temple in Jerusalem]." One school holds that Ezekiel did go back to Jerusalem the year after he had received his call to service and remained there until 587/6 B.C.E., when he returned with the new exiles to Babylonia. A second point of view contends that Ezekiel remained permanently in Babylonia. Having lived at one time in Jerusalem, he was familiar with its names and places so that he could speak of them as though he were personally present.

The Book of Ezekiel, unlike the Book of Jeremiah, is arranged in an orderly fashion:

1. Prophecies given before the fall of Jerusalem (593–587/6 B.C.E.)

    a. Ezekiel's opening vision and call (1–3)

    b. Oracles of doom against Judah and Jerusalem (4–24)

2. Oracles against the neighboring nations (25–32) †

3. Prophecies given after the fall of Jerusalem (587/6–573 B.C.E.)

    a. Oracles of Promise (33–39)

    b. The New Jerusalem (40–48)

† Scholars differ as to whether Ezekiel was the author or whether these oracles were written by one or more unknown prophets and later attached to the writings of Ezekiel. Since the content of these oracles does not affect the story of the birth of the Torah, a discussion of their contents will be omitted.

In 592 B.C.E., five years after the first exiles had gone to Babylonia, Ezekiel, already thirty years of age, had a vision in which he felt Yahweh had called him to become a prophet. Like Isaiah before him, Ezekiel, too, felt himself suddenly transported into the very presence of Yahweh. He beheld a strange mixture of symbols taken both from the tradition of the Temple in Jerusalem and from the religious emblems of his new home in Babylonia.

The vision described Yahweh's heavenly chariot as it approached from the north. The chariot itself was mounted on four weird creatures, called cherubim. They were like the half-animal and half-human figures so familiar in Babylonian archaeological excavations. Each cherub was in perfect coordination with the others, as though a divine spirit directed them. The chariot itself could move easily in all directions, for it worked as though it were a "wheel within a wheel." Each cherub, in turn, supported upon its wings what seemed to be a platform, or a "firmament." Above the "firmament" Ezekiel felt that he beheld "a likeness as the appearance of a man" (Ezek. 1:26), "the appearance of the likeness of the glory of Yahweh" (Ezek. 1:28).

Overwhelmed by what he saw, Ezekiel fell with his face to the ground. He realized fully that he was only a "son of man," a mortal being, and that he was in the presence of the immortal Yahweh. When Yahweh spoke with him, however, he stood up. The words came clear and sure. Ezekiel was to warn the people of their rebelliousness. Even if they were "brazenfaced and stiff-necked," he was to remind them of their unfaithfulness to Yahweh and to warn them of their impending doom. Whether they listened or not was of little concern to him, because Yahweh would remain faithful by continuing to send a prophet, no matter what the shortcomings of the people might be. The people could never protest that they had not been warned. Finally, a hand, holding a scroll, reached out to

Ezekiel, and he was commanded to eat the book. Here was written the people's shortcomings, and though the scroll was filled with "lamentations and moaning, and woe," he ate it as though it were "honey for sweetness." His commission, however, was too overwhelming, and for seven days Ezekiel sat dazed by the river Chebar.

Like Jeremiah prior to the complete destruction of Jerusalem in 597 B.C.E., Ezekiel, too, preached a message of doom. He also used many signs to punctuate the urgency of his message. On one occasion he drew a picture of the siege of Jerusalem on a clay brick. He then lay for thirty-nine days on his left side and for forty days on his right side to point out the respective number of years of punishment for the kingdoms of Israel and Judah (Ezek. 4:1–3). Even as he lay there, he weighed out small portions of food and water to indicate the sufferings which he anticipated the siege would bring (Ezek. 4:4–8). On another occasion, he prepared food that looked revolting, and he ate it sparingly to signify the starvation which would come with the impending siege (Ezek. 4:9–17). On still another occasion, he cut off his hair with a sword, and, dividing it into three parts, indicated that the people of Jerusalem would be punished by fire, sword, and exile (Ezek. 5:1–12). Again, he would eat and drink with quaking and trembling to symbolize the state of fear which would obtain when the siege would come (Ezek. 12:17–20). In still another instance, he beat himself violently because he believed a glittering sword was hanging over the head of his people (Ezek. 21:9–15). Even when his wife, whom he loved dearly, died, he refused to mourn for her to indicate to the exiles that their own mourning over the imminent destruction of Jerusalem would be too bitter and tragic for tears (Ezek. 24:15–27).

The people, however, paid little attention either to his words or to his signs. They neither repented nor turned upon him in hostility as they had upon Jeremiah. In fact, some even enjoyed his messages; Ezekiel's words became as "a love song of one that hath a pleasant voice" (Ezek. 33:30–33).

Nonetheless, Ezekiel persisted, and in two eloquent sermons (Ezek. 16 and 23), using the figure of the harlot as Hosea and Jeremiah had done before him, he sketched in bold strokes the extent of Israel's ‡ rebelliousness. From her very birth Israel had been faithless to the covenant, for she was herself an illegitimate child. Only the continuing faithfulness of Yahweh had maintained the covenant. In fact, Yahweh was anxious to renew the covenant on an everlasting basis. First, however, Israel would need to become an object of reproach before the nations. Israel's sins were too many for Yahweh to forgive without a judgment. In the Temple the people worshiped the sun with their faces to the east; the women wept for Tammuz, the Babylonian fertility god; they filled the Holy of Holies with forbidden pictures of beasts, idols, and men (Ezek. 8–11). Israel's harlotry included not only ritual abuses but also ethical crimes. There was bloodshed, adultery, extortion, dishonor of parents, and violation of the rights of the orphan, widow, and traveler (Ezek. 22). Everyone, Ezekiel believed, was involved in the harlotry. Not a righteous person was to be found anywhere. Not even Noah, Daniel, and Job, the three men who were thought to be above reproach, could now save Jerusalem, in Ezekiel's opinion (Ezek. 14:12–20). For all this Israel needed to be punished.

Once Jerusalem came under siege, however, Ezekiel's message changed rapidly from doom to hope. Before, when nationalistic feelings ran high, his task was to shatter the people's illusions; now, when his people were thrown into the depths of despair, his responsibility was to give them assurance of a

‡ Ezekiel throughout used the term Israel to denote the entire people, not just the northern kingdom of Israel as distinct from the southern kingdom of Judah, which had entered into the original covenant in the Sinai desert-wilderness.

new hope. Therefore, he took up the theme to which he had
alluded earlier, the promise of a new beginning. Yahweh was
prepared to establish a new covenant of the heart. The message of hope took a threefold direction: (1) the concept of
individual retribution; (2) the restoration of Judah and Israel;
and (3) the doctrine of the new covenant.

The concept of individual retribution was not new with
Ezekiel. Jeremiah had developed it as part of his own message
of hope. The concept of individual retribution, stated simply,
taught that a person was responsible for his own sins. He was
not to blame others, particularly those who lived in previous
generations, for his own shortcomings. Each person had to answer for himself to Yahweh. This was the meaning which both
Jeremiah and Ezekiel applied to the current proverb: "The
fathers have eaten sour grapes, and the children's teeth are set
on edge" (Jer. 31:29; Ezek. 18:1–4).

While scholars may differ as to whether Ezekiel began to
emphasize the concept of individual retribution before or
after the fall of Jerusalem, the ultimate significance of Ezekiel's teachings has remained timeless. Like Jeremiah, Ezekiel
felt that the people of Jerusalem were trying to place the
blame for their present predicament upon their forefathers by
claiming that their ancestors, not they, had broken the covenant through their ritual and ethical abuses. The people believed that they were the helpless victims of inheritance. Ezekiel, however, was not misled by these sidestepping tactics.
Instead, he challenged them to assume their responsibility:

Cast away from all your transgressions, wherein you have
transgressed; and make you a new heart and a new spirit;
for why will you die, O house of Israel? For I have no
pleasure in the death of him who dies, says the Lord God;
wherefore turn yourselves, and live (Ezek. 18:31–32)
(cf. Ezek. 33:10–20).

Ezekiel tried not only to strengthen the moral fiber of the individual but also to bolster the collapsing morale of the nation. In a masterful vision of the valley of dry bones, he spoke of the restoration of the nation (Ezek. 37). To those in Jerusalem and in Babylonia who wailed, "our bones are dried up, and our hope is lost," he replied that the bones would live again. Before their very eyes, they would see the bones both clothed with sinews and animated by the spirit of Yahweh. Renewed life was to be Israel's destiny.

> Thus says the Lord God: Behold I will open your graves, and cause you to come up out of your graves, O my people; and I will bring you into the land of Israel (Ezek. 37:12).

As though this were not enough, Ezekiel took two sticks, writing upon one the name of Judah and upon the other the name of Joseph (the sons of Joseph became part of the northern kingdom of Israel). Then he took the sticks and placed them together and proclaimed in the name of Yahweh:

> Behold, I will take the children of Israel from among the nations, whither they are gone, and will gather them on every side, and bring them into their own land . . . (Ezek. 37:21).

In Ezekiel's judgment, Yahweh would restore not only the nation but also Judah and Israel as one nation.

Finally, Ezekiel held forth to the defeated and disillusioned exiles the hope of a new covenant. Israel from its very birth may have played the part of the harlot; however, Yahweh now was prepared to receive her back. It would be another sign to the nations of the world that Yahweh, as God, would restore a helpless and hopeless people. As much as the people needed Yahweh, Yahweh, in turn, needed them.

> A new heart also will I give you, and a new spirit will I
> put in you; and I will take away the stony heart out of
> your flesh, and I will give you a heart of flesh. And I will
> put my spirit within you, and cause you to walk in My
> statutes, and you shall keep My ordinances and do them
> (Ezek. 36:26–27; also 11:19–20).

Once the reconciliation had been made, then Israel, of its own
volition and in appreciation for Yahweh's everlasting faithfulness, would drive from her life all forms of idolatry. Israel
would repent her former evil ways and accept the responsibilities of the covenant. At that time, Yahweh would dwell
among his people in the Temple in Jerusalem. Thus, the book
of Ezekiel came to a close with an elaborate description of the
new Temple in a new Jerusalem (Ezek. 40–48).

Although the Temple in Jerusalem lay in ruins and many
of the priests had gone into exile, the priestly influence was
able to re-establish itself quickly in Babylonia. This influence
was evident already in Ezekiel, who lived at the very beginning of the Exile. In his description of the new Temple, Ezekiel's priestly background came to the fore. The restored community, as he envisaged it, would be centered in the priesthood
and the activities of the Temple. This new priestly emphasis
which took hold in Babylonia proved to be of tremendous significance for the birth of the Torah. To this last phase we now
turn.

XVIII

The P School

THE years of the Babylonian captivity represented an era of intense religious activity. Prophet and priest alike felt destined to strengthen the sense of covenant between Israel and Yahweh. The people, too, recognizing that they were no longer held together by a common national allegiance, devoted themselves to the twofold task of (1) studying their ancient traditions to discover their meaning for the new age, and (2) committing their heritage to writing so that it might be preserved for the future. The Babylonian Exile, thus, became a period of continuous creativity. This was the age in which the Synagogue came into being; also, it was the time when the Torah in its completed form may have been born.

Among those who had come to Babylonia were the priests of Jerusalem. Although King Josiah, during the Deuteronomic Reformation, had tried to emphasize the ritual role of the priests, the people still remembered them as teachers, as the transmitters of the rules and procedures by which Yahweh was to be worshiped and served. To the priests, therefore, the people turned for leadership, for many of them not only had learned the tradition by heart but also had brought along copies of the ancient writings.

While scholars differ about how familiar the priests were

with the JE and particularly the D traditions, they are agreed on the fact that they did have a tradition of their own. Therefore, the priests undertook a twofold task: (1) to preserve and teach the various traditions as they knew them, and (2) to record their own priestly heritage. Out of this creative urge emerged a series of writings which modern scholars have assigned to the P School, after their priestly authors and editors.

The P material is found in large blocks throughout the Torah, especially in the books of Genesis, Exodus, Leviticus, and Numbers. These writings can be recognized readily because of their emphasis upon ritual observance and concern for detail. For example, the Book of Leviticus, with its elaboration of the sacrificial system, and chapters 25 to 31, and 35 to 40 of the Book of Exodus, which describe the procedures for the building of the Tabernacle, the vestments and practices of the priests, as well as the procedures of the holy days, are examples of the P writers' concern for ritual observance. Their careful consideration of details is demonstrated further by their interest in genealogies (Gen. 5; 10; 25:12–18; 36; 46:8–27).

Above all, however, the P writings can be detected because of a point of view. First of all, an atmosphere of worship pervaded their work. There were no dramatic narratives about human affairs like those found in J and E. P was concerned with instructing the people how to worship Yahweh—as worship was understood, of course, by the Jersualem priests. Second, the P writings were governed by a theological purpose. From the P School's point of view, Yahweh's revelation followed a prearranged, systematic plan. There were four successive stages to this plan, each one marked by the granting of certain privileges and the placing of responsibilities. Revelation for the P writers emphasized what Yahweh gave to man instead of what man discovered in seeking his God. This preference was to have far-reaching implications for the future of

Judaism. Since the P writers were the last editors to rework
the text of the Torah, it was their imprint which became the
dominating influence in Jewish life. For example, their strong
Yahweh-centered emphasis upon revelation ultimately grew
in later years into the belief that the entire Torah, and not
just the commandments, had been delivered by Yahweh to
Moses at Sinai. In their time, however, the P writers noted
four successive stages in the process of revelation, each of
which portrayed Yahweh's purpose: the selection of Israel for
special service. The four stages of the revelation were: (1) the
Creation; (2) the covenant with Noah; (3) the covenant with
Abraham; and (4) the covenant at Mt. Sinai.

The Creation

Like the J writers, the P School was familiar with the creation stories of ancient Babylonia. Today, thanks to archaeological discoveries, we have the text of one of the Babylonian
accounts. On March 4, 1875, more than two years after he
had found the now-famous clay tablets containing the Gilgamesh Epic and its flood story, the English archaeologist
George Smith told the scientific world that he had discovered
in addition seven tablets describing the creation of the world.
Although there were many gaps in the original text of the
Seven Tablets of Creation, recently discovered fragments have
made Smith's account more complete.

The Babylonian story of creation was contained in a long
poem which was recited each year during the New Year's
celebration. It began with a picture of the earliest imaginable
period of time when only two gods were in existence. They
were Apsu, the fresh water, and Tiamat, the salt water. In
time, several generations of gods sprang from the first pair.
Soon enmity arose between the generations, until finally Apsu

decided to destroy his descendants. Under the leadership of Ea, the wise earth-and-water god, however, the younger gods joined together and slew Apsu. The bereaved mother-goddess, Tiamat, planned her revenge, but the younger gods were prepared. They had chosen Marduk, the principal god of the city of Babylon, as their champion. In the ensuing battle Marduk was victorious, and immediately thereafter he undertook the process of creation.

First, Marduk split Tiamat's body, like a shellfish, into two parts. From one half he made the sky, and from the other half he established the firmament. Then he caused the moon to shine at night, after which he set the constellations in their courses. Finally, Marduk proclaimed that he would bring blood and bone together and establish a "savage." This savage would be called "man," and it was to be savage-man's destiny to serve the gods so that they might be at ease. To draw the blood for savage-man, Marduk and the gods chose the god Kingu, who had undertaken to lead Tiamat's revenge. Since he was guilty, they severed his blood vessels and from his blood fashioned mankind. When all was done, the gods sat down at a banquet and feasted, and then the gods took over their assigned stations of heaven and earth, over which they were to rule.

The P account of the Creation Story is found in Genesis 1:1–2:4a. While both the P and Babylonian versions contain materials not found in the other (Genesis tells of the creation of animals, fish, and fowl; the Babylonian story, the building of the temple of Esagila), the reader will recognize immediately many elements which they do hold in common.[1]

The P writers, however, like their earlier predecessors, were not indiscriminate borrowers. They, too, adapted what they needed, but, in turn, they then poured into the material their own interpretation and emphasis. For the P writers, a conflict

Babylonian	Genesis
1. The watery chaos of Apsu and Tiamat.	1. The unformed earth and the deep.
2. Birth of Marduk, "Sun of the heavens."	2. Creation of light.
3. Sky is fashioned from half of Tiamat's body.	3. Creation of the firmament and the sky.
4. Forming of the earth from other part of Tiamat's body.	4. Gathering of water together to form the earth.
5. Setting up the constellatons.	5. Creation of the lights in the firmament.
6. Making man for the service of the gods.	6. Creation of man to have dominion over animal life.
7. The divine banquet.	7. Resting of God on the seventh day.

between gods was incomprehensible. Yahweh, to them, was the undisputed sovereign of the universe. He alone was not created, and without His supporting power the world would return immediately to primeval and meaningless chaos. Carefully, therefore, the P writers detailed the account of creation, emphasizing the creative act of Yahweh.

As the climax of all creative acts came man. In the P writers' conception of creation, man was to be created "in the image of Yahweh," and not, as in the Babylonian account, to be a "savage-man" fashioned from the material of the most guilty of the gods. Man was to be Yahweh's "image" or representative on earth, in the same way as the image or statue of a king was regarded as the symbol of the ruler's power wherever it was set up throughout a kingdom. Thus, Yahweh blessed man so that he could multiply and have dominion over all other living creatures (Gen. 1:28).

As a fitting conclusion, and in keeping with their emphasis upon ritual observance, the P writers closed the account of creation with the Sabbath day. Since the Sabbath was one of the basic institutions of Israel, they sought to enhance its meaning for their generation by making Sabbath rest the goal of Yahweh's creative work.

The Covenant with Noah

The P writers were familiar not only with the Creation epics but also with the Flood stories so characteristic of the ancient world. The present text of the Torah preserves the P account of the Flood. Unlike the Creation story, which was placed side by side with the earlier J account, the P Flood story is interlaced with the J version. Only the skillful scholarly eye can often detect the differences.

The P version gives the following account of the Flood. The generation in which Noah lived was corrupt; he alone was considered a righteous man. When Yahweh decided to destroy the earth which "was filled with violence," therefore, He commanded Noah to build an ark. The measurements of the ark and those people and animals to be saved were carefully outlined. Only Noah and his family and two of each kind of animal, male and female, were to survive in order that Yahweh after the flood might establish a covenant with them (Gen. 6:9–22). Noah was six hundred years old (Gen. 7:6) when he and his family and the designated animals entered the ark (Gen. 7:11, 13–16a). For 150 days the waters covered the earth, and all perished except Noah and those who were with him in the ark (Gen. 7:18–21, 24). Finally Yahweh remembered Noah, and he stopped "the fountains also of the deep and the windows of heaven" so that the waters began to recede (Gen. 8:1–2a). The ark rested on Mount Ararat (Gen. 8:3b–5). When the earth had dried sufficiently, Noah, his family, and all the animals went out from the ark (Gen. 8:13a, 14–19).

Yahweh then established a covenant with the survivors, promising them never again to destroy the earth. As a token of his promise, Yahweh placed the rainbow in the sky (Gen. 9: 1–17).

In setting forth their interpretation of the flood story, the P writers sought to impress upon their generation ideas which they felt were fundamental. For example, they emphasized the basic importance of the sacrificial system by describing how Yahweh through the new covenant gave man the privilege of eating meat, providing it was bloodless and had been properly sacrificed or slaughtered (Gen. 9: 1–5). Previously, man had been forbidden, according to some scholarly interpretations of the P school, to eat any meat at all; man was to be a vegetarian (Gen. 1: 29–30). Also, the dignity of man, that he had been created in "the image of Yahweh" and that Yahweh's creation was good, was emphasized by the P writers when they prohibited the wanton shedding of a man's blood. Finally, they pointed out that Yahweh originally had made his covenant with all men and not merely with Israel. All the nations of the world were descended from Noah and his sons; thus, the covenant with Noah was universal in its scope.

Jewish tradition has continued to emphasize the universal significance of the laws of Noah. There are seven altogether, and they have been called "The Seven Laws of the Sons of Noah" or simply the "Noachian Covenant" or "Noachian Laws." They are binding upon all men. Those who wish to take on the additional responsibilities of Judaism may do so; however, the seven laws of Noah represent for Judaism the minimum essentials for the establishment of a civilized society and from which no man or nation is exempt.

The rabbis who lived after the Torah was completed did not differentiate between the different schools of writers. For them, the Torah was all of one piece. For them, six of the seven laws were enjoined upon Adam and are found in Genesis 2:16 (which we would call a product of the J school). They are: (1) not to worship idols; (2) not to blaspheme the name of God; (3) to establish courts of justice; (4) not to kill; (5) not to commit adultery; and (6) not to rob. A seventh commandment, they believed, was added after the Flood and is found in Genesis 9:4 (which we would assign to the P writers): not to eat flesh that had been cut from a living animal.

The Covenant with Abraham

Like their predecessors, the P school believed that Abraham would be the father of many nations, and, more particularly, to him and his descendants the land of Canaan would be given as an everlasting possession. Thus, with Abraham, too, Yahweh had established a covenant (Gen. 17). As a consequence, Abraham's name was changed from Abram, meaning "may the (divine) father be exalted," to Abraham, which, according to the P writers, meant "father of a multitude." The covenant, moreover, was to be sealed by the rite of circumcision which the priests regarded as a basic institution of the priestly religion. Whoever refused to be circumcised broke, in their opinion, the covenant. He was to be excluded from the community of Israel and the claim that his heirs would inherit the land would automatically be forfeited.

By recounting the story of the Cave of Machpelah (Gen. 23), the P writers also sought to encourage their people in exile. Abraham and Sarah had been buried, they taught, in a cave near Hebron. Even though the promise was not fulfilled in their own lifetime, at least in death the patriarchs would come to inherit the land with their posterity. In this way the P writers sought to impress upon the exiles the ultimate fulfillment of the promise.

The Covenant at Sinai

The P writers believed that Yahweh's special revelation had been given to Israel at Mount Sinai. In the beginning, Yahweh had established the Sabbath for all men. The covenant with Noah also was universal in its emphasis. Mankind, however, did not wish to accept the responsibility of a covenant relationship. It was necessary, therefore, for Yahweh to pick a special people with whom His covenant could be established. He began with Abraham, the father of all peoples; finally, he selected only Israel to be a holy people, separated from all the other nations in order that He might dwell in their midst (Exod. 29:43–46). At Mount Sinai, moreover, Yahweh revealed the laws and institutions which were to be followed if Israel were to be a holy people. Thus, the P writers carefully detailed all procedures, for neither ethical nor ritual impurity would be permitted to defile the holy people. This material, constituting part of the Book of Exodus and all of the Book of Leviticus, was introduced into the JE account between the story of the making of the covenant (Exod. 24) and the departure from Sinai (Num. 10:29 ff.).

The version of the Ten Commandments as they are best known to us today also comes from the period of the P school (Exod. 20:1–14). Not all scholars agree with this view; however, generally it can be said that the P writers took the original shortened form of the Commandments and elaborated upon it in keeping with their own point of view. The D writers had done the same thing before them. Apparently, a common tradition had grown up around the original commandments, so that both the D and P schools were familiar with the same interpretations and developments. It is in the fourth commandment particularly that the P point of view was emphasized. The D writers had based the setting aside of the Sabbath as a day of rest upon the fact that Israel once had

been enslaved in Egypt; therefore, as a free people it was now
fitting for them to observe a day of rest. The P writers, on
the other hand, concerned with the ritual purity of Israel,
ascribed the Sabbath as a day of rest to the fact that such was
Yahweh's intention in the very act of creation.

Each of the four stages of Yahweh's systematic plan of revelation, according to the P writers, used its own special name
for Yahweh. In fact, it was not until the fourth phase—the
revelation at Sinai—that they introduced the name Yahweh
itself (Exod. 6:2–3). In the first two stages, the P writers used
the name Elohim, which has been translated as "God." When
the revelation was given to Abraham, Yahweh was made
known by the name of El Shaddai, often translated as "God
Almighty." Only when the revelation was directed to Israel
alone at Sinai did the name Yahweh appear.

Sometime during the Babylonian Exile, or shortly thereafter, the practice developed of not pronouncing the holy
name Yahweh because it might be taken in vain. For example, the popular belief existed that if one could pronounce the
name in exactly the proper manner, he could coerce Yahweh
and thus persuade him to do his bidding. In order to avoid
profaning Yahweh's name and to eliminate these elements of
superstition, the pronouncing of the name Yahweh was re-
served only for the most holy occasions and was entrusted,
when the Temple was rebuilt after the end of the Babylonian
Exile, only to the High Priest. In place of the name of Yahweh, a form made up of two separate words was substituted.
The consonants from the name Yahweh, namely Y, H, W, H,
were added to the vowels from the noun "Adonai" or "Lord."
Although the newly blended form reads "Jehovah," it was
pronounced "Adonai" and is to this day translated as "Lord."

The term Jehovah became popular around the fourteenth
century c.e., when a Christian, not understanding the process

of blending which had taken place, mistakenly read the vowels of "Adonai" together with the consonants of "Yahweh." The Jewish tradition, however, has never used the name "Jehovah," nor does it still make use of the name "Yahweh." From the fourth or fifth century B.C.E. to the present, the terms "Elohim" (God) and "Adonai" (Lord) have been used instead.

CHAPTER XIX

The Birth of the Torah

T HE Babylonian Exile witnessed the birth of the Torah book. Ever since King Josiah had established the "Book of the Covenant" as the basis of national life, the thought of a "constitution," as it were, continued to pervade the thoughts of the people. Out of the religious ferment of the exile, this constitution was to emerge.

After the destruction and exile, remorse and contrition seized the people, rising out of their sense of sin and estrangement from God. The simple faith in God's nearness and immanence in Israel's history was shattered. It was as if the ancient covenant had been broken. By acts of repentance the people sought to heal the breach that had opened between them and God and to renew the covenant. This meant, first, to observe the Torah that was given the people as the basis of the ancient covenant. By this alone could Israel hope to be reinstated in divine favor. The idea of collecting all the ancient traditions into one book which could serve as the constitution of the penitent community came into being. The leaders of the community undertook to finish the task begun by the creator of Deuteronomy: to compile and complete the Torah book.[1]

Scholars disagree concerning both the process and the exact date of this fulfillment. The early modernist position contended that P, as the latest school of writers, edited the earlier

JE and D materials and reworked them into their present form. For them, JED and P are known as successive schools or traditions, each of which built upon the foundation stones laid by its predecessors. The contemporary modernists, on the other hand, prefer to look upon JED and P as parallel schools, each of which developed simultaneously from antiquity until they were brought together in the Torah book. The contemporary view has been explained by Yehezkel Kaufmann in these words:

> The ideas, the religious and political symbols of the Torah were fully formed by the time of the early monarchy. The literature continued, of course, to develop and pass through successive formulations; but, the symbols and ideals of early times remained intact.[2]

The following charts will indicate further the different views of the early and contemporary modernists.

EARLY MODERNISTS
Successive Schools

850	750	721	621	600	550	550–450
J						
	E					
		JE				
			D			
				JED		
					P	
						JEDP

CONTEMPORARY MODERNISTS[3]
Parallel Schools

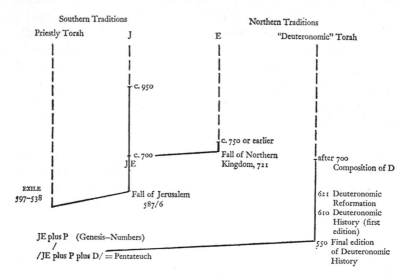

In the above chart the broken lines signify the informal tradition in its oral and written forms, while the solid lines signify the transmission of the formal tradition in written form. Notice that all the traditions are parallel developments growing out of the ancient period, although each was subject to a special development in the circle which preserved it. Like several streams flowing into one river, these traditions were joined and unified in a priestly edition, thus forming the Pentateuch.

The contemporary modernists, too, believe that the unifier of the Torah book was a representative of the priestly group. Who he was, however, remains shrouded in the mystery of history. This anonymous editor began by taking the J and E versions of the tradition which had been blended together shortly after the fall of the northern kingdom of Israel in 721. Into this narrative he inserted at various points his priestly tradition, which had grown up among the Jerusalem priests. Finally, he inserted the Book of Deuteronomy into the priestly edition of JE just before the story of Moses' death

(Deut. 34). Thus, the Pentateuch took shape, and the Torah was born.

During the Exile the Torah was born, but nearly 150 years were to elapse before the Torah was to be recognized fully as the Torah constitution of Israel.

In 539 B.C.E. the Babylonian Empire, already faltering from within because of corruption and abuse, fell before the mighty onrush of Cyrus, King of the Medes and the Persians. With his entry into Babylon, the Exile for the Judeans came to an end. Cyrus was an extraordinarily benevolent and humane monarch. Among his many acts of generosity was the granting of permission for the Judean exiles to return to their former homeland. In the very first year of his reign (538 B.C.E.) he issued an edict of liberation, which has been preserved both in Aramaic (Ezra 6:3–5) and in Hebrew (Ezra 1:1–4), permitting the exiles to return to Judah. Thus, the Exile that had begun nearly half a century before came to an end. The descendants of the original exiles were free once again to return to Jerusalem to rebuild the destroyed Temple.

At this time, there also appeared an anonymous prophet whose words have been attached to the book of Isaiah (Isa. 40–55) and who is therefore called Deutero-Isaiah or the Second Isaiah. He encouraged all to return, for Yahweh would be glorified once again. This was a new era of hope. Yahweh would forgive Israel's past sins; the exile would be brought to an end, and once again Israel would be Yahweh's people and Yahweh would be its God. Thus, the old covenant motif was revived by the prophet as he gave encouragement to his generation. Moreover, Yahweh not only would redeem Israel but also give Israel a special role in the redemption of mankind. Israel was to be "a light unto the nations" who by her example would lead the nations. Israel's election as Yahweh's servant was for responsibility. There would be times when the task would involve hardship and even suffering. Yet Israel would not fail, for Yahweh was indeed the universal God; Yahweh's majesty and might, testified the prophet, were the very foundations of creation and were revealed in the destinies of nations.

> Behold My servant, whom I uphold;
> My elect, in whom My soul delights;
> I have put My spirit upon him,
> He shall make the right to go forth to the nations.
> He shall not cry, nor lift up,
> Nor cause his voice to be heard in the street.
> A bruised reed shall he not break,
> And the dimly burning wick shall he not quench;
> He shall make the right to go forth according to the truth.
> He shall not fail nor be crushed,
> Till he have set the right in the earth;
> And the isles shall wait for his teaching.
> Thus says God the Lord
> He that created the heavens, and stretched them forth,
> He that spread forth the earth and that which comes
>   out of it,
> He that gives breath unto the people upon it,
> And spirit to them that walk therein:
> I the Lord have called you in righteousness,
> And have taken hold of your hand,
> And kept you, and set you for a covenant of the people,
> For a light of the nations;
> To open the blind eyes,
> To bring out the prisoners from the dungeon,
> And them that sit in darkness out of the prison house.
>   (Isa. 42:1-7)

Despite the generosity of Cyrus and the inspiring words of Deutero-Isaiah, it should not be assumed that everyone welcomed the return with equal enthusiasm. Although the Bible tells us that fifty thousand did choose to make the journey, scholars are more inclined to believe that this figure was expanded by a later writer. A much smaller group made the first return, and gradually over the years others joined them. At no time, however, was there a mass migration from fertile, prosperous Babylon to poor, desolate Jerusalem. The first returnees, moreover, found much to disillusion them with the result that others were deterred further from following in their footsteps. In fact, many exiles had so prospered that they were quite loath to give up their hard-earned gains. For others, the thought of returning to an impoverished and devastated Jerusalem seemed like a foolhardy venture.

In Jerusalem, the returnees met with resistance not only from the local inhabitants but also from the Samaritans, who were descendants of the survivors who had remained in the northern kingdom of Israel after its fall in 721 B.C.E. They had intermarried, however, with the people whom the Assyrians had transported to Israel and had begun to follow practices foreign to the covenant with Yahweh. When the returned exiles refused the Samaritans permission to participate in the rebuilding of the Temple because they had not remained faithful to the covenant, the Samaritans undertook a campaign to hinder the resettlement. They complained to the Persians, accusing the returned exiles of disloyalty. Because of these and other obstacles, it was not until the year 515 B.C.E., some eighteen years after Cyrus' decree and following the constant admonitions of the prophets Haggai and Zechariah, that a very modest Temple structure finally was completed. Even then life in Jerusalem was filled with constant struggle. The Bible preserves for us three pictures of the burdened community. For example, the Book of Obadiah reflects the pressure of neighboring Edom, which resented strongly the re-emergence of Judah, whose territory it coveted. Also, the prophets Joel and

Malachi preserve for us the story of the inner struggle born of poverty, disillusionment, and the inevitable religious apathy which followed.

For nearly a century, the community was only a shadow of its former greatness. Suddenly, there appeared two leaders, Nehemiah and Ezra. Scholars are sharply divided concerning who was the first to come to Jerusalem. The Book of Ezra leads us to conclude that Ezra preceded. The inclination of scholars, however, is to assume that Nehemiah arrived in 445 B.C.E., followed shortly after by Ezra. Nehemiah was a military governor who had been appointed by the Persian king to repair the city defenses so that the people of Jerusalem could defend themselves from their neighboring enemies. He also instituted many reforms to strengthen the community. Ezra, on the other hand, was a priest or, perhaps better, a scribe. He has been called "the Father of Judaism." His was the task of renewing the covenant and reorganizing the community religiously, just as Nehemiah had done militarily. Ezra brought with him from Babylonia a copy of "the book of the law of Moses." One day he read the law before the people. This event proved to be a turning point in Jewish history.

And when the seventh month was come, and the children of Israel were in their cities, all the people gathered themselves together as one man into the broad place that was before the water gate; and they spoke unto Ezra the scribe to bring the book of the law of Moses, which the Lord had commanded to Israel. And Ezra the priest brought the Law before the congregation, both men and women, and all that could hear with understanding, upon the first day of the seventh month. And he read therein before the broad place that was before the water gate from early morning until midday, in the presence of the men and the women, and of those that could under-

stand; and the ears of all the people were atentive unto
the book of the Law. And Ezra the scribe stood upon a
pulpit of wood, which they had made for the purpose;
... And Ezra opened the book in the sight of all the
people—for he was above all the people—and when he
opened it, all the people stood up.

... even the Levites, caused the people to understand
the Law; and the people stood in their place. And they
read in the book, in the Law of God, distinctly; and they
gave the sense, and caused them to understand the reading.

And Nehemiah, who was the Tirshatha, and Ezra the
priest the scribe, and the Levites that taught the people,
said unto all the people: "This day is holy unto the Lord
your God; mourn not, nor weep." For all the people
wept, when they heard the words of the Law. Then he
said unto them: "Go your way, eat the fat, and drink the
sweet, and send portions unto him for whom nothing is
prepared; for this day is holy unto our Lord; neither be
you grieved; for the joy of the Lord is your strength." So
the Levites stilled all the people, saying: "Hold your
peace, for the day is holy; neither be you grieved." And
all the people went their way to eat, and to drink, and to
send portions, and to make great mirth, because they had
understood the words that were declared unto them.

And on the second day were gathered together the
heads of fathers' houses of all the people, the priests, and
the Levites, unto Ezra the scribe, even to give attention
to the words of the Law. And they found written in the
Law, how that the Lord had commanded by Moses, that
the children of Israel should dwell in booths in the feast
of the seventh month; and that they should publish and
proclaim in all their cities, and in Jerusalem, saying: "Go
forth unto the mount, and fetch olive branches, and
branches of wild olive, and myrtle branches, and palm

branches, and branches of thick trees, to make booths, as it is written." So the people went forth, and brought them, and made themselves booths, every one upon the roof of his house, and in their courts, and in the courts of the house of God, and in the broad place of the water gate, and in the broad place of the gate of Ephraim. And all the congregation of them that were come back out of the captivity made booths, and dwelt in the booths; for since the days of Joshua the son of Nun unto that day had not the children of Israel done so. And there was very great gladness (Neh. 8).

The event was nothing less than a ceremony of renewal, reminiscent of those which had taken place nearly two centuries before in the days of Josiah and nearly six hundred years prior in the time of Joshua.

Was the "book of the law of Moses" which Ezra read the Torah as we know it today? This is difficult to say. Scholars themselves are not agreed.

What law Ezra brought is a question to which there is no certain answer. There is no reason to assume that it was altogether a new law entirely unknown to the people. Since it was already accepted by Babylonian Jews as the law of Moses, much of it at least may have been long known by Jews in Palestine as well. Some have supposed that it was the Priestly Code, which preserves the official traditions of the pre-exilic Temple as these had been handed down, collected, and given fixed form, presumably in the exile. Others think that it was the completed Pentateuch, which, all its components having long been in existence, had almost certainly been compiled in roughly its present form before Ezra's day, although no one standard recension as yet existed. Still others believe that it was a collection of laws, perhaps including various cultic and other regulations secondarily attached to the Priestly narrative, the exact limits of which can no longer be determined. We cannot, of course, say which laws Ezra actually read aloud. But it is most probable that the completed Pentateuch was in his possession, and that it was he who imposed it on the community, as the normative rule of faith and practice. The Torah certainly had this status soon after Ezra's time, and it is plausible to suppose that this was the law which he brought. The law, in any event, was accepted by the people in solemn covenant before Yahweh and thus became the constitution of the community.[4]

Thus, we bring our story of the birth of the Torah to a close. We have pursued the account from the embryonic days of Torah literature to fulfillment in the form of a Torah book or constitution. Those who wish to understand the role of the Torah in Jewish life, however, need to carry the story further. Once the Torah was born, it continued to grow into a Torah tradition. The two are inseparable. The "book" and the "tradition," these are the heart of Israel's very life. Judaism is the product both of the "book" and the "tradition."

He who knows only the book knows only the childhood of Judaism; he who ignores the book and treasures only the tradition forgets the admonition of the poet that "the child is father of the man." [5]

Appendix

The following Bible selections are suggested as parallel readings for each of the chapters. (All references are to the Jewish Publication Society version of the Bible.) [1]

Chapter 1: Archaeology and the Science of Bible Study   (none)

Chapter 2: Mesopotamian Beginnings
Genesis 13–14

Chapter 3: The Egyptian Sojourn
Exodus 1–15

Chapter 4: The Covenant at Sinai
Exodus 19–20
Exodus 24
Exodus 31:18–34:10
Exodus 34:27–35

Chapter 5: Entrance into Canaan
Exodus 16–17
Numbers 11–14
Numbers 20–24
Joshua 1–12
Judges 1

Chapter 6: The Covenant Reaffirmed
Exodus 21:1–23:19
Exodus 34:10–26
Joshua 24

Chapter 7: Years of Transition
Judges 2:6–16:31
I Samuel 1–26

Chapter 8:   The Golden Age
              I Samuel 27–31
              II Samuel
              I Kings 1–11

Chapter 9:   The Covenant Is Challenged   (none)

Chapter 10:   The J School: The Primeval Tradition
              The Traditions of the Beginnings: Genesis 2:4b–11

              The Creation and Fall of Man   2:4b–3:24
              The First Murderer (Cain and
                Abel)   4:1–16
              The Origins of Nomadic Society   4:17–26
              The Fall of the Divine Beings   6:1–8
              The Flood (Noah and his Sons)   7:1–10, 12, 16b–17,
                                                     22–23; 8:2b–3a,
                                                     6–12, 13b, 20–22
              The First Drunkard (Noah)   9:18–27
              The Descendants of Noah   10:8–19, 21, 24–30
              The Tower of Babel   11:1–9

Chapter 11:   The J School: The Patriarchal Tradition
              The Traditions of the Patriarchs: Genesis 12–50

              The Call and Journey of Abraham
                to Canaan   12:1–4a
              Abraham in Egypt   12:10–20
              Abraham and Lot Separate   13:1–18
              The Birth of Ishmael to Hagar   16:1–2, 4–14
              The Destruction of Sodom and
                Gomorrah   18:1–19:28, 30–38
              The Birth of Isaac   21:1a, 2a (... in his
                                                     old age)
              The Renewal of the Promise to
                Abraham   22:16–18, 20–24
              Rebekkah Obtained for Isaac   24:1–67
              Later Sons of Abraham   25:1–6
              The Birth of Esau and Jacob   25:21–34
              Isaac's Relations with Abimelech
                of Gerar   26:1–33
              Jacob Obtains Isaac's Blessing   27:1–45
              Yahweh Appears to Jacob at Bethel   28:13–16
              Jacob Meets Rachel and Laban   29:2–14

Comparative Readings in J, E, and P

Some readers may wish to pursue the J, E, and P writings beyond the passages dealing with the early beginnings and the patriarchs. The following table carries the outline through the several traditions of the Bondage, the Exodus, and the Wilderness Wanderings.[2]

I. J School

The Traditions of Bondage and Exodus: Exodus 1–14

Oppression of Israel After the Death of Joseph	1:6, 8–12
Moses' Flight to Midian	2:15–23a
The Call of Moses to Deliver Israel	3:2–3, 5, 7–8, 16–18; 4:1–16, 19–20a, 22
The "Bridegroom of Blood"	4:24–26
Moses' Demand to Pharaoh, Persecution and Discontent of Israel	4:30–31; 5:3, 5–6:1
The Plague Stories	
Nile Turned to Blood	7:14–15a, 16, 18, 21a, 23–25
Frogs	7:26–29; 8:4–11
Swarms of Flies	8:16–28
Cattle Disease	9:1–7
Hail	9:13–21, 23b, 25b–34
Locusts	10:1–11, 13b (and Yahweh brought an east wind . . .), 15–19
Death of Egyptian First-Born	11:4–8; 12:29–30
Festival of Passover and Unleavened Bread	12:21–27; 13:3–16
Flight of Israel and the Crossing of the Red Sea	13:21–22; 14:5–7, 10–14, 19b–20, 21b (from "and Yahweh drove

the sea" through
"made the sea dry
land"), 24–25, 27b,
30–31

The Traditions of the Wilderness Wan-
derings (Sinai-Kadesh):   Exodus 15–Numbers 34

From the Sea to the Mountain   15:22–27; 16:4, 5, 25–30;
                                           17:1b–2, 7
The Revelation at Sinai   19:3b–9 (and Yahweh
                                           called him out of the
                                           mountain...)
The Covenant Feast   24:1–2, 9–11
Moses Prays for Israel and Purges the
    Apostates   32:9–14, 25–34
Yahweh Reveals His Glory to Moses   33:1–4, 12–23
Tablets Reinscribed with "Ritual"
    Decalogue   34:1–28

(In Numbers it becomes difficult to disentangle J and E so that
many scholars treat them as a unity, JE.)

Departure from Sinai with Hobab   10:29–33, 35–36
Provision of Quails   11:1–35
Miriam and Aaron Criticize Moses   12:1–16
Spies Sent to Canaan   13:17b–20 (Go up into
                                           the South...), 22–24
                                           26b–33
Forty-Year Wandering Decreed   14:3–4, 8–9, 11–25, 31–
                                           33, 39–45
Revolt of Dathan and Abiram   16:12–15, 25–34 (omit
                                           Korah)
Moses Excluded from Canaan   20:1–13
Edom Refuses Israel Passage   20:14–21
Defeat of Sihon and Og   21:1–35
Balaam's Oracles   22:2–24: 25
Israelite Apostasy to Baal Peor   25:1–6
Reuben and Gad Settled in Trans-
    Jordan   32:1–17, 20–27, 34–42

II. E School

The Traditions of Bondage and Exodus: Exodus 1–15

Birth of Moses and Introduction to
    Court   1:15–2:10

Moses Kills an Egyptian	2:11–14
"I AM" Calls Moses to Deliver Israel	3:1, 4, 6, 9–15, 19–22
Moses Enlists Aid of Jethro and Aaron	4:17–18, 21, 27–28
Pharaoh Refuses to Free Hebrews	5:1–2, 4
The Plagues	
Nile Turned to Blood	7:15b, 17, 20b (... he lifted)
Hail	9:22–25 (except for 23b and 25b which are J), 35
Locusts	10:12–13a, 14, 20
Darkness	10:21–23, 27
The "Expulsion" from Egypt	11:1–3; 12:31–39, 42a; 13:17–19
The Songs of Moses and Miriam	15:1–18, 20–21
The Traditions of the Wilderness Wanderings (Horeb-Kadesh):	Exodus 17–Numbers 34
Water from the Rock at Horeb	17:3–6
Israel Wars wth Amalak	17:8–16
Moses Reunited with Jethro, the Covenant Meal	18:1–27
Israel Consecrated for the Covenant	19:2b–3a (from "and there Israel encamped" through "went up to God"), 10–11a, 14–17, 19
Ethical Decalogue	20:1–20
The Covenant Code (Canaanite Civil Code)	21:1–23:19
Covenant Sealed with Blood Ceremony	24:3–8
Moses Receives the Tables of Stone	24:12–14, 18b; 31:18b (the tables of stone ...)
The Golden Calf	32:1–8, 15–24, 35
The People Discard Their Amulets	33:4–6
Moses and the Tent of Meeting	33:7–11

III. P School

The Traditions of the Beginnings:	Genesis 1–11
The Creation Story (Sabbath)	1:1–2:4a
Genealogy from Adam to Noah	5:1–28, 30–32
The Flood	6:9–22

APPENDIX

The Mosaic Covenant Traditions[3]

Source	Location	Act of Establishment	Stipulations
J	Mt. Sinai	Exodus 24:1–2, 9–11	Ritual Decalogue Exodus 34:11–26
E	Mt. Horeb	Exodus 24:3–8	Ethical Decalogue Exodus 20:1–17 Covenant Code or Canaanite Civil Code Exodus 21:1–23:19
D	Mt. Horeb	Deuteronomy 4:9–14 5:1–5, 19–30	D Decalogue Deuteronomy 5:6–21
	Moab	Deuteronomy 29	Book of the Covenant Deuteronomy 12–28
P	Mt. Sinai	Exodus 19:1–2 24:15–18 34:29–35 40:34–38	Exodus 25–31; 35–40:33 Holiness Code Leviticus 17–26 (27) Priestly Code Leviticus 1–16 Numbers 1–10:10

Notes

Chapter 1:

1 The author has preferred to use the terms B.C.E. and C.E. instead of B.C. and A.D. B.C.E. stands for "Before Common Era" and C.E. for "Common Era."

2 Eugene B. Borowitz, "Solving the Theological Problems in Teaching Bible," *Jewish Teacher* (Union of American Hebrew Congregations), Vol. 29, No. 4 (April, 1961), p. 12.

3 John Bright, "Modern Study of Old Testament Literature," in *The Bible and the Ancient Near East*, ed. G. Ernest Wright (New York: Doubleday & Co., Inc., 1961), p. 17.

4 *Webster's New World Dictionary* (Cleveland and New York: The World Publishing Co., 1960), p. 75.

5 Frederic Kenyon, *Our Bible and the Ancient Manuscripts* (London, 1939), p. 48, quoted in Pritchard, J. B., *Archaeology and the Old Testament* (Princeton, N.J.: Princeton University Press, 1958), p. 43.

6 Yigael Yadin, *The Message of The Scrolls* (New York: Simon and Schuster, 1957), p. 22.

7 All biblical references are to *The Holy Scriptures according to the Massoretic Text, A New Translation* (Philadelphia: Jewish Publication Society, 1917).

8 In the summer of 1961, the author was in Israel, where he had the opportunity of discussing the Megiddo findings with a noted Israeli archaeologist. This authority was of the opinion that the stables belonged not to Solomon but to King Ahab of the northern kingdom of Israel, who ruled approximately sixty years after Solomon. He believed that if archaeologists were to dig deeper they would unearth Solomon's stables also. From all indications, however, he felt that the Solomonic finds would be sufficiently similar to the Ahab stables not to justify continued digging. Cf., "City of Ahab," *Time*, 75:54 (February 1, 1960).

9 Nelson Glueck, *The River Jordan* (Philadelphia: Jewish Publication Society, 1946), p. 146.

10 Nelson Glueck, "The Effect of Modern Discoveries on Judaism," in the *Report of The Twelfth International Conference of The World Union For Progressive Judaism* (July, 1961), pp. 84–85. Another significant statement summarizing the contribution of archaeology to the study of the Bible is found in Harry M. Orlinsky, *Ancient Israel* (Ithaca, N.Y.: Cornell University Press, 1954), pp. 6–7:

"Until the eighteenth century the Bible was universally accepted as a trustworthy history book of antiquity. Indeed, the Book was regarded as being literally true, the Creation, the Flood, Noah's Ark, the walls of Jericho, and all. But as the Age of Reason dawned and in turn gave way to nineteenth-century philosophies of evolution and scientific materialism, the Bible, in common with the New Testament and all records of antiquity, Greek, Roman, and the rest, came to be very considerably discounted as a reliable basis for the reconstruction of history.

"The heroic doings of the patriarchs, Abraham, Isaac, and Jacob, as described in the Book of Genesis, were discounted as mere myth. The very existence of Moses was doubted. Joshua was believed to have had little or nothing to do with the Israelite conquest of Canaan. David and Solomon were considered greatly overrated. Extensive parts of the prophetic books were attributed not to the prophets themselves but to redactors and disciples who lived several centuries later in different circumstances. The story of the Babylonian Exile was relegated to the realm of fiction. . . .

"Today, in considerable degree, the pendulum has swung the other way. Modern historians do not, to be sure, accept every part of the Bible equally as literal fact. Yet they have come to accept much of the Biblical data as constituting unusually reliable historical documents of antiquity, documents which take on new meaning and pertinence when they are analyzed in the light of the newly discovered extra-Biblical sources. Indeed, even the mythical parts of the Bible are now generally regarded as reliable reflection of fact, empirically grounded, and logical in their way. It is a question of understanding the perspective and circumstances involved."

Chapter 2:

[1] John Bright, *A History of Israel* (Philadelphia: The Westminster Press, 1959), p. 139.
[2] Nelson Glueck, "The Archaeological History of the Negev," in the *Hebrew Union College Annual,* Vol. 37 (1961).
[3] Nelson Glueck, *Rivers in the Desert* (New York: Farrar, Straus & Cudahy, Inc., 1959), pp. 68–75.
[4] W. F. Albright, *From the Stone Age to Christianity* (2d ed.; New York: Doubleday & Co., Inc., 1957), pp. 61 ff.
[5] C. Ernest Wright, *Biblical Archaeology* (Philadelphia: The Westminster Press, 1957), p. 40. Also abridged edition (1960), pp. 21–22.

Chapter 3:

[1] Bright, *A History of Israel,* pp. 32–33.
[2] Bernhard W. Anderson, *Understanding the Old Testament* (Englewood Cliffs, N.J.: Prentice-Hall, Inc., © 1957), p. 29.
[3] Norman K. Gottwald, *A Light To The Nations* (New York: Harper & Brothers, 1959), p. 113.
[4] Bright, *op. cit.,* p. 116.
[5] Abba Hillel Silver, *Moses and the Original Torah* (New York: The Macmillan Co., 1961), p. 19.
[6] Yehezkel Kaufmann, *The Religion of Israel,* trans. Moshe Greenberg (Chicago: University of Chicago Press, 1960), pp. 226–28.
[7] Wright, *Biblical Archaeology,* p. 54.

8 Gottwald, *op. cit.*, p. 121.
9 Bright, *op. cit.*, p. 115.

Chapter 4:

1 Julian Morgenstern, "Decalogue" in Universal Jewish Encyclopedia (New York: Universal Jewish Encyclopedia, Inc., 1939–44).
2 Anderson, *op. cit.*, p. 56.
3 This chart is adapted from the conclusions of George E. Mendenhall, *Law and Covenant in Israel and the Ancient Near East* (Pittsburgh: The Biblical Colloquim, 1955), pp. 32–34.
4 Anderson, *op. cit.*, pp. 56–57.
5 Mendenhall, *op. cit.*, p. 36.
6 Kaufmann, *op. cit.*, pp. 233–34.

Chapter 5:

1 Glueck, *Rivers In The Desert*, p. 109.
2 Anderson, *op. cit.*, p. 92.
3 W. F. Albright, "The Role of the Canaanites in the History of Civilization" in Wright, *The Bible and the Ancient Near East*, pp. 339, 351.
4 Bright, *op. cit.*, p. 108.

Chapter 6:

1 Mendenhall, *op. cit.*, p. 42.
2 Mendenhall, *op. cit.*, p. 44.

Chapter 7:

1 W. F. Albright, "The Biblical Period," in *The Jews: Their History, Culture and Religion,* ed. Louis Finkelstein (New York: Harper & Brothers, 1949).
2 Albright, *ibid.*, p. 23.

Chapter 8:

1 Anderson, *op. cit.*, p. 143.

Chapter 10:

1 Jack Finegan, *In The Beginning* (New York: Harper & Brothers, 1961), pp. 78–79.

Chapter 11:

1 Gerhard Von Rad, *Genesis* (Philadelphia: The Westminster Press, 1956), p. 36.

Chapter 12:

1 Gottwald, *op. cit.*, p. 260.
2 Bright, *op. cit.*, p. 65.
8 Albright, "The Biblical Period," p. 11.

Chapter 13:

[1] J. M. Powes Smith, *The Prophet and His Problems* (New York: Charles Scribner's Sons, 1914), p. 104. A more recent statement concerning the prophet's role is found in Sheldon H. Blank, *Jeremiah: Man and Prophet* (Cincinnati: Hebrew Union College Press, 1961), pp. 4–5:

"A prophet deserves honor not because he foresees the coming event but because he sees the meaning within the current event. It is the prophet's gift of insight, not his foresight, that sets him apart. Although Amos rightly foresaw the Assyrian conquest of the Northern Kingdom in 722 B.C. and although Jeremiah correctly foresaw the Babylonian conquest of the Southern Kingdom in 587 B.C., neither prophet's honor derives from the accuracy of his political predictions. It derives from his gained recognition of the fundamental causes making for his nation's impending collapse. The prophet saw a pattern in human society (he called it God), according to which pattern a rotting social structure, like a condemned building, must collapse. An Amos, or later a Jeremiah, saw fatal decay in his own society and experienced concern. (An active concern always impregnates a prophet's insight.) So he sounded the alarm. Like Amos and the others, Jeremiah sounded frantic warnings, not in anger but in pain, and appealed for measures designed to buttress the tottering structure. What he was given to see and what he was moved to do for his people made Jeremiah a prophet."

Chapter 14:

[1] For a complete study of Isaiah see Sheldon H. Blank, *Prophetic Faith In Isaiah* (New York: Harper & Brothers, 1958).

Chapter 15:

[1] Kaufmann, *op. cit.*, pp. 174–5.

Chapter 18:

[1] This chart is taken from James B. Pritchard, *Archaeology and the Old Testament* (Princeton, N.J.: Princeton University Press, 1958), p. 192.

Chapter 19:

[1] Kaufmann, *op. cit.*, pp. 210–11.
[2] Kaufmann, *op. cit.*, p. 204.
[3] The following chart is taken from Anderson, *op. cit.*, p. 383.
[4] Bright, *op. cit.*, pp. 374–75.
[5] William Wordsworth, "My Heart Leaps Up When I Behold," *The Home Book of Verse* ed. Burton Stevenson (New York: Henry Holt & Company).

Appendix:

[1] Based upon Gottwald, *op. cit.*, pp. 215–18; 248–49; 450–53.
[2] Based upon Gottwald, *op. cit.*, pp. 215–18; 248–49; 450–53.
[3] Based upon Gottwald, *op. cit.*, p. 111.

Index